Using Analytics to Detect Possible Fraud

Founded in 1807, John Wiley & Sons is the oldest independent publishing company in the United States. With offices in North America, Europe, Asia, and Australia, Wiley is globally committed to developing and marketing print and electronic products and services for our customers' professional and personal knowledge and understanding.

The Wiley Corporate F&A series provides information, tools, and insights to corporate professionals responsible for issues affecting the profitability of their company, from accounting and finance to internal controls and performance management.

Using Analytics to Detect Possible Fraud

Tools and Techniques

PAMELA S. MANTONE

WILEY

Cover image: Wiley
Cover design: © iStockphoto.com/Artur Figurski

Library of Congress Cataloging-in-Publication Data:

ISBN 978-1-118–58562-7 (Hardcover); ISBN 978-1-118–71595-6 (ebk)
ISBN 978-1-118–71598-7 (ebk)

10 9 8 7 6 5 4 3 2 1

To all who cherish the opportunity to continue to learn and excel in whatever they may do.

Contents

Preface   xi

Acknowledgments   xv

Chapter 1:   Overview of the Companies   **1**

The Four Companies   2
    Company 1   2
    Company 2   5
    Company 3   8
    Company 4   10
Summary   16

Chapter 2:   The "Norm" and the "Forensic" Preliminary
Analytics: Basics Everyone Should Know   **19**

Liquidity Ratios   20
    Working Capital   21
    Working Capital Index   21
    Working Capital Turnover   22
    Current Ratio   22
Case Studies: Liquidity Ratios   22
Profitability Ratios   25
    Gross Profit   26
    Gross Profit Margin   26
    Stock Sales   26
    Return on Equity   27
Case Studies: Profitability Ratios   27
    Company 1   31
Horizontal Analysis   36
    Company 1   36
    Company 2   43
    Company 3   50

Company 4   61
Vertical Analysis   66
  Company 1   66
  Company 2   70
  Company 3   73
  Company 4   79
Summary   79

Chapter 3: The Importance of Cash Flows and Cash Flow Statements   **83**

Cash Flows and Net Income   85
  Company 1   87
  Company 2   89
  Company 3   92
  Company 4   97
Other Cash Flow Techniques   100
  Company 1   101
  Company 2   104
  Company 3   107
  Company 4   114
Summary   117

Chapter 4: The Beneish M-Score Model   **119**

Company 1   124
Company 2   133
Company 3   143
  Indices of the Primary Government   145
  Indices of the Governmental Funds   151
Company 4   158
Summary   166
Notes   170

Chapter 5: The Accruals   **171**

Dechow–Dichev Accrual Quality   173
  The Four Companies: Dechow–Dichev Model   175
Sloan's Accruals   184
  The Four Companies: Sloan's Model   185
Jones Nondiscretionary Accruals   191
  The Four Companies: Jones Model   192
Summary   196
Notes   198

Chapter 6: Analysis Techniques Using Historical Financial Statements and Other Company Information   **199**

The Piotroski F-Score Model	200
Company 1	203
Company 2	205
Company 3	207
Company 4	212
Lev–Thiagarajan's 12 Signals	215
Company 1	220
Company 2	222
Company 3	225
Company 4	230
Summary	233
Notes	235

Chapter 7: Benford's Law, and Yes—Even Statistics   **237**

Benford's Law	239
Company 1	243
Company 2	249
Company 3	255
Company 4	267
Simple Statistics	272
Company 1	277
Company 2	281
Company 3	284
Company 4	289
Summary	290
Note	292

Chapter 8: Grading the Four Companies   **293**

Company 1	294
Company 2	302
Company 3	310
Company 4	320
Summary	326

Bibliography   **329**

About the Author   **331**

Index   **333**

Preface

THE CONCEPT of writing this book goes back to June 2012, when, as a presenter at the Annual Consultant's Conference, I was asked if I would consider writing a book over the content of the presentation. There have been many times since then that I questioned my sanity over the decision to continue this task while still working full time. However, even today, I still recognize the need for providing information to those who want to learn more about forensic accounting, since there is little information available about this "new field" in accounting. My purpose in writing this book is to provide information written in plain language, using case studies as the prime source for learning the material. I hope that I have succeeded in this task. I have used the term *financial forensic examiner* in the book to define anyone who wants to understand financial statement changes from year to year, so the tools and techniques are useful not only to practitioners, but also to investors, brokers, management, valuators, and attorneys.

This book is a practical overview of a "first stage" of forensic accounting in that it provides a common source of analytical tools and techniques that sort out and define anomalies in financial information. It is both impractical and ineffective to begin a forensic accounting investigation using a hunt-and-peck methodology in trying to find fraudulent information. Many practitioners use tools and techniques that they are familiar with but that may not be essential for this type of engagement. The tools and techniques covered in this book allow anyone analyzing financial statements to find *anomalies* in the information that require additional investigative techniques. More importantly, these tools and techniques provide both efficiency and effectiveness in forensic accounting investigations by offering a roadmap to areas of unusual variations or unusual relationships. This allows one to focus attention on those questionable areas.

The various techniques included in this book start from the very basic, simple analytics that most are familiar with and continue to more advanced analytical tools and techniques that enable the financial forensic examiner to tweak further investigative work. These tools and techniques include:

- Liquidity ratios
- Profitability ratios
- Horizontal analysis
- Vertical analysis
- Cash realized from operations
- Analyzing cash realized from operations to net income from operations
- The Beneish M-Score model
- Dechow-Dichev Accrual Quality
- Sloan's Accruals
- Jones Nondiscretionary Accruals
- The Piotroski F-Score model
- Lev-Thiagarajan's 12 Signals
- Benford's Law
- Z-score analysis
- Correlation
- Regression analysis

To make the application of these techniques easy to learn and follow, the book also includes four different companies as case studies providing practical application of the tools and techniques within the book. The case studies also allow the reader to understand how to interpret the results of the testing. Three of these companies' financial statements include fraudulent activity resulting from both embezzlement and financial statement fraud. The fourth company is a model of what "normal" should look like, yet also provides some interesting anomalies related to unusual events occurring within the operation cycles of the company.

Many charts and graphs are included so the reader may begin to develop visual interpretation skills, noticing even the minute changes that may occur from year to year. Visual aids allow the reader to focus on changes that are often overlooked when dealing with just numbers, but may be important signals to someone performing a forensic accounting engagement. Learning the correct type of visual aid is also important when defining the outcomes of tests, since these may become evidence for prosecution.

It is important to remember that these tools and techniques alone are not sufficient for prosecution. In each of these case studies, additional investigative work included drilling down to detailed documentation to support the conclusions of the analytical testing, along with conducting interviews. Another important factor to remember is that financial information may not include all of the financial activity of a company, so even if there are no unusual variations or anomalies in the financial statements, there still may be fraudulent activity occurring. Finally, not every anomaly or unusual relationship means that fraud is occurring, but these changes also require additional work to determine the cause of the variations.

The crux of this book is to provide information that leads to an efficient forensic accounting engagement without sacrificing effectiveness. In fact, efficiency leads to a more successful engagement by allowing the financial forensic examiner to focus attention on items significant to the engagement.

Acknowledgments

THERE HAVE been so many practitioners over the years who have influenced and shaped my career that it would be difficult to list them here, but all of them in one way or another provided insight and guidance relating to a career in public accounting.

Bryan Bean, CPA, actually began my career path in public accounting by offering me my very first position in his public accounting firm, and for that I am extremely grateful. Little did I know back then that I would end up having so much fun working in this field, much less write a book!

I have also had the opportunity and pleasure to work with many talented people at my current place of employment, Joseph Decosimo and Company, PLLC. My admiration for their abilities and knowledge reminds me that I still have much to learn.

Finally, leaving the best for last, I cannot begin to thank my family, especially my husband, for their support while I was working those very long hours and ignoring everything else. I cannot begin to express my love and thanks to my husband, who has always encouraged me in every aspect of my life by saying "Yes, you can" when I say "I can't do this." This book is for him.

Using Analytics to Detect Possible Fraud

CHAPTER ONE

Overview of the Companies

B EFORE BEGINNING any analytical testing of financial information, a financial forensic examiner needs to consider preliminary discussions with management to gather information that may become useful in analyzing financial information. For use within this book, a *financial forensic examiner* is any individual who wants to pursue a detailed analysis of a set of financial statements to determine not only the *consistency* of the financial information but also possible *anomalies* that may suggest the possibility of fraudulent activity. Discussions should provide information relating to general company operations, allowing the financial forensic examiner to understand management's philosophy and general operating style. These discussions should also include financial matters, such as profit margins built into pricing products and any unusual transactions or changes that might have occurred during the period under examination. These discussions may reveal information that the financial forensic examiner will need to assess in determining the results of analytical testing of financial information.

Herein lies a lesson for the financial forensic examiner: *Anomalies in financial information may occur and may not be representative of fraudulent activity.*

 THE FOUR COMPANIES

Before beginning any of the analytics noted in future chapters, this chapter is dedicated to providing general information about each company, including basic financial information and an overview of each company's general operations. Specific information for each case is available so the financial forensic examiner may follow each case study through the analytical process of finding anomalies in the financial information. This chapter will provide the foundation for interpretations made from the various tools and techniques shown throughout the book.

Company 1

Company 1 is a communications company whose primary revenues relate to advertising. The company is an S-corporation and includes three shareholders. Shareholder 2 maintained the financial information for the company. Throughout the history of the corporation, various shareholders sold their shares to new shareholders, with the exception of Shareholder 2, who would add any rounding of shares to Shareholder 2's total shares, increasing the total shares over time. Shareholder 2 was also the corporate secretary and treasurer, even though both corporate positions were not to be held by the same person, according to the Articles of Incorporation. The other two shareholders did not protest this arrangement.

Even though Company 1 filed annual tax returns, management did not review monthly, quarterly, or even annually prepared financial statements. Shareholder 3 suspected the financial information was flawed and began retaining information related to the company for an independent external review. Having gathered sufficient information, Shareholder 3 presented the documents to an external auditor for review.

Since formal financial statements had never been prepared for management, information subject to examination included sales journals, customer ledger cards, tax returns, bank statements, cash disbursement journals, and payroll journals. Even though an accounting software package maintained the financial information, Shareholder 2 would not supply a backup of the files. Financial information shown in the following tables came from the tax returns provided by the client and adjusted to book basis using the M-1 reconciliations on the tax returns.

Figure 1.1 illustrates the reconstructed balance sheet for the periods under investigation and condensed for presentation purposes.

Figure 1.2 shows the reconstructed income statements for the periods under investigation and condensed for presentation purposes. More detail has been included for additional discussions in Chapter 2.

After the recomputation of the financial statements, an integral part of the investigative planning stage used various analytical tools and techniques employed to determine specific focus areas for further investigations. Due to the nature of inconsistent postings of similar expenses in various categories during a fiscal year, the income statement presented contains some reclassifications among account balances for comparisons. The results of these tools

	YR 1	YR 2	YR 3	YR 4	YR 5
Assets					
Cash	$ 13,478	$ 1,195	$ 3,519	$ 330	$ (5,299)
Accounts Receivable	18,011	24,345	29,994	33,807	28,138
Total Current Assets	31,489	25,540	33,513	34,137	22,839
Fixed Assets (net)	122,019	121,058	116,855	113,473	114,437
Total Assets Liabilities	$153,508	$146,598	$150,368	$147,610	$137,276
Accounts Payable	$ 12,545	$ 10,612	$ 5,447	$ 7,642	$ 10,441
Total Current Liabilities	12,545	10,612	5,447	7,642	10,441
Notes Payable	—	17,641	31,192	30,554	32,862
Total Liabilities	$ 12,545	$ 28,253	$ 36,639	$ 38,196	$ 43,303
Shareholders Equity	140,963	118,345	113,729	109,414	93,973
Total Liabilities & SE	$153,508	$146,598	$150,368	$147,610	$137,276

FIGURE 1.1 Condensed Balance Sheets for Company 1

	YR 1	YR 2	YR 3	YR 4	YR 5
Sales	$145,246	$121,842	$130,859	$128,344	$138,443
Less Purchases	9,017	12,249	17,248	5,752	5,820
Less Labor Costs	4,542	8,143	6,115	10,292	2,988
Gross Profit	131,687	101,450	107,496	112,300	129,635
Expenses					
Selling Expenses	$ 1,712	$ 2,657	$ 2,001	$ 8,939	$ 12,730
General & Administrative	41,946	38,122	36,668	40,829	30,378
Salaries	9,820	15,592	8,266	4,234	43,490
Repairs & Maintenance	5,842	6,453	1,132	6,243	3,603
Bad Debt	—	—	—		4,280
Rent	2,976	2,000	5,000	7,504	1,615
Taxes & Licenses	5,937	10,312	5,791	6,149	8,284
Insurance	2,570	7,072	4,883	5,371	5,242
Utilities	15,782	16,487	16,823	18,131	17,177
Supplies	4,590	7,190	8,368	4,956	4,066
Depreciation	4,863	4,664	10,805	5,882	6,831
Accounting Fees	1,050	2,036	1,320	1,470	1,110
Vehicle Expense	2,291	4,929	—	—	—
Civic Donations	580	1,070	770	520	130
Legal Fees	709	—	—	—	—
Internet Fees	161	—	21	—	—
Office Expenses	689	—	—	—	—
Freight	78	—	—	22	—
Postage	209	—	244	403	386
Lodging & Travel	—	—	—	300	625
Commissions	522	—	54	380	870
Total General Expenses	100,615	115,927	100,145	102,394	128,087
Total Expenses	102,327	118,584	102,146	111,333	140,817
Interest Income	949	—	752	374	—
Interest Expenses	5,360	5,484	5,083	5,656	4,259
Net Profit	$ 24,949	$(22,618)	$ 1,019	$ (4,315)	$(15,441)

FIGURE 1.2   Condensed Income Statements for Company 1

and techniques are the focus of the case study for Company 1 throughout the remaining chapters.

Other developments in the examination included the finding of a checking and savings account that was in the company's name but not recorded in the financial information, and another entity set up as a partnership for the three shareholders to maintain the rental property owned by the S-corporation.

Herein lies a lesson for the financial forensic examiner: *Financial records are not always entirely conclusive for all transactions.*

Although the rental property was not vacant during the periods under investigation, the company did not complete tax returns for the partnership and did not keep financial records for the partnership. The use of *off-book* bank accounts allowed Shareholder 2 to remove funds from these accounts and then deposit these funds into the company, recording a note payable to Shareholder 2, although the funds in these accounts were actually revenues from advertising sales and rental income for the partnership.

As the investigation progressed, interviews with Shareholder 2 revealed that the intent of the fraud was to reduce the net worth of the company so that Shareholder 1 and Shareholder 2 would be able to purchase the shares of the heir of Shareholder 3 at a fraction of their true net worth. The local district attorney received a report of the examination findings and ultimately the shareholders' attorney negotiated the case before any court appearance. The plea-bargain arrangements removed the note payable to Shareholder 2 from the company's financial records, and required the hiring of an additional employee to manage the finances of the company, thus removing all operational and corporate authority from Shareholder 2.

Company 2

Company 2 is a manufacturing company with a niche in the market as the sole source for specific parts for large equipment, such as excavators, wheel loaders, cranes, and so forth. As a sole-source provider of these specific products, the company has a select customer base, maintaining a good working relationship with its customers and recording very little, if any, bad debt. The company monitored its receivables continuously and many of its customers paid their balances within the 30-day period, or the amounts due were collected at the time of delivery. Due to the nature of its manufacturing products, cost of sales and gross margins are consistent among the various models of its product lines.

The company is a C-corporation and did not have external audits of its financial records, just external compilations and reviews of its financial information. The financial information compiled for management's reviews consisted of specific ratios requested by management relating to liquidity, such as the current ratio, the quick ratio, income before tax to net worth, the debt coverage ratio, and the leverage ratio. The financial information related to the reviews did not include cash flow statements as part of the basic reports, nor did it include ratios relating to performance, such as gross margins and measurements of profitability.

Only the accounting staff had access to the financial information maintained through a commercial accounting software package. The accounting staff had access to various modules of the software, but not the complete accounting package. The office manager and the chief financial officer (CFO) both had unrestricted access to the accounting software. Other basic internal controls in place included appropriate segregation of duties relating to receiving cash, depositing cash, writing checks, and performing bank reconciliations. The CFO would use the signature stamp (kept locked in a filing cabinet in the office) to sign the checks. The CFO would ensure that each check had all support documentation attached before the checks were stamped. Only the office manager and the CFO were able to record manual journal entries in the accounting system.

The company issued hundreds of checks monthly, so staff did not sort the canceled checks in numerical order but relied on the bank statement listing of cleared checks to reconcile the financial records. By not sorting the canceled checks, staff did not notice whether any canceled checks were missing from the stack. When performing the reconciliations, staff would tick and tie check

Herein lies a lesson for the financial forensic examiner: *Internal control systems and documented procedures have inherent limitations to consider in the overall investigative process.*

numbers and amounts in the bank statement to the accounting records, using only the listing in the bank statement and not the individual canceled checks supplied in the bank statements.

Knowing the operational procedures of the accounting department, the office manager took advantage of the "opendoors," or weak areas within the company's internal control structure, and for many years embezzled monies from the firm. By having unrestricted access to backing up and restoring the financial records, the office manager was able to write personal checks, restore a backup of the financial records, and record fictitious vendor checks in the financial records, thus replacing the personal checks in the financial records with the fictitious checks. By removing the canceled personal checks from the monthly bank statements prior to giving the statements to the appropriate staff for reconciling, no one noticed any canceled checks missing. The company suspected fraudulent activity based on one transaction the office manager posted to the fixed assets in the general ledger in covering up one of the personal checks. In reviewing the general ledger transactions, the CFO noticed the posting of a purchase to fixed assets and knew that he had not authorized the purchase.

Figure 1.3 shows the balance sheets for the periods under investigation, condensed for presentation purposes.

Figure 1.4 illustrates the income statements for the periods under investigation, condensed for presentation purposes.

Due to the nature of the fraudulent activity and the attempted cover-up of lost funds, various analytical tools and techniques used in the planning stages of the investigation defined areas in the financial information that would require further inspection and detailed analysis. Further investigations of detailed documents revealed that a second, unauthorized signature stamp had been used to process personal checks. The office manager destroyed all backup copies of the financial records saved to the office manager's personal computer, along with the signature stamp. E-Discovery techniques were not successful in recreating all of the backup copies, but sufficient information recovered included excessive personal purchases, revealing a rather extravagant lifestyle.

Common in cases of embezzlement, the company owners respected and trusted the office manager, considered the office manager to be an excellent employee, and gave quarterly bonuses for outstanding performance. Although at first management was reluctant to press charges and prosecute the office manager, management did change its views as the office manager did not return any of the embezzled funds as promised. In the end, the court convicted the office manager and sentenced the individual to 10 years in prison, but the court

	YR 1	YR 2	YR 3	YR 4	YR 5
Assets					
Cash	$ 6,037	$ 219,408	$ 409,620	$ 1,615,708	$ 866,801
Accounts Receivable	1,388,977	2,905,601	2,282,772	2,158,034	2,275,985
Allowance for Bad Debts	(1,000)	(60,000)	(37,172)	(100,000)	(100,000)
Refundable Income Taxes	—	—	21,205	47,000	40,000
Inventory	1,866,785	3,904,040	3,282,898	3,887,568	5,159,037
Prepaid Expenses	256,677	309,566	176,110	73,826	75,412
Total Current Assets	3,517,476	7,278,615	6,135,433	7,682,136	8,317,235
Other Assets	—	—	—	—	963,459
Fixed Assets (net)	1,786,908	2,210,753	2,472,082	2,501,071	2,421,222
Total Assets	$5,304,384	$9,489,368	$8,607,515	$10,183,207	$11,701,916
Liabilities					
Accounts Payable	$1,186,293	$2,987,894	$1,902,907	$ 1,951,605	$ 1,352,480
Deferred Income Taxes	—	—	—	30,000	—
Other Liabilities	26,150	124,856	64,452	86,796	461,000
Total Current Liabilities	1,212,443	3,112,750	1,967,359	2,068,401	1,813,480
Deferred Income Taxes	488,762	873,317	1,270,317	424,317	604,000
Notes Payable	619,508	17,19,098	—	—	—
Total Liabilities	2,320,713	5,705,165	3,237,676	2,492,718	2,417,480
Stockholders Equity	2,984,671	3,784,203	5,369,839	7,690,489	9,284,436
Total Liabilities & SE	$5,305,384	$9,489,368	$8,607,515	$10,183,207	$11,701,916

FIGURE 1.3   Condensed Balance Sheets for Company 2

also allowed probation, so the office manager did not serve any time in prison. As part of the sentence, the office manager had to pay restitution to the company for the diverted funds. The company never received payments; the office manager moved out of state, and no other court intervention occurred.

Company 3

Company 3 is a local governmental entity requiring specific financial reporting. The magnitude of the embezzlement makes this a great case study for the

	YR 1	YR 2	YR 3	YR 4	YR 5
Sales	$10,950,180	$28,188,122	$40,214,834	$38,780,333	$30,397,677
Less Cost of Sales	8,737,104	23,312,675	33,082,011	31,270,725	24,613,108
Gross Profit	2,213,076	4,875,447	7,132,823	7,509,608	5,784,569
Expenses					
General & Administrative	1,764,716	3,534,123	4,555,539	3,722,301	3,358,667
Depreciation	203,295	240,233	306,697	339,156	375,978
Income Tax Expense	162,287	523,542	950,439	1,313,500	890,000
Total Expenses	2,130,298	4,297,898	5,812,675	5,374,957	4,624,645
Misc Income	117,305	221,983	265,491	185,999	434,023
Net Profit	$ 200,083	$ 799,532	$ 1,585,639	$ 2,320,650	$ 1,593,947

FIGURE 1.4 Condensed Income Statements for Company 2

analytical tools and techniques examined in this text, especially since external auditors also audited the local government's financial information annually and never found the embezzlement activities. Another reason for including this company is to show the financial forensic examiner that the analytical tools and techniques discussed in this book are applicable to all types of entities and types: public or nonpublic entities, corporations, partnerships, sole proprietorships, manufacturing, and government, nonprofit, and even financial institutions.

The local government's treasurer and comptroller maintained the financial records. The comptroller, accused of embezzling anywhere from $30 to $50 million or more from the local government, has pleaded guilty to all charges of stealing funds from the government. The audited financial statements completed by an external auditor noted no findings of internal control deficiencies or instances of noncompliance. The local government filed a lawsuit against its auditors for professional negligence and negligent misrepresentations in the auditor reports. However, one important factor overlooked was the effectiveness of the local government's management in monitoring the activities of the local government.

Since governmental financial statements require special presentation, both at the fund level and at the primary government level, the financial statements for Company 3 require presentation at both levels, totals only. The total governmental funds financial statements require presentation using the modified cash basis of accounting and include only the governmental funds. These funds included a general fund, special revenue funds, debt service funds, and a capital projects fund. The business-type activities (proprietary funds and enterprise funds) in the financial statements require presentation using the full accrual basis. Statements of cash flows are required for proprietary funds but not for governmental funds.

The primary government financial statements also include both governmental activities and business activities. The governmental activities financial statements, presenting the local government as a whole, included the general government, public safety, highways and streets, traffic development, welfare, culture and recreation, and airport and cemetery services. The business-type activities included a landfill, sewer, and water services.

The difference is that governmental activities require presentation using the full accrual method. The financial statements must include reconciliations of the modified cash basis of presentation to the accrual basis of accounting.

Figure 1.5 shows the primary government balance sheets and Figure 1.6 shows the governmental funds balance sheets for the periods under investigation.

Figure 1.7 shows the primary government income statements while Figure 1.8 shows the governmental funds income statements for the period under investigation. The structure of the income statements differs from the required structure, making the analytical tools easier to follow.

As with Company 1, diverted funds went to a specific bank account not recorded in the financial statements. By transferring governmental funds through the various bank accounts into this off-book bank account, the manager embezzled governmental funds for many years. The manager also created fictitious invoices to hide the embezzled funds, recording fictitious expenses in general expenses and capital outlay.

Company 4

No analytical study would be complete without having some sort of benchmark to use for comparison with the results of data analyses. Company 4 is the benchmark used in this book because the financial information for the

	YR 1	YR 2	YR 3	YR 4	YR 5
Assets					
Cash	$ 7,127,424	$ 5,829,038	$ 3,503,752	$ 1,282,307	$ 1,299,373
Investments	3,026,409	6,883,554	5,376,081	802,697	550,593
Accounts Receivable	6,193,387	5,675,948	5,770,644	6,221,333	7,481,059
Allowance for Bad Debts	(2,500)	(2,500)	(2,500)	(52,500)	(77,500)
Inventory	176,657	181,274	140,525	148,483	183,381
Prepaid Expenses	172,006	181,279	222,326	103,951	104,732
Total Current Assets	16,693,383	18,748,593	15,010,828	8,506,271	9,541,638
Restricted Cash	166,608	192,647	209,721	287,989	289,919
Notes Receivable	67,528	38,837	33,202	10,368	7,726
Restricted Investments	222,359	225,587	227,670	163,779	170,170
Fixed Assets (net)	67,637,960	69,924,748	79,045,344	85,833,195	91,983,964
Total Assets	$84,787,838	$89,130,412	$94,526,765	$94,801,602	$101,993,417
Liabilities					
Accounts Payable	$ 563,946	$ 761,336	$ 1,332,591	$ 643,130	$ 1,422,480
Accrued Liabilities	664,625	664,470	750,486	858,797	944,611
Due to Pension Fund	—	—	—	—	264,032
Long Term Due in 1 Year	1,579,370	2,861,106	2,350,037	2,580,092	6,454,289
Total Current Liabilties	2,807,941	4,286,912	4,433,114	4,082,019	9,085,412
Deferred Revenues	4,651,080	4,020,322	4,109,313	4,169,035	4,324,932
Long Term Liabilities	24,126,024	28,850,525	32,039,458	30,943,153	29,059,876
Total Liabilities	31,585,045	37,157,759	40,581,885	39,194,207	42,470,220
Net Assets	53,202,793	51,972,653	53,944,880	55,607,395	59,523,197
Total Liabilities & Net Assets	$84,787,838	$89,130,412	$94,526,765	$94,801,602	$101,993,417

FIGURE 1.5   Primary Government Balance Sheets for Company 3

company is clean. A "clean" set of financial statements indicates that the financial information of the company is free from material misstatements and free from fraudulent transactions. To ensure that Company 4 is a suitable benchmark for comparison, the company is a publicly traded entity with

	YR 1	YR 2	YR 3	YR 4	YR 5
Assets					
Cash	$ 2,305,503	$ 3,073,334	$ 2,134,862	$ 816,508	$ 594,169
Investments	2,839,407	6,688,938	5,174,742	532,041	284,067
Accounts Receivable	4,514,877	4,966,972	5,060,185	5,373,058	5,679,331
Due from Other Funds	3,288,257	3,924,350	4,719,495	7,739,995	9,472,608
Inventory	23,331	38,520	20,316	48,458	60,221
Prepaid Expenses	140,855	146,444	166,472	53,949	57,488
Total Current Assets	13,112,230	18,838,558	17,276,072	14,564,009	16,147,884
Notes Receivable	67,528	38,837	33,202	10,368	7,726
Total Assets	$13,179,758	$18,877,395	$17,309,274	$14,574,377	$16,155,610
Liabilities					
Accounts Payable	$ 298,718	$ 297,522	$ 899,478	$ 450,921	$ 295,905
Accrued Liabilities	323,311	377,450	404,528	522,458	597,552
Due to Other Funds	2,328,257	3,404,495	4,234,495	7,434,497	8,908,530
Total Current Liabilties	2,950,286	4,079,467	5,538,501	8,407,876	9,801,987
Deferred Revenues	3,359,531	3,659,683	3,732,514	3,777,793	3,926,262
Total Liabilities	6,309,817	7,739,150	9,271,015	12,185,669	13,728,249
Total Fund Balances	6,869,941	11,138,245	8,038,259	2,388,708	2,427,361
Total Liabilities & Fund Balances	$13,179,758	$18,877,395	$17,309,274	$14,574,377	$16,155,610

FIGURE 1.6 Governmental Funds Balance Sheets for Company 3

audited financial statements and subjected to the requirements of the Sarbanes-Oxley Act of 2002, meaning that the internal controls of the company are tested not only for the effectiveness of design, but also for operating effectiveness. The financial statements presented for comparison contained no material weaknesses or significant control deficiencies in the years tested.

Herein lies a lesson for the financial forensic examiner: *Results of analytical testing must be applied to benchmarks for concluding on the testing.*

	YR 1	YR 2	YR 3	YR 4	YR 5
Revenues					
Charges for Services	$6,084,880	$5,704,315	$6,139,777	$5,828,204	$6,923,015
Taxes	9,129,602	10,461,415	10,500,843	10,073,437	10,603,535
Interest Income	577,099	410,530	370,676	149,676	86,778
Other Revenues	869,006	403,249	494,776	1,347,473	700,999
Transfer from Private Trust Fund	—	—	—	—	200,000
Grants & Contributions	30,421	69,478	2,463,413	1,183,513	3,341,682
Total Revenues	16,691,008	17,048,987	19,969,485	18,582,303	21,856,009
Expenses					
General & Administrative	10,488,090	13,021,732	13,080,004	11,560,648	12,360,554
Depreciation Expense	3,702,017	3,966,022	4,333,368	4,810,923	5,303,901
Interest Expense	93,559	410,930	583,886	548,217	275,752
Total Expenses	14,283,666	17,398,684	17,997,258	16,919,788	17,940,207
Change in Net Assets	$2,407,342	$ (349,697)	$1,972,227	$1,662,515	$3,915,802

FIGURE 1.7   Primary Government Income Statements for Company 3

Company 4 is a C-corporation with consolidated subsidiaries, including foreign subsidiaries. For future reference, the notes to the financial statements included these comments:

▪ The external auditor issued a going-concern opinion in YR 1.
▪ The subsidiary (not one of the foreign subsidiaries) filed for liquidation in YR 3.
▪ Trustee's final report for the subsidiary's liquidation approved the liquidation in YR 4 and allowed the company to deconsolidate the subsidiary from the financial statements with a non-cash gain.
▪ The effective tax rate increased in YR 5 from an average over the prior years of 10.5 to 36.3%.

Company 4 is an industry leader in a specialized market manufacturing specific types of products for sale. In contrast to Company 2, Company 4 has a large customer base, using a network of domestic and foreign independent

	YR 1	YR 2	YR 3	YR 4	YR 5
Revenues					
Charges for Services	$ 431,025	$ 453,688	$ 446,319	$ 453,633	$ 428,142
Taxes	3,137,291	3,339,281	3,524,222	3,716,189	3,756,412
Licenses, Permits, Fees	283,344	281,260	266,924	270,910	282,192
Fines & Penalties	159,788	181,919	148,360	159,894	129,461
Other Revenues	620,379	537,394	667,642	1,306,048	614,931
Intergovernmental Revenues	6,493,027	7,191,612	9,440,034	6,507,210	8,333,667
Total Revenues	11,124,854	11,985,154	14,493,501	12,413,884	13,544,805
Expenses					
General & Administrative	7,398,658	9,123,875	8,625,966	9,738,780	9,736,115
Pension and SS Payments	970,971	1,012,097	1,042,311	1,109,795	1,123,927
Capital Outlay	5,171,038	6,032,238	8,645,654	7,634,565	5,376,412
Debt Service	623,000	397,000	691,000	647,000	1,154,666
Interest Expense	375,710	346,640	523,556	558,295	264,032
Total Expenses	14,539,377	16,911,850	19,528,487	19,688,435	17,655,152
Excess (Deficiency)	(3,414,523)	(4,926,696)	(5,034,986)	(7,274,551)	(4,110,347)
Operating Transfers In	6,350,000	7,815,000	7,341,000	5,935,000	6,479,000
Bond Proceeds	—	6,500,000	—	—	1,679,000
Operating Transfers Out	4,753,000	5,120,000	5,406,000	4,310,000	4,009,000
Changes in Fund Balance	$(1,817,523)	$4,268,304	$(3,099,986)	$(5,649,551)	$ 38,653

FIGURE 1.8   Governmental Funds Income Statements for Company 3

distributors. Since the consolidated financial statements included the consolidation of foreign subsidiaries, both the balance sheets and the income statements of these subsidiaries required conversion to the functional currency of U.S. dollars. The equity section of the balance sheet shows the effect of this currency translation.

Figure 1.9 shows the condensed balance sheets for Company 4 and Figure 1.10 illustrates the condensed income statements for the company.

(in thousands)	YR 1	YR 2	YR 3	YR 4	YR 5
Assets					
Cash	$ 5,240	$ 2,812	$ 6,147	$ 8,204	$ 23,282
Accounts Receivable	39,052	50,452	67,626	86,674	68,675
Allowance for Bad Debts	(1,062)	(1,116)	(1,834)	(2,488)	(1,640)
Inventory	26,715	34,994	38,318	43,155	39,313
Prepaid Expenses	1,783	1,525	739	2,079	1,775
Total Current Assets	71,728	88,667	110,996	137,624	131,405
Other Assets	39,113	20,393	16,131	32,281	23,830
Fixed Assets (net)	20,977	18,762	17,443	27,527	33,807
Total Assets	$131,818	$127,822	$144,570	$197,432	$189,042
Liabilities					
Accounts Payable	$ 34,164	$ 36,224	$ 45,352	$ 58,620	$ 39,926
Other Liabilities	37,680	18,416	16,065	13,269	10,623
Current Portion of Debt	2,050	2,052	1,595	1,623	1,802
Total Current Liabilities	73,894	56,692	63,012	73,512	52,351
Notes Payable	29,927	24,345	16,803	10,537	4,203
Total Liabilities	$103,821	$ 81,037	$ 79,815	$ 84,049	$ 56,554
Shareholders Equity	27,997	46,785	64,755	1,13,383	1,32,488
Total Liabilities & SE	$131,818	$127,822	$144,570	$197,432	$189,042

FIGURE 1.9 Condensed Balance Sheets for Company 4

Based on the general information of each company, the following characteristics apply:

- Company 1 did not provide financial information for any type of review, nor were they audited.
- Company 1 and Company 2 did not calculate cash flow statements.
- Company 2 had an independent review of financial information.
- Company 3 provided only the required cash flow statements at the business-activities level only.
- Company 3 had financial statements audited by an external auditor.

(in thousands)	YR 1	YR 2	YR 3	YR 4	YR 5
Revenues					
Sales	$205,996	$236,308	$351,884	$409,421	$400,032
Less Cost of Sales	179,008	205,021	301,943	349,639	343,885
Gross Profit	26,988	31,287	49,941	59,782	56,147
Expenses					
General & Administrative	13,841	15,812	21,533	24,229	23,971
Depreciation	3,570	3,092	2,760	2,608	3,134
Other Expense	6,291	4,657	4,012	3,518	3,392
Income Tax Expense	1,216	740	2,936	2,454	9,319
Total Expenses	24,918	24,301	31,241	32,809	39,816
Misc Income	(16,223)	(1,511)	(114)	18,370	-
Net Profit (Loss)	$(14,153)	$ 5,475	$ 18,586	$ 45,343	$ 16,331

FIGURE 1.10 Condensed Income Statements for Company 4

- Company 1 and Company 3 did not have appropriate segregation of duties.
- Company 2 represents inherent risks in a weak internal control structure.
- Company 3 poses the question of appropriate governance and oversight.
- Company 4 is a benchmark for comparing the analyses of the other companies.

SUMMARY

The basic information for the various entities forms the foundation for the analytical techniques used throughout the following chapters. These techniques provide the financial forensic examiner with a roadmap of where anomalies exist in the financial information that may indicate possible fraudulent activity. These tools, by themselves, are not sufficient evidence for prosecution but allow the financial forensic examiner to focus further investigative work in specific areas, allowing the financial forensic examiner to be both efficient and effective in the investigative process. From the perspective of a reader and user of financial statements, the tools provide insight to prepared financial statements presented for review. These tools may indicate that additional information or explanation may be required for certain areas of the financial statements.

Not every investigation requires all of the analytical tools discussed within these chapters; therefore, the financial forensic examiner can be selective and tailor the tools and techniques to meet the needs of the engagement. Applying the results of these tests to benchmarks is a requirement for interpreting the results of these tests. Visual aids give a clearer picture of the test results compared to just using the numbers and are often needed in presenting case information to juries. The benefits of visual aids will become quite apparent as the various tools and techniques are applied to the case studies in the following chapters.

The next chapter focuses on common preliminary analytics and preliminary forensic analytics applied to each of the companies' financial information.

CHAPTER TWO

The "Norm" and the "Forensic" Preliminary Analytics

Basics Everyone Should Know

A S DISCUSSED in the previous chapter, analytical tools reveal anomalies in financial statement information that may indicate possible fraudulent transactions that will require the use of further investigative techniques to provide detailed evidence required for prosecution. Some of the more basic preliminary analytics that almost everyone is familiar with include *liquidity-to-debt ratios, profitability ratios,* and *horizontal analysis* of accounts by comparing current-year results to prior-year results. A less recognized tool, *vertical analysis,* is extremely important in understanding account relationships. These basic tools allow the forensic financial examiner to focus on *big-picture concepts* before applying more enhanced analytical tools and techniques that drill down to specific areas for detailed investigation. When using Excel for calculating formulas, remember to use the "evaluate formula" function to make certain that the calculations are correct when numbers are negative.

One noteworthy item for the financial forensic examiner to remember is that sometimes the financial statements do not contain all of the financial transactions of the company. As in the case of Company 1 and Company 3, the transactions of the off-book bank accounts in the companies' names are not part of the financial transactions provided for examination. In addition, not all analytical tests will be applicable for every engagement, so choose techniques that meet the needs of the engagement and remember to apply the results of the tests to benchmarks of similar companies.

Also noted in the previous chapter, Company 2 used basic liquidity ratios in its annual compilations, and these were not successful in uncovering the fraudulent transactions in the financial statements. Originally developed by lenders emphasizing the importance of collateral, capacity, and a company's ability to pay off its debt, these ratios by themselves are seldom sufficient for forensic investigations, but provide the financial forensic examiner with basic concepts of the financial operations of the company. Because ratios alone are seldom sufficient for a complete forensic analysis, indices that calculate changes from period to period are better choices for more advanced forensic techniques.

Since these basic tools tend to be more unpredictable in forensic investigations, they require additional examination with a forensic preliminary analytic such as vertical analysis, and then the more advanced forensic tools and techniques provided in future chapters. The use of various benchmarks from similar companies found in assorted publications will provide more substance to the basic preliminary analytics, as well as using visual aids to enhance interpretations of the outcomes of the tests.

Even though these are basic tools, as the studies continue, the financial forensic examiner should pay particular attention to the following signs:

- Abnormal profitability when similar companies are not making profits within the same parameters
- Recurring negative cash flows from operations while reporting earnings and growth
- Abnormal growth in days sales in receivables when compared to benchmarks of similar companies
- Abnormal increase in growth of profit margins
- The growth in profit margins that are in excess of industry standards
- Unusual account relationships

 ## LIQUIDITY RATIOS

The liquidity ratios focused on in this section include *working capital*, *working capital index*, *working capital turnover*, and the *current ratio*. Since these ratios focus on a company's ability to pay its debt, companies may have to meet debt covenants' required calculations to prevent the debt from becoming due immediately; therefore, these ratios should interest anyone analyzing financial information when concerned about debt. These are of particular interest to a forensic investigation relating to financial statement presentation, especially when a company must meet debt covenants annually.

The liquidity ratios listed next provide additional insight to the financial forensic examiner relating to the operations of a company.

Working Capital

Current Assets minus Current Liabilities

$$(CA - CL)$$

Working capital is a measure of both a company's efficiency and its short-term health. A company uses working capital to pay off its short-term liabilities, which provides insight to the company's operations. If, over a period of time, the working capital ratio declines, further analysis is required. The company may have both decreasing sales and decreasing accounts receivable, or it may have excess inventory and/or slow collections. Decreases in working capital from one period to another may signal underlying problems in its operations.

The working capital index is a method of analyzing working capital from period to period and follows working capital.

Working Capital Index

Current Year Working Capital minus Prior Year Working Capital

$$(CY\ WC - PY\ WC)$$

The working capital index is a means of comparing changes in working capital from one period to another. In view of the fact that working capital relates to both current assets and current liabilities, the working capital index is a means of measuring the changes in these items from year to year, which is a more appropriate forensic tool compared to the other liquidity ratios. The working capital index works similarly to working capital. Decreases from one year to another may indicate an underlying problem in the company's operations.

Working Capital Turnover

Net Sales divided by (Current Assets minus Current Liabilities)

$$Net\ S \div (CA - CL)\ or\ Net\ S \div WC$$

Working capital turnover shows how a company is using its working capital to fund operations and the sales generated from these operations. Generally, larger values are desirable, so a financial forensic examiner should pay special attention to significant increases that occur from one period to another since they could be a symptom of revenue-related fraud. Benchmarks from similar companies, along with other forensic analyses, provide comparisons so that judgment alone does not determine the "significant increase."

Current Ratio

Current Assets divided by Current Liabilities

$$CA \div CL$$

The current ratio measures the ability of a company to pay back its short-term liabilities and, in a sense, the effectiveness of the company's operating cycle. Financing obtained by a company that requires it to maintain certain covenants often has this ratio stipulated as part of the requirements that a company must maintain. A current ratio *less than 1* suggests that a company would not be able to pay off its obligations if they came due at that point in time and is considered to be a sign of a company's poor financial health. It would be in the best interest of the company to maintain a current ratio of at least 1. Because operations differ between industries, a financial forensic examiner must apply benchmarks of similar companies for proper analysis.

 ## CASE STUDIES: LIQUIDITY RATIOS

The working capitals calculated for each company from the financial information found in Chapter 1 follow. For presentation purposes, Company 3 working capital calculations are for the primary government financial statements only, since this presentation is full-accrual and records the debt of the governmental entity. Later in the chapter, the studies will include both the primary government and the fund financial statements. Table 2.1 illustrates the working capital calculations for each company.

TABLE 2.1 Working Capital Calculations

	YR 1	YR 2	YR 3	YR 4	YR 5
Company 1	$ 18,944	$ 14,928	$ 28,066	$ 26,495	$ 12,398
Company 2	2,305,033	4,165,865	4,168,074	5,613,735	6,503,755
Company 3	13,885,442	14,461,681	10,577,714	4,424,252	456,226
Company 4	−2,166,000	31,975,000	47,984,000	64,112,000	79,054,000

From the calculations for the companies, Company 1 appears to be inconsistent in its ability to manage operations effectively, since working capital amounts are fluctuating from year to year. Company 2 seems as though management is effectively managing the operations of the company. Company 3 seems to be facing financial trouble, as the working capital is decreasing from year to year, showing a significant decrease in the fifth year of operations. Company 4 looks as though management is solving its operational issues since the working capital calculations are increasing from year to year.

Building a forensic analytical conclusion from these calculations is premature, but Company 1 and Company 3 stands out as having operational issues since working capital is either fluctuating or decreasing over time. Both Company 2 and Company 4 appear to be managing operations effectively, but remember, Company 2's financial statements were riddled with fraudulent transactions covering up an embezzlement that continued throughout the years under study. Therefore, a more appropriate way to measure these differences would be to use the working capital index calculations shown in Table 2.2.

TABLE 2.2 Working Capital Index Calculations

	YR 2	YR 3	YR 4	YR 5
Company 1	$ −4,016	$ 13,138	$ −1,571	$ −14,097
Company 2	1,860,832	2,209	1,445,662	890,020
Company 3	576,239	−3,883,967	−6,153,462	−3,968,026
Company 4	34,141,000	16,009,000	16,128,000	14,952,000

Since the working capital indices' calculations must use prior-year numbers and the case studies are for a five-year period, these indices cover a four-year period. As discussed in Chapter 1, Company 4 was experiencing financial difficulties in YR 1 and the auditor's opinion expressed a going-concern issue, so anyone reviewing these indices should expect a significant change in YR 2 if the company were to stay in operations. The indices for Company 1, Company 2, and Company 3 follow the same patterns as the working capital calculations.

The working capital turnover calculations, although not indices, do provide some valuable information relating to the management of inventory and accounts receivable and are useful in preliminary analysis related to possible revenue-related fraud. Remember that this calculation is a very basic tool, and more advanced analytical procedures are necessary if the preliminary analysis indicates peculiarities in the financial information. Table 2.3 illustrates the working capital turnover calculations for the four companies.

TABLE 2.3 Working Capital Turnover Calculations

	YR 1	YR 2	YR 3	YR 4	YR 5
Company 1	6.95	8.16	4.66	4.84	11.17
Company 2	4.75	6.77	9.65	6.91	4.67
Company 3	1.20	1.18	1.89	4.20	5.58
Company 4	95.10	7.39	7.33	6.39	5.06

Once again, the variance in Company 4 is easy to deduce from the preceding comments related to the going-concern issues. Thus far, Company 1 still exhibits fluctuations in the calculations from year to year with a significant increase from YR 4 to YR 5, but Company 3 is now showing increases from year to year. Once more, Company 2 is showing oscillation from year to year similar to the working capital index calculations. Of these calculations, the increases in Company 3, especially from YR 3 to YR 4, are significant changes when compared to decreases in both working capital and working capital indices.

The final liquidity ratio calculations are the calculations related to the current ratio, which generally tells an analyst whether a company is able to pay off its debt should it become due. Generally, as long as the calculation equals at least 1, investors and financial analysts consider that a company is able to pay off its debt when it becomes due. One problem relating to the current ratio is associated with the timing in recording the transactions, especially with end-of-month transactions, whereby the current ratio may provide inaccurate information.

The results of the current ratio calculations should be a concern for the financial forensic examiner if other liquidity studies suggest a different pattern. Table 2.4 illustrates the current ratio calculations for the four companies.

For the first time, the calculations for Company 4 are not excessive or significantly different when compared to the other companies. Company 1 is

TABLE 2.4 Current Ratio Calculations

	YR 1	YR 2	YR 3	YR 4	YR 5
Company 1	2.51	2.41	6.15	4.47	2.19
Company 2	2.90	2.34	3.12	3.71	4.59
Company 3	5.95	4.37	3.39	2.08	1.05
Company 4	.97	1.56	1.76	1.87	2.51

still showing variations from year to year, whereas Company 3 is showing decreases from year to year. Company 2 is showing increases from year to year. The liquidity ratios indicate the following patterns for each company:

- Company 1 shows significant variations from year to year in all of the liquidity ratios.
- Company 2 shows increases in both the working capital calculations and the current ratio calculations while showing variations in both the working capital index and the working capital turnover.
- In essence, Company 3 shows decreases in the working capital calculations, the working capital index, except for YR 5, and the current ratio calculations while showing significant increases in the working capital turnover from YR 3 to YR 4.
- Company 4 shows increases from year to year in the current ratio calculations and working capital. The cause of the significant flux in the working capital index is explainable. Otherwise, Company 4 had decreases from year to year in working capital turnover while the current ratio increased, indicating increased liquidity as issues related to the bankrupt subsidiary disappeared.

The liquidity ratios are just the first step in performing preliminary analytical procedures in analyzing financial statements. Profitability ratios are the required second step in preliminary analytical testing. The following section provides facts relating to profitability ratios.

 ## PROFITABILITY RATIOS

The profitability ratios focused on here include *gross profit, gross margin, stock sales,* and *return on equity.* These are the more common ratios used in financial analysis, given that these ratios measure the ability of a company to make a profit. Generally, a company wants these ratios to have higher values, representing that the company is doing well. For an efficient analysis, though, it is important to remember that some companies experience seasonality in their revenues, so comparing the same time frame from year to year would provide more useful information for the analyst than comparing different time frames that introduce seasonality in the analytics. The definitions and formulas for the profitability ratios follow.

Gross Profit

$$\text{Sales minus Cost of Sales}$$
$$S - COS$$

Gross profit measures how efficiently a company uses both labor and supplies in the production process. Likewise, gross profit is the measurement of a company's profit after deducting the costs associated with the production of the sales item. In addition, it provides management a tool to determine the financial success of its products. When prepared using general accepted accounting principles (GAAP), the income statement shows the gross profit of a company. Furthermore, gross profit is a very important component of the calculation of the gross profit margin as shown next.

Gross Profit Margin

$$\text{(Sales minus Cost of Sales) divided by Sales}$$
$$S - COS \div S$$

While gross profit measures the efficiency of a company's use of both labor and supplies in the production process, the gross profit margin assesses the financial health of a company and is an important measure for investors and potential investors. If a company is being efficient and managing its resources effectively, the gross profit margin will remain comparatively stable over time, or increase as the company gains efficiencies in the production process or adds additional sales products. Significant changes or variations in this ratio may indicate potential fraud or accounting irregularities.

Stock Sales

$$\text{Ending Inventory divided by Net Sales}$$
$$EI \div S$$

The stock sales ratio is a means of determining the efficiency of a company in maintaining its inventory and a quick-and-easy way to look at recent changes in inventory levels. For the financial forensic examiner, the movement of this ratio is important in view of the fact that increases in this ratio indicate either that inventory is growing more rapidly than sales or that sales are dropping. Likewise, a decrease in this ratio indicates either that inventory is shrinking in relation to sales or that sales are increasing without a corresponding increase in inventory.

Return on Equity

Net Income divided by ((Beginning Shareholder Equity + Ending Shareholder Equity) divided by 2)

$$NI \div ((Beginning\ SE + Ending\ SE) \div 2)$$

Or

Net Income divided by Shareholder Equity

$$NI \div SE$$

Based on numerous articles and books relating to financial ratios, the return on equity ratio may be calculated by either method noted and still be appropriate for financial analysis. Some variations exclude preferred dividends as well. This ratio measures a company's profits with monies invested from shareholders; in general, the higher the better, especially when compared to its competitors. Investors use this tool frequently to measure the worth of their investments in companies, so a company wants to maintain a higher return on equity. A company wants to make sure that its investors realize that their monies are being used effectively and not being squandered.

CASE STUDIES: PROFITABILITY RATIOS

The profitability ratios calculated for each company are from the financial information found in Chapter 1. For presentation purposes, Company 3 profitability ratio calculations are for the primary government financial statements only, since this presentation is full-accrual and provides total revenues and expenses. Since governmental entities do not have "gross profit" per se, the calculations in Table 2.5 come from total sales less grant revenues minus general and administrative expenses, which will be sufficient for the calculations of the profitability ratios. Table 2.5 illustrates the gross profit calculations, the first of the profitability ratios.

TABLE 2.5 Gross Profit

	YR 1	YR 2	YR 3	YR 4	YR 5
Company 1	$ 131,687	$ 101,450	$ 107,496	$ 112,300	$ 129,635
Company 2	2,213,076	4,875,447	7,132,823	7,509,608	5,784,569
Company 3	6,172,497	3,957,777	4,426,068	5,838,142	6,153,773
Company 4	26,988,000	31,287,000	49,941,000	59,782,000	56,147,000

Company 1's gross profit varies from year to year, decreasing in YR 2 and then increasing for the other years. Since Company 1 is a service company, the expenses allocated to cost of sales was actually salaries of the employees in advertising sales. Since there was no employee turnover during the time under investigation, gross profits should remain comparatively stable with only small changes related to increases in salaries. The gross profit for Company 2 increases until YR 5, when it decreases but is still higher when compared to YR 1 and YR 2, whereas Company 4 follows the same trend except that the decrease in YR 5 is still higher when compared to YR 1, YR 2, and YR 3. Company 3 is the only company whose gross profits increase each year, beginning from YR 2.

These calculations imply that Company 1 is either inefficient or its products were not successful in the market, whereas Company 3 is quite efficient and its services are financially successful. Since the gross profits of Company 1 are unrelated to the production of products, the financial forensic examiner may not analyze its gross profit in those terms. Knowing that both Company 2 and Company 4 produce specific products for a selected group of customers, the increases point to efficiency and financial success of their products even though both companies saw declines in YR 5.

Table 2.6, showing the gross profit margin calculations, measures the financial health of each company and should have results comparable to the gross profit calculations.

TABLE 2.6 Gross Profit Margin Calculations

	YR 1	YR 2	YR 3	YR 4	YR 5
Company 1	.91	.83	.82	.87	.94
Company 2	.20	.17	.18	.19	.19
Company 3	.37	.23	.22	.31	.28
Company 4	.13	.13	.14	.15	.14

Knowing that if management is running a company efficiently and effectively the gross margin will change very little over time, the variations for both Company 2 and Company 4 suggest that management is doing all the right things and the companies are in good financial health. On the other hand, the calculations for the other companies show greater variations, suggesting that management is not doing a good job of running the company, which seems contradictory to the gross margin calculations in Table 2.5.

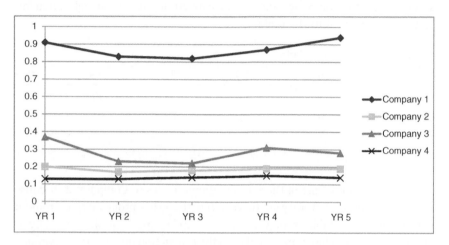

FIGURE 2.1 Gross Margin Profit Calculations

The variations in the gross profit margin calculations seem minor when looking at each individual number, but using a visual aid such as the graph in Figure 2.1 will better point out the variations from year to year.

When presenting the gross profit margin calculations using a visual aid, the changes in Company 2 appear a bit more dramatic when compared to Company 4, particularly in the first three years under study. Sometimes the most effective tool to use in analyzing data is a visual aid. Another interesting aspect of this particular visual aid is the ability to see the significance of the variances by the slopes of the lines from one year to the other. Those experienced in testifying understand that "a picture is worth a thousand words." For the financial forensic examiner, the use of visual aids assists in reaching a proper conclusion to the analytical testing.

Along with the gross profit margin calculations, the stock sales ratio may provide more insight into a company's operations and, indirectly, the cost of goods sold component of the gross profit calculations. One of the basic components of cost of sales includes beginning inventory, the addition of purchases and costs associated with the purchases, and the subtraction of ending inventory. This is one area where possible fraudulent activity may occur, especially if fictitious entries put into the inventory financial information reduce the expenses of cost of sales. Table 2.7 provides the results of the stock sales ratio calculations for the four companies under study. For Company 3, the calculation of the stock sales ratio uses only the revenue account charges for services revenue. Company 1 did not have inventory in its financial statement, so it is not included in the table.

TABLE 2.7 Stock Sales Ratios

	YR 1	YR 2	YR 3	YR 4	YR 5
Company 2	.17	.14	.08	.10	.17
Company 3	.03	.03	.02	.03	.03
Company 4	.13	.15	.11	.11	.10

The interesting part of these calculations relates to Company 2, because the stock sales vary from year to year but the gross profit margins remain somewhat more stable from year to year, indicating that the company is efficient in its use of labor and supplies in the production process. Has a paradox been exposed? This is a question for the financial forensic examiner to answer. Remember also that decreases from year to year indicate either increasing sales or shrinking inventory, whereas increases suggest decreased sales or increasing inventory. Company 3 remains comparatively stable from year to year, along with Company 4.

One last profitability ratio to be calculated is the return-on-equity ratio that measures a company's profit with its shareholders' (investors') monies. These calculations use the more simplified version discussed previously: $NI \div SE$ Table 2.8 illustrates the results of these calculations for the four companies.

TABLE 2.8 Return on Equity

	YR 1	YR 2	YR 3	YR 4	YR 5
Company 1	.18	−.19	.01	−.04	−.16
Company 2	.07	.21	.30	.30	.17
Company 3	.05	−.01	.04	.03	.07
Company 4	−.51	.12	.29	.40	.12

Company 4 demonstrates the classic example of knowing when to apply and when not to apply an analytical technique established during those preliminary discussions with management providing knowledge of the overall company operations. Chapter 1 revealed that Company 4 is a consolidated entity with foreign subsidiaries, and those financial statements require conversion to the functional currency of U.S. dollars. Because a component of stockholders' equity reflects these adjustments, the results of the foreign currency translation adjustments distort the return-on-equity calculations unless removed from the calculations. The return-on-equity calculations for the other companies are not surprising and follow similar trends of the other calculations.

Before beginning discussions related to the study of horizontal and vertical analyses, the profitability ratios indicated the following patterns for each company:

■ Calculations for Company 1 consistently indicate variations from year to year.
■ The stock sales ratio for Company 2 is inconsistent with the other calculations.
■ The calculations for Company 3 follow similar trends and patterns.
■ With the exception of the return-on-equity calculations already discussed, the other calculations for Company 4 are reasonably consistent.

While the liquidity and the profitability ratio findings follow individually in the preceding paragraphs, a prudent financial forensic examiner will combine those findings to search for universal trends that require additional examination. The following sections summarize the combined findings for each company.

Company 1

■ Working capital calculations vary from year to year with decreases from YR 1 to YR 2 and YR 3 through YR 5 and an increase from YR 2 to YR 3.
■ Working capital index increases from YR 2 to YR 3, with decreases from YR 3 through YR 5.
■ Working capital turnover increases from YR 1 to YR 2 and again from YR 3 through YR 5, with a decrease from YR 2 to YR 3.
■ Current ratios decrease from YR 1 to YR 2 and again from YR 3 through YR 5 while increasing from YR 2 to YR 3.

- Gross profit decreases from YR 1 to YR 2, with increases from YR 3 through YR 5.
- Gross profit margins decrease from YR 1 through YR 3 and increase from YR 4 through YR 5.
- The company records no inventory.
- Return-on-equity decreases from YR 1 to YR 2, increases from YR 2 to YR 3, and then decreases from YR 3 through YR 5.

Analyzing the information by the above method makes it difficult to follow all of the changes. Figure 2.2 shows a better method for analyzing all of the pieces of the puzzle that have been examined thus far.

Using "+" for increases, "=" for no change, and "−" for decreases, the chart not only makes the changes easy to see, it also provides an enhanced view of the relationships that become very important to the financial forensic examiner. Noteworthy items in the chart include the changes and relationships from YR 3 to YR 4 and from YR 4 to YR 5 with gross profit and gross profit margins increasing while working capital and the current ratios are decreasing. Since inventory is not a factor in the working capital (current assets minus current liabilities), the driving force for these changes relates to either cash, accounts receivable, or accounts payable.

From the information relating to the balance sheet of Company 1 in Figure 1.1, from YR 3 to YR 4 cash decreased, accounts receivable increased, and accounts payable increased, logically explaining the differences. Yet from

	From YR 1 to YR 2	From YR 2 to YR 3	From YR 3 to YR 4	From YR 4 to YR 5
Working Capital	−	+	−	−
Working Capital Index	n/a	+	−	−
Working Capital Turnover	+	−	+	+
Current Ratio	−	+	−	−
Gross Profit	−	+	+	+
Gross Profit Margin	−	−	+	+
Stock Sales Ratio	n/a	n/a	n/a	n/a
Return on Equity	−	+	−	−

FIGURE 2.2 Company 1 Testing Results

YR 4 to YR 5, when gross profits and gross profit margins increased, cash and accounts receivable decreased while accounts payable increased. To bring the pieces of the puzzle together, the financial forensic examiner should also review the drivers of the gross profit and gross profit margins, sales and cost of sales, for the same period. From YR 3 to YR 4 sales decreased, but so did cost of sales. From YR 4 to YR 5 sales increased while cost of sales continued to decrease.

Using the big-picture concept in exploring the changes, the financial forensic examiner is able to begin putting the outside-edge pieces of the puzzle in place. In YR 4 sales increased, accounts receivable decreased, cash decreased, and cost of sales decreased, making the relationships mismatched. These changes will be more apparent once the horizontal and the vertical analyses are completed.

Moving on to Company 2, Figure 2.3 provides the testing results for Company 2.

	From YR 1 to YR 2	From YR 2 to YR 3	From YR 3 to YR 4	From YR 4 to YR 5
Working Capital	+	+	+	+
Working Capital Index	n/a	−	+	−
Working Capital Turnover	+	+	−	−
Current Ratio	−	+	+	+
Gross Profit	+	+	+	−
Gross Profit Margin	−	+	+	=
Stock Sales Ratio	=	−	+	=
Return on Equity	+	+	=	−

FIGURE 2.3   Company 2 Testing Results

Studies of the basic relationships for the preliminary analytical studies of the liquidity and profitability ratios will be included in the review of both the horizontal and vertical analyses, since the balance sheet for this company is more complex than the balance sheet of Company 1. Nonetheless, the question relating to stock sales and gross profit, especially for the changes from YR 3 through YR 5, requires additional study. Remember that increases in the stock sales ratio indicate that either inventory is increasing or sales are decreasing. Looking at Figure 1.3, inventory increased from YR 3 throughout YR 5, and Figure 1.4 also shows sales decreasing during the same period, suggesting that management may not be effectively managing its inventory or using the higher inventory values to manage its working capital and current ratios.

Since this question arose in the analyses of the profitability ratios, the answers become more apparent when using a graph to picture the movements of the items in question. Figure 2.4 shows the relationship between the gross profit margin calculations and the stock sales ratios.

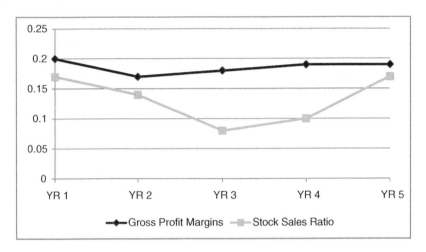

FIGURE 2.4   Company 2 Profitability Ratio Inconsistency

From the graphical representation, the changes from YR 1 to YR 2 look as if they are comparable; even the lines in the chart appear to be parallel at this point. On the other hand, the changes from YR 2 through YR 5 show movement in different directions with increases in gross profit margins and decreases in the stock sales ratios. At the same time, the gross profit margin lines show seemingly reasonable changes with greater variations in the stock sales ratio. Seeing the results of combing and reviewing two different analytical tests that show indications of divergence, the financial forensic examiner needs to do a more detailed analysis of the components of the gross margin calculations, both sales and cost of sales.

Figure 2.5 provides the combined analysis for Company 3.

Probably the most apparent result in the figure relates to the changes in working capital and the current ratio, since both of these decreases from YR 2 through YR 5. These decreases indicate that the government has some serious concerns with its ability to continue operations under the current trends.

	From YR 1 to YR 2	From YR 2 to YR 3	From YR 3 to YR 4	From YR 4 to YR 5
Working Capital	+	−	−	−
Working Capital Index	n/a	−	−	+
Working Capital Turnover	−	+	+	+
Current Ratio	−	−	−	−
Gross Profit	−	+	+	+
Gross Profit Margin	−	−	+	−
Stock Sales Ratio	=	−	+	=
Return on Equity	+	+	+	−

FIGURE 2.5   Company 3 Testing Results

Figure 2.6 illustrates the testing results for Company 4.

Since the changes from YR 1 to YR 2 recount the ability of management to turn around the company from the going-concern opinion from the external auditor in YR 1, further examination indicates that management is making determined efforts to maintain the company's momentum. Both working

	From YR 1 to YR 2	From YR 2 to YR 3	From YR 3 to YR 4	From YR 4 to YR 5
Working Capital	+	+	+	+
Working Capital Index	n/a	−	+	−
Working Capital Turnover	−	−	−	−
Current Ratio	+	+	+	+
Gross Profit	+	+	+	−
Gross Profit Margin	=	+	+	−
Stock Sales Ratio	+	−	=	−
Return on Equity	+	+	+	−

FIGURE 2.6   Company 4 Testing Results

capital and the current ratio increased from YR 2 throughout YR 5, even though gross profit and gross profit margins declined in YR 5.

Even with the calculations of these ratios complete, there is another basic preliminary test needed for all of the companies, and that is the horizontal analysis. Almost everyone is familiar with and quite often uses the horizontal analysis of financial statements. In the following section, the horizontal analysis of each company presents additional facts about each.

 ## HORIZONTAL ANALYSIS

Horizontal analysis is a common technique used by investors, auditors, financial analysts, and other interested parties to examine the changes in the line items of the balance sheet and the income statement from year to year. Often the term *trend analysis* also applies to horizontal analysis, since it presents the changes from year to year in either dollars or percentages, and either term is acceptable. Here, *horizontal analysis* is more appropriate, since the comparison calculations are shown horizontally for both the balance sheets and the income statements for each company, allowing comparison for current and past performance.

From the financial forensic examiner's perspective, using percentages to analyze the trends in the line items of the financial statements more appropriately determines changes from year to year and allows the financial forensic examiner to examine each line item of the balance sheet and income statement. For this reason, each company's horizontal analysis displays changes in percentages only and does not include the dollar amount of the changes. To calculate the percentages of changes for each line item, subtract the prior-year amount from the current-year amount and divide the outcome by the prior-year amount. Here is the equation for the calculation:

$$(CY - PY) \div PY$$

Company 1

Figure 2.7 illustrates the balance sheet horizontal analysis for Company 1, while Figure 2.8 illustrates the horizontal analysis for the income statement of Company 1.

	YR 1	YR 2		YR 3		YR 4		YR 5	
Assets									
Cash	$ 13,478	$ 1,195	-91.13%	$ 3,519	194.48%	$ 330	-90.62%	$ (5,299)	-1705.76%
Accounts Receivable	18,011	24,345	35.17%	29,994	23.20%	33,807	12.71%	28,138	-16.77%
Total Current Assets	31,489	25,540	-18.89%	33,513	31.22%	34,137	1.86%	22,839	-33.10%
Fixed Assets (net)	122,019	121,058	-0.79%	116,855	-3.47%	113,473	-2.89%	114,437	0.85%
Total Assets	$153,508	$146,598	-4.50%	$150,368	2.57%	$147,610	-1.83%	$137,276	-7.00%
Liabilities									
Accounts Payable	$ 12,545	$ 10,612	-15.41%	$ 5,447	-48.67%	$ 7,642	40.30%	$ 10,441	36.63%
Total Current Liabilities	12,545	10,612	-15.41%	5,447	-48.67%	7,642	40.30%	10,441	36.63%
Notes Payable	—	17,641		31,192	76.82%	30,554	-2.05%	32,862	7.55%
Total Liabilities	$ 12,545	$ 28,253	125.21%	$ 36,639	29.68%	$ 38,196	4.25%	$ 43,303	13.37%
Shareholders Equity	140,963	118,345	-16.05%	113,729	-3.90%	109,414	-3.79%	93,973	-14.11%
Total Liabilities & SE	$153,508	$146,598	-4.50%	$150,368	2.57%	$147,610	-1.83%	$137,276	-7.00%

FIGURE 2.7 Balance Sheet Horizontal Analysis for Company 1

	YR 1	YR 2		YR 3		YR 4		YR 5	
Sales	$145,246	$121,842	−16.11%	$130,859	7.40%	$128,344	−1.92%	$138,443	7.87%
Less Purchases	9,017	12,249	35.84%	17,248	40.81%	5,752	−66.65%	5,820	1.18%
Less Labor costs	4,542	8,143	79.28%	6,115	−24.90%	10,292	68.31%	2,988	−70.97%
Gross Profit	131,687	101,450	−22.96%	107,496	5.96%	112,300	4.47%	129,635	15.44%
Expenses									
Selling Expenses	$ 1,712	$ 2,657	55.20%	$ 2,001	−24.69%	$ 8,939	346.73%	$ 12,730	42.41%
General & Administrative	41,946	38,122	−9.12%	36,668	−3.81%	40,829	11.35%	30,378	−25.60%
Salaries	9,820	15,592	58.78%	8,266	−46.99%	4,234	−48.78%	43,490	927.16%
Repairs & Maintenance	5,842	6,453	10.46%	1,132	−82.46%	6,243	451.50%	3,603	−42.29%
Bad Debt	—	—		—				4,280	
Rent	2,976	2,000	−32.80%	5,000	150.00%	7,504	50.08%	1,615	−78.48%
Taxes & Licenses	5,937	10,312	73.69%	5,791	−43.84%	6,149	6.18%	8,284	34.72%
Insurance	2,570	7,072	175.18%	4,883	−30.95%	5,371	9.99%	5,242	−2.40%
Utilities	15,782	16,487	4.47%	16,823	2.04%	18,131	7.78%	17,177	−5.26%
Supplies	4,590	7,190	56.64%	8,368	16.38%	4,956	−40.77%	4,066	−17.96%
Depreciation	4,863	4,664	−4.09%	10,805	131.67%	5,882	−45.56%	6,831	16.13%
Accounting Fees	1,050	2,036	93.90%	1,320	−35.17%	1,470	11.36%	1,110	−24.49%
Vehicle Expense	2,291	4,929	115.15%	—	−100.00%	—		—	

Civic Donations	580	1,070	84.48%	770	-28.04%	520	-32.47%	130	-75.00%
Legal Fees	709	—	-100.00%	—		—		—	
Internet Fees	161	—	-100.00%	21		—	-100.00%	—	
Office Expenses	689	—	-100.00%	—		—		—	
Freight	78	—	-100.00%	—		22		—	-100.00%
Postage	209	—	-100.00%	244		403	65.16%	386	-4.22%
Lodging & Travel	—	—		—		300		625	108.33%
Commissions	522	—	-100.00%	54		380	603.70%	870	128.95%
Total General Expenses	100,615	115,927	15.22%	100,145	-13.61%	102,394	2.25%	128,087	25.09%
Total Expenses	102,327	118,584	15.89%	102,146	-13.86%	111,333	8.99%	140,817	26.48%
Interest Income	949	—	-100.00%	752	-7.31%	374	-50.27%	—	-100.00%
Interest Expenses	5,360	5,484	2.31%	5,083		5,656	11.27%	4,259	-24.70%
Net Profit	$ 24,949	$(22,618)	-190.66%	$ 1,019	104.51%	$ (4,315)	-523.45%	$(15,441)	-257.84%

FIGURE 2.8 Income Statement Horizontal Analysis for Company 1

In the case of Company 1, the horizontal analysis for the balance sheet shows several interesting facts when reviewing the variations year over year:

- Cash changes dramatically year over year with decreases from YR 4 to YR 5 of 1,706%.
- Accounts receivable changes fall each year, decreasing from 35% to negative 17%.
- Accounts payable fluctuates from year to year, either increasing or decreasing in significant amounts.
- The notes payable (to Shareholder 2) materializes in YR 2, and increases significantly from YR 2 to YR 3 with following changes somewhat insignificant.

Now, for the income statement horizontal analysis, remember that currently, the financial forensic examiner must focus attention on the big-picture concept and compare the changes in the income statement to the changes in the balance sheet, looking at the reasonableness of the changes. For example, if sales are decreasing, accounts receivable is decreasing, and accounts payable is increasing while expenses are decreasing, then the reasonable conclusion would be that cash is increasing. In the event that cash is decreasing as well, that is a red flag, suggesting further analysis and study.

- The changes in sales vary, so from YR 1 to YR 2 sales decrease, from YR 2 to YR 3 sales increase, from YR 3 to YR 4 sales decrease, and from YR 4 to YR 5 sales increase again.
- Selling expenses change dramatically from year to year, with the changes ranging from a negative 16% to 8%.
- General expenses change significantly from year to year, ranging from a negative 14% to 25%.
- Interest expense relates to interest paid on past-due invoices only and it varies from year to year, ranging from 11% to a negative 25%.
- Interest income is inconsistent from year to year.
- The line item detail of account balances that make up the total amount general and administrative expenses is especially interesting in that some of the line items vary significantly from year to year. One would expect these costs not to vary significantly from year to year, especially if the company records expenses consistently from year to year in the same account classifications.

To assist in developing the big-picture concepts required for this particular analysis, Figure 2.9 illustrates the changes in cash, accounts receivable,

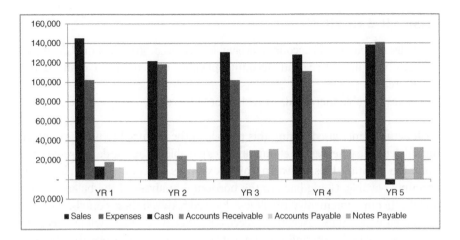

FIGURE 2.9 Big-Picture Concepts for Company 1

accounts payable, notes payable, sales, and expenses. A visual picture of account relationships is quite valuable in making preliminary judgments of areas that require additional investigative procedures as compared to listing the changes as in the noted items.

Using this technique, a financial forensic examiner can quickly determine not only the relationships associated with the income statement and the balance sheet, but also the changes within those relationships to determine if the changes are reasonable. This technique is quite useful for small companies whose financial statements are not complex. In Figure 2.9, a financial forensic examiner should note the following changes in the relationships.

From YR 1 to YR 2

- Sales decreased and accounts receivable increased, so cash should decrease.
- Expenses decreased and accounts payable decreased, so cash should decrease.
- Notes payable increased, so cash should increase.

Cash decreased, suggesting that the inflow of cash in the form of notes payable was probably necessary to improve the company's cash flow problems. Therefore, the changes in the relationships appear reasonable.

From YR 2 to YR 3

▪ Sales increased and accounts receivable increased, so cash should decrease.
▪ Expenses decreased and accounts payable decreased, so cash should decrease.
▪ Notes payable increased, so cash should increase.

Cash actually increased during this period, so the financial forensic examiner must determine whether the change in notes payable offsets the decreases in cash from the relationships between sales, expenses, accounts receivable, and accounts payable. Going back to the horizontal analyses of the balance sheet and the income statement, cash almost doubled between these periods, showing an increase of 194%. Accounts receivable increased 23%, while accounts payable decreased 49% and notes payable increased 77%. Since the changes in accounts receivable and accounts payable decrease cash, the increase in notes payable is definitely not large enough to explain the increase in cash. If you factor in the decrease changes, then the inconsistency is even greater.

The horizontal analysis for the income statement adds to the inconsistency since sales increased only 7% in comparison to the change in accounts receivable of 23%. Expenses decreased 5% while accounts payable decreased 49%, leaving a difference of 44% that would decrease cash. These changes also add to the fact that the relationships appear to be at odds with each other.

From YR 3 to YR 4

▪ Sales decreased and accounts receivable increased, so cash should decrease.
▪ Expenses increased and accounts payable increased, so cash should increase.
▪ Notes payable decreased, so cash should decrease.

Cash decreased during the period, so the primary factors relating to the decrease relate to notes payable and accounts receivable. Once again, horizontal analysis provides a way to determine whether the change in cash is reasonable. Cash decreased 91% while the decrease in notes payable was only 2%, clearly insignificant when compared to the decrease of 91% for cash. The only other factor decreasing cash is accounts receivable, which increased only 13%. Again, these changes are not consistent.

When looking at the horizontal analysis of the income statement, sales decreased only 2% while total expenses increased 22% and accounts payable increased 40%. Now, two years' worth of changes in the account relationships do not complement each another.

From YR 4 to YR 5

- Sales increased and accounts receivable increased, so cash should increase.
- Accounts payable increased, so cash should increase.
- Notes payable increased, so cash should increase.

Cash decreased during this period, which totally contradicts all of the account relationships in the balance sheet without even looking at the horizontal analysis. As for the changes in the income statement, the horizontal analysis indicates that sales increased 8% while total expenses increased 17%, with accounts payable decreasing 4%. When reviewing this information and looking at the trends presented, a financial forensic examiner should easily be able to determine the financial statement information to be contradictory.

Company 1's lack of complexity in the financial statements provides a good example for the use of a simpler analytic technique that supplies sufficient documentation of inconsistency in the financial statements. The use of more intricate techniques will supply the financial forensic examiner with a roadmap to follow for further analysis, but even the most basic of analytical tests provide the financial forensic examiner with the basic assumption that the financial information is troublesome.

In the next company, the financial forensic examiner will be able to understand why even the basic preliminary analytical techniques require minor changes to assist the financial forensic examiner with further investigative studies.

Company 2

The financial statements for Company 2 are somewhat more intricate with the addition of inventory, allowance for bad debts, and deferred income taxes, so the analytical techniques will require some fine-tuning in the preliminary stages compared to those used in the examination of Company 1's financial statements. (See Figures 2.10 and 2.11.)

Because a financial forensic examiner needs to focus on account relationships, beginning with Company 2, diagnostic trends for both the balance sheet and the income statement will center on those relationships in order to develop and enhance critical thinking skills as to how each account balance trend influences other account balance trends.

	YR 1	YR 2	%	YR 3	%	YR 4	%	YR 5	%
Assets									
Cash	$ 6,037	$ 219,408	3534.4%	$ 409,620	86.7%	$ 1615,708	294.4%	$ 866,801	−46.4%
Accounts Receivable	1,388,977	2,905,601	109.2%	2,282,772	−21.4%	2,158,034	−5.5%	2,275,985	5.5%
Allowance for Bad Debts	(1,000)	(60,000)	5900.0%	(37,172)	−38.0%	(100,000)	169.0%	(100,000)	0.0%
Refundable Income Taxes	—	—		21,205		47,000	121.6%	40,000	−14.9%
Inventory	1,866,785	3,904,040	109.1%	3,282,898	−15.9%	3,887,568	18.4%	5,159,037	32.7%
Prepaid Expenses	256,677	309,566	20.6%	176,110	−43.1%	73,826	−58.1%	75,412	2.1%
Total Current Assets	3,517,476	7,278,615	106.9%	6,135,433	−15.7%	7,682,136	25.2%	8,317,235	8.3%
Other Assets	—	—		—		—		963,459	
Fixed Assets (net)	1,786,908	2,210,753	23.7%	2,472,082	11.8%	2,501,071	1.2%	2,421,222	−3.2%
Total Assets	$ 5,304,384	$ 9,489,368	78.9%	$ 8,607,515	−9.3%	$10,183,207	18.3%	$11,701,916	14.9%
Liabilities									
Accounts Payable	$ 1,186,293	$ 2,987,894	151.9%	$ 1,902,907	−36.3%	$ 1,951,605	2.6%	$ 1,352,480	−30.7%
Deferred income taxes	—	—		—		30,000		—	−100.0%
Other Liabilities	26,150	124,856	377.5%	64,452	−48.4%	86,796	34.7%	461,000	431.1%
Total Current Liabilities	1,212,443	3,112,750	156.7%	1,967,359	−36.8%	2,068,401	5.1%	1,813,480	−12.3%
Deferred Income Taxes	488,762	873,317	78.7%	1,270,317	45.5%	424,317	−66.6%	604,000	42.3%
Notes Payable	619,508	1,719,098	177.5%	—	−100.0%	—		—	
Total Liabilities	2,320,713	5,705,165	145.8%	3,237,676	−43.3%	2,492,718	−23.0%	2,417,480	−3.0%
Stockholders Equity	2,984,671	3,784,203	26.8%	5,369,839	41.9%	7,690,489	43.2%	9,284,436	20.7%
Total Liabilities & SE	$ 5,305,384	$ 9,489,368	78.9%	$ 8,607,515	−9.3%	$10,183,207	18.3%	$11,701,916	14.9%

FIGURE 2.10 Balance Sheet Horizontal Analysis for Company 2

	YR 1	YR 2		YR 3		YR 4		YR 5	
Sales	$ 10,950,180	$ 28,188,122	157.4%	$ 40,214,834	42.7%	$ 38,780,333	-3.6%	$ 30,397,677	-21.6%
Less Cost of Goods Sold	8,737,104	23,312,675	166.8%	33,082,011	41.9%	31,270,725	-5.5%	24,613,108	-21.3%
Gross Profit	2,213,076	4,875,447	120.3%	7,132,823	46.3%	7,509,608	5.3%	5,784,569	-23.0%
Expenses									
General & Administrative	1,764,716	3,534,123	100.3%	4,555,539	28.9%	3,722,301	-18.3%	3,358,667	-9.8%
Depreciation	203,295	240,233	18.2%	306,697	27.7%	339,156	10.6%	375,978	10.9%
Income Tax Expense	162,287	523,542	222.6%	950,439	81.5%	1,313,500	38.2%	890,000	-32.2%
Total Expenses	2,130,298	4,297,898	101.8%	5,812,675	35.2%	5,374,957	-7.5%	4,624,645	-14.0%
Misc Income	117,305	221,983	89.2%	265,491	19.6%	185,999	-29.9%	434,023	133.3%
Net Profit	$ 200,083	$ 799,532	299.6%	$ 1,585,639	98.3%	$ 2,320,650	46.4%	$ 1,593,947	-31.3%

FIGURE 2.11 Income Statement Horizontal Analysis for Company 2

From YR 1 to YR 2

- Gross accounts receivable increased, so cash should decrease.
- The change in the allowance for bad debts is a non-cash transaction.
- Inventory also increased, so cash should decrease.
- Prepaid expenses increased 21%, so cash should decrease.
- Net fixed assets increased 24%, but the effect on cash may require more analysis, since both purchases and sales affect both components of the net fixed asset balance, as well as a non-cash component relating to depreciation expense and accumulated depreciation. Generally, the cash flow statement provides the detailed information of the change in cash related to fixed assets. Here, the general assumption is that cash increased.
- Accounts payable more than doubled, so cash should increase.
- Other liabilities increased 377%, so cash should increase.
- Changes in deferred taxes are non-cash transactions.
- Notes payable increased 177%, so cash should increase.
- Sales increased 157%, but although cost of sales increased 167%, gross profit increased 120%.
- All general and administrative expenses increased 102%. Both depreciation and income tax expense are non-cash transactions.

Since both cost of sales and the total other expenses increased, the increase in inventory, accounts payable, and other liabilities is reasonable. Therefore, the increase in cash is also a reasonable assumption. Since both sales and accounts receivable increased, the assumption that cash decreased is also reasonable, unless a portion of the increase in sales relates to cash payments. When looking at the increase in gross accounts receivable compared to the increase in sales, a financial forensic examiner is able to determine that part of this increase could relate to cash sales (157% –109%). Notes payable directly increases cash. Cash increased significantly and, at first glance, the increase appears reasonable.

From YR 2 to YR 3

- Gross accounts receivable decreased, so cash should increase.
- Inventory decreased, so cash should increase.
- Prepaid expenses decreased, so cash should increase.
- Fixed assets increased, so cash should decrease.
- Accounts payable and other liabilities both decreased, so cash should decrease.

- Notes payable decreased, so cash should decrease.
- Sales, cost of goods sold, and the total of general and administrative expenses all increased.

During this period, since sales increased and accounts receivable decreased, the financial forensic examiner does not need to address whether any of the sales are cash sales because the effect of decreases in accounts receivable also increases cash, just as the cash sales would. Because cost of sales increased and inventory decreased, the assumption here is that sales generated in this period consumed previously bought inventory and no additional purchases of inventory were required in the production process, so the increase in cash is a reasonable assumption. Even though general and administrative expenses increased during this period, both the decreases in accounts payable and other liabilities make up for the difference (85% − 29%), so the decrease in cash is a reasonable assumption. If the decreases in the asset accounts are greater than the decreases in the liability accounts, then an increase in cash is a reasonable assumption.

A much easier approach is to look at the changes in the current assets less cash and the allowance for bad debt compared to changes in current liabilities. Here, the decreases in the current asset totals, excluding cash and the allowance, amount to 17%, while the decreases in the current liabilities amount to 37%. Since cash increased 87%, either the changes are not congruent or something is missing from the analysis, especially since decreases in cash related to the changes in notes payable and net fixed assets are not yet accounted for in the analysis. Reviewing the income statement, the miscellaneous income increase of 20% would increase cash and this is the only other account balance missing from the analysis. At this point in the testing, the financial forensic examiner should realize that some of the account relationships are to some extent mismatched.

From YR 3 to YR 4

- Gross accounts receivable decreased, so cash should increase.
- Inventory increased, so cash should decrease.
- Prepaid expenses decreased, so cash should increase.
- Fixed assets increased, so cash should decrease.
- Both accounts payable and other liabilities increased, so cash should increase.
- Sales, cost of sales, and general and administrative expenses decreased while miscellaneous income increased.

Given that gross receivables decreased, an increase in cash is a reasonable assumption. Increases in accounts payable and other liabilities compared to decreases in general and administrative expenses and cost of sales also suggest an increase in cash. Since there are no transactions in notes payable, cash amounts neither increase nor decrease. During this time, cash increased 294%.

Since changes in the current assets are not consistent with how cash changes, the simple comparison used for the prior years is not effective because inventory increases decrease cash and a gross accounts receivable decrease increases cash. Yet, looking at Figure 2.10, the changes in the account balances do not support the significant increase in cash.

From YR 4 to YR 5

▪ Gross accounts receivable increased, so cash should decrease.
▪ Both inventory and prepaid expenses increased, so cash should decrease.
▪ Fixed assets decreased, so cash should increase.
▪ Accounts payable decreased, so cash should decrease.
▪ Other liabilities increased, so cash should increase.
▪ Sales, cost of sales, and general and administrative expenses decreased while miscellaneous income increased.

Just the simple statements above present a Catch-22 in the first round of understanding how transactions in one individual account affect another account; inventory may either increase or decrease if costs of sales decrease, depending on how much inventory stock is required for future scheduled production. When looking at the decrease for cost of sales, the decrease of 21% is not comparable to the inventory increase of 33%. The question for the financial forensic examiner then becomes defining the possibilities for this change. One plausible answer connects the difference to increases in costs for materials used in the production process; another possibility relates to the amount of inventory maintained for future scheduled production.

Using the simple approach again, since the changes are flowing in the same direction, current liabilities decreased 11% while current assets increased 23%. Cash decreased 46%, so the first round of testing is not showing obvious signs of the relationships with the account balances contrasting each other.

In all of the horizontal analysis studies, for the periods where cash changes and accounts receivable changes were somewhat mismatched, the answer lies in comments made in Chapter 1 relating to the company's customers generally paying within a 30-day time span. This practice definitely affects how the changes in gross receivables influence cash. From our studies of changes above, the questionable relationships among the account balances did not disclose anything unusual that could not be explained from materials and information provided by the company in Chapter 1.

So, have all of these studies been for naught? Maybe not, for in the horizontal analysis of the income statement there is a trend that appears unusual and is not explained; it might require looking at the information in another manner to see it, unless the financial forensic examiner is quite perceptive. Figure 2.12 provides the clues.

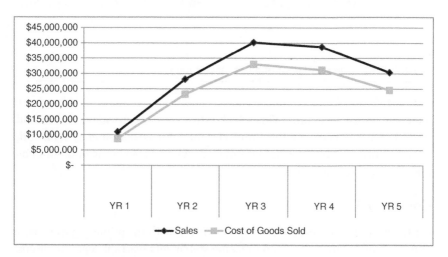

FIGURE 2.12   Sales and Cost of Sales for Company 2

In the graph, the space between sales and cost of sales is the gross profit. Our previous studies of liquidity and profitability ratios indicate that the management of Company 2 is effectively managing operations, with increases occurring in both working capital and current ratio calculations and comparatively stable gross profit margins while stock sales ratios had more variability compared to the other profitability ratios. Since the majority of these ratios were consistent and management is effectively managing the company operations, then should the lines in the graph be parallel? Figure 2.13 presents the same information for Company 4. Although there are variances in the gross profit, the lines for the sales and cost of sales correspond to each other better than the sales and cost of sales lines in Figure 2.12. Although this analysis is very basic, the studies for this company have thus far provided two clues for the

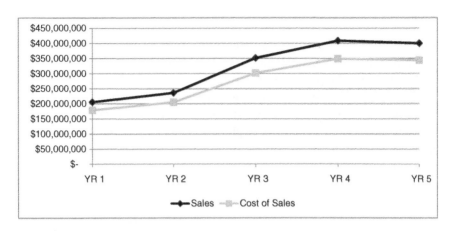

FIGURE 2.13   Sales and Cost of Sales for Company 4

financial forensic examiner: First, stock ratios are not consistent, and second, the relationship between sales and cost of sales is not similar, indicating inconsistencies in the financial information, which is obviously enough information to pursue further testing.

Company 3

For the horizontal analysis study of Company 3, both the primary government and the fund balance sheets and income statements warrant separate discussions. Since Company 3 is a governmental entity, there will be differences between the balance sheet and income statements for the primary government and fund financial statements. As discussed in Chapter 1, the primary government financial statements require full accrual presentation and inclusion of the business activities, while the fund financial statements require modified cash presentation. It is important for the financial forensic examiner to know these differences and look for variances in either of the financial statement presentations. The horizontal analyses for the primary government balance sheets and the income statements are given in Figures 2.14 and 2.15.

Although the financial statements present both cash and restricted cash, for the purposes of examining the horizontal analysis, both of these accounts are actually cash in the bank, only the restricted amount requires holding and spending the funds for the designated purpose. In the income horizontal analysis, grants and contributions generally vary from year to year and the financial forensic examiner should understand this when beginning the

	YR 1	YR 2		YR 3		YR 4		YR 5	
Assets									
Cash	$ 7,127,424	$ 5,829,038	−18.2%	$ 3,503,752	−39.9%	$ 1,282,307	−63.4%	$ 1,299,373	1.3%
Investments	3,026,409	6,883,554	127.4%	5,376,081	−21.9%	802,697	−85.1%	550,593	−31.4%
Accounts Receivable	6,193,387	5,675,948	−8.4%	5,770,644	1.7%	6,221,333	7.8%	7,481,059	20.2%
Allowance for Bad Debts	(2,500)	(2,500)	0.0%	(2,500)	0.0%	(52,500)	2000.0%	(77,500)	47.6%
Inventory	176,657	181,274	2.6%	140,525	−22.5%	148,483	5.7%	183,381	23.5%
Prepaid Expenses	172,006	181,279	5.4%	222,326	22.6%	103,951	−53.2%	104,732	0.8%
Total Current Assets	16,693,383	18,748,593	12.3%	15,010,828	−19.9%	8,506,271	−43.3%	9,541,638	12.2%
Restricted Cash	166,608	192,647	15.6%	209,721	8.9%	287,989	37.3%	289,919	0.7%
Notes Receivable	67,528	38,837	−42.5%	33,202	−14.5%	10,368	−68.8%	7,726	−25.5%
Restricted Investments	222,359	225,587	1.5%	227,670	0.9%	163,779	−28.1%	170,170	3.9%
Fixed Assets (net)	67,637,960	69,924,748	3.4%	79,045,344	13.0%	85,833,195	8.6%	91,983,964	7.2%
Total Assets	$84,787,838	$89,130,412	5.1%	$94,526,765	6.1%	$94,801,602	0.3%	$101,993,417	7.6%
Liabilities									
Accounts Payable	$ 563,946	$ 761,336	35.0%	$ 1,332,591	75.0%	$ 643,130	−51.7%	$ 1,422,480	121.2%
Accrued Liabilities	664,625	664,470	0.0%	750,486	12.9%	858,797	14.4%	944,611	10.0%
Due to Pension Fund	—	—		—		—		264,032	
Long Term Due in 1 Year	1,579,370	2,861,106	81.2%	2,350,037	−17.9%	2,580,092	9.8%	6,454,289	150.2%
Total Current Liabilities	2,807,941	4,286,912	52.7%	4,433,114	3.4%	4,082,019	−7.9%	9,085,412	122.6%

(continued)

	YR 1	YR 2		YR 3		YR 4		YR 5	
Deferred Revenues	4,651,080	4,020,322	−13.6%	4,109,313	2.2%	4,169,035	1.5%	4,324,932	3.7%
Long Term Liabilities	24,126,024	28,850,525	19.6%	32,039,458	11.1%	30,943,153	−3.4%	29,059,876	−6.1%
Total Liabilities	31,585,045	37,157,759	17.6%	40,581,885	9.2%	39,194,207	−3.4%	42,470,220	8.4%
Net Assets	53,202,793	51,972,653	−2.3%	53,944,880	3.8%	55,607,395	3.1%	59,523,197	7.0%
Total Liabilities & Net Assets	$84,787,838	$89,130,412	5.1%	$94,526,765	6.1%	$94,801,602	0.3%	$101,993,417	7.6%

FIGURE 2.14   Primary Government Balance Sheet Horizontal Analysis for Company 3

	YR 1	YR 2		YR 3		YR 4		YR 5	
Revenues									
Charges for Services	$ 6,084,880	$ 5,704,315	−6.3%	$ 6,139,777	7.6%	$ 5,828,204	−5.1%	$ 6,923,015	18.8%
Taxes	9,129,602	10,461,415	14.6%	10,500,843	0.4%	10,073,437	−4.1%	10,603,535	5.3%
Interest Income	577,099	410,530	−28.9%	370,676	−9.7%	149,676	−59.6%	86,778	−42.0%
Other Revenues	869,006	403,249	−53.6%	494,776	22.7%	1,347,473	172.3%	700,999	−48.0%
Transfer from Private Trust Fund	—	—		—		—		200,000	
Grants & Contributions	30,421	69,478	128.4%	2,463,413	3445.6%	1,183,513	−52.0%	3,341,682	182.4%
Total Revenues	16,691,008	17,048,987	2.1%	19,969,485	17.1%	18,582,303	−6.9%	21,856,009	17.6%
Expenses									
General & Administrative	10,488,090	13,021,732	24.2%	13,080,004	0.4%	11,560,648	−11.6%	12,360,554	6.9%
Depreciation Expense	3,702,017	3,966,022	7.1%	4,333,368	9.3%	4,810,923	11.0%	5,303,901	10.2%
Interest Expense	93,559	410,930	339.2%	583,886	42.1%	548,217	−6.1%	275,752	−49.7%
Total Expenses	14,283,666	17,398,684	21.8%	17,997,258	3.4%	16,919,788	−6.0%	17,940,207	6.0%
Change in Net Assets	$ 2,407,342	$ (349,697)	−85.5%	$ 1,972,227	664.0%	$ 1,662,515	−15.7%	$ 3,915,802	135.5%

FIGURE 2.15 Primary Government Income Statement Horizontal Analysis for Company 3

analysis. Interest expense relates to outstanding debt, usually bonds, and this, too, varies from year to year.

From YR 1 to YR 2

- Accounts receivable decreased, so cash should increase. At the same time, charges for services decreased and tax revenues increased, indicating the possibility of a higher percentage of accounts receivable balances related to charges for services, although generally tax receivables is the majority of the balance.
- Both inventory and prepaid expenses increased, so cash should decrease.
- Notes receivable decreased, so cash should increase.
- Fixed assets increased, so cash should decrease.
- Investments increased significantly, so cash from operations should decrease, especially if the increase was merely a transfer.
- Both accounts payable and long-term liabilities increased, so cash should increase. At the same time, general and administrative expenses increased.
- Both deferred revenues related to tax revenues and accrued liabilities decreased, so cash should increase.

Cash decreased 18%. Since investments increased over 127%, the concept of a cash transfer from operating cash appears reasonable due to the magnitude of the change. The other changes related to cash, both increases and decreases, were minor, with the change in debt the highest at 23%.

From YR 2 to YR 3

- Accounts receivable decreased, so cash should increase. Both charges for services and tax revenues increased while accounts receivable decreased, indicating the possibility that these revenue accounts included cash sales.
- Inventory decreased, so cash should increase.
- Prepaid expenses increased, so cash should decrease.
- Notes receivable decreased, so cash should increase.
- Investments decreased, so cash should increase.
- Fixed assets increased, so cash should decrease.
- Accounts payable, accrued liabilities, and deferred revenues increased, so cash should increase. General and administrative expenses also increased.
- Debt also increased, so cash should increase.

Cash decreased approximately 40%. Fixed assets increased 13%, and the only other major player decreasing cash is prepaid expenses at 23%. When taking the dollar amount of the change in fixed assets compared to the decrease in both cash and investments, the change in cash appears reasonable.

From YR 3 to YR 4

- Investments decreased significantly, so cash should increase.
- Both charges for services and tax revenues decreased while accounts receivable increased, indicating the possibility of delinquent receivables playing a major role in the increase in receivables, definitely supporting the decrease in cash.
- Inventory increased slightly, so cash should decrease.
- Both prepaid expenses and notes receivable decreased, so cash should increase.
- Fixed assets increased, so cash should decrease.
- Both debt and accounts payable decreased, so cash should decrease. In addition, general and administrative expenses decreased.
- Accrued liabilities and deferred revenues increased, so cash should increase.

Cash decreased 63%. Major changes taking away from cash include fixed assets (9%), accounts payable (52%), and debt (3%), so it is plausible that the decrease in cash is realistic. To be confident that the changes include the significant decrease in investments assumed transferred into cash operations, the financial forensic examiner needs to look also at the numbers, which may be necessary when transfers of funds are included in the analysis. For instance, cash decreased $2.2 million, fixed assets increased $6.8 million, and the transfer of funds from the investments amounted to $4.5 million. In this particular instance, following the dollars also supported the decrease in cash as reasonable.

From YR 4 to YR 5

- Investments decreased, so cash should increase.
- Accounts receivable increased as well as both charges for services and tax revenues, so cash should decrease.
- Both inventory and prepaid expenses increased, so cash should decrease.
- Notes receivable decreased, so cash should increase.
- Fixed assets increased, so cash should increase.
- Debt increased, so cash should increase.
- Accounts payable, accrued liabilities, and deferred revenues increased, so cash should increase. General and administrative expenses also increased.

Cash increased 1%. Considering the increase in fixed assets amounting to 7% or $6.1 million, the increase in cash may not be realistic. Debt only increased $2 million and there was an additional $1 million increase in accounts payable. These changes do not support the change in cash. Additionally, the financial statements provide another glitch in the analysis related to the due-to-pension-fund account. This account is highly unusual and immediately warrants further investigation. Thus, the horizontal analysis of the primary government financial statements provides a few items requiring further study: changes of cash in YR 5, the due-to-pension-fund account, and the wide variances of both the charges for services and tax revenue accounts, especially the tax revenue as it tends to be somewhat stable.

In addition to the primary government financial statements, the fund financial statements also need reviewing for possible inconsistencies. Just like the primary government financial statements, the fund financial statements also have peculiar account terms related to governmental entities. The *due-to* and *due-from* accounts represent transfers of funds between the funds that are eliminated in the consolidated primary government financial statements. *Capital outlay* refers to expenses classified as fixed assets in the primary government financial statements. *Debt service expense* refers to payments on debt. *Bond proceeds* refers to monies received from the issuance of new debt. *Intergovernmental revenues* consist of grant revenues that may fluctuate significantly from year to year. Finally, *operating transfers in and out* refers to transfers of cash between government funds. Figures 2.16 and 2.17 show the horizontal analyses of both the fund balance sheets and the fund income statements.

From YR 1 to YR 2

- Accounts receivable increased, so cash should decrease. Total revenues increased 8%, with the main increase related to intergovernmental revenues.
- Notes receivable decreased, so cash should increase.
- The net effect between the due-to and due-from accounts relates to the change recorded in the business-type activities and properly eliminated in the primary government financial statements.
- Inventory and prepaid expenses increased, so cash should decrease.
- Accrued liabilities and deferred revenues increased, so cash should increase.
- Accounts payable decreased, so cash should decrease. General and administrative expenses and associated payroll expenses increased as well.

	YR 1	YR 2		YR 3		YR 4		YR 5	
Assets									
Cash	$ 2,305,503	$ 3,073,334	33.3%	$ 2,134,862	−30.5%	$ 816,508	−61.8%	$ 594,169	−27.2%
Investments	2,839,407	6,688,938	135.6%	5,174,742	−22.6%	532,041	−89.7%	284,067	−46.6%
Accounts Receivable	4,514,877	4,966,972	10.0%	5,060,185	1.9%	5,373,058	6.2%	5,679,331	5.7%
Due from Other Funds	3,288,257	3,924,350	19.3%	4,719,495	20.3%	7,739,995	64.0%	9,472,608	22.4%
Inventory	23,331	38,520	65.1%	20,316	−47.3%	48,458	138.5%	60,221	24.3%
Prepaid Expenses	140,855	146,444	4.0%	166,472	13.7%	53,949	−67.6%	57,488	6.6%
Total Current Assets	13,112,230	18,838,558	43.7%	17,276,072	−8.3%	14,564,009	−15.7%	16,147,884	10.9%
Notes Receivable	67,528	38,837	−42.5%	33,202	−14.5%	10,368	−68.8%	7,726	−25.5%
Total Assets	$13,179,758	$18,877,395	43.2%	$17,309,274	−8.3%	$14,574,377	−15.8%	$16,155,610	10.8%
Liabilities									
Accounts Payable	$ 298,718	$ 297,522	−0.4%	$ 899,478	202.3%	$ 450,921	−49.9%	$ 295,905	−34.4%
Accrued Liabilities	323,311	377,450	16.7%	404,528	7.2%	522,458	29.2%	597,552	14.4%
Due to Other Funds	2,328,257	3,404,495	46.2%	4,234,495	24.4%	7,434,497	75.6%	8,908,530	19.8%
Total Current Liabilities	2,950,286	4,079,467	38.3%	5,538,501	35.8%	8,407,876	51.8%	9,801,987	16.6%
Deferred Revenues	3,359,531	3,659,683	8.9%	3,732,514	2.0%	3,777,793	1.2%	3,926,262	3.9%
Total Liabilities	6,309,817	7,739,150	22.7%	9,271,015	19.8%	12,185,669	31.4%	13,728,249	12.7%
Total Fund Balances	6,869,941	11,138,245	62.1%	8,038,259	−27.8%	2,388,708	−70.3%	2,427,361	1.6%
Total Liabilities & Fund Balances	$13,179,758	$18,877,395	43.2%	$17,309,274	−8.3%	$14,574,377	−15.8%	$16,155,610	10.8%

FIGURE 2.16 Governmental Funds Balance Sheet Horizontal Analysis for Company 3

	YR 1	YR 2		YR 3		YR 4		YR 5	
Revenues									
Charges for Services	$ 431,025	$ 453,688	5.3%	$ 446,319	-1.6%	$ 453,633	1.6%	$ 428,142	-5.6%
Taxes	3,137,291	3,339,281	6.4%	3,524,222	5.5%	3,716,189	5.4%	3,756,412	1.1%
Licenses, Permits, Fees	283,344	281,260	-0.7%	266,924	-5.1%	270,910	1.5%	282,192	4.2%
Fines & Penalities	159,788	181,919	13.9%	148,360	-18.4%	159,894	7.8%	129,461	-19.0%
Other Revenues	620,379	537,394	-13.4%	667,642	24.2%	1,306,048	95.6%	614,931	-52.9%
Intergovernmental Revenues	6,493,027	7,191,612	10.8%	9,440,034	31.3%	6,507,210	-31.1%	8,333,667	28.1%
Total Revenues	11,124,854	11,985,154	7.7%	14,493,501	20.9%	12,413,884	-14.3%	13,544,805	9.1%
Expenses									
General & Administrative	7,398,658	9,123,875	23.3%	8,625,966	-5.5%	9,738,780	12.9%	9,736,115	0.0%
Pension & SS Payments	970,971	1,012,097	4.2%	1,042,311	3.0%	1,109,795	6.5%	1,123,927	1.3%
Capital Outlay	5,171,038	6,032,238	16.7%	8,645,654	43.3%	7,634,565	-11.7%	5,376,412	-29.6%
Debt Service	623,000	397,000	-36.3%	691,000	74.1%	647,000	-6.4%	1,154,666	78.5%
Interest Expense	375,710	346,640	-7.7%	523,556	51.0%	558,295	6.6%	264,032	-52.7%
Total Expenses	14,539,377	16,911,850	16.3%	19,528,487	15.5%	19,688,435	0.8%	17,655,152	-10.3%
Excess (Deficiency)	(3,414,523)	(4,926,696)		(5,034,986)		(7,274,551)		(4,110,347)	
Operating Transfers In	6,350,000	7,815,000	23.1%	7,341,000	-6.1%	5,935,000	-19.2%	6,479,000	9.2%
Bond Proceeds	—	6,500,000		—		—		1,679,000	
Operating Transfers Out	4,753,000	5,120,000	7.7%	5,406,000	5.6%	4,310,000	-20.3%	4,009,000	-7.0%
Changes in Fund Balance	$(1,817,523)	$4,268,304	334.8%	$(3,099,986)	-172.6%	$5,649,551	82.2%	$ 38,653	-100.7%

FIGURE 2.17 Governmental Funds Income Statement Horizontal Analysis for Company 3

- The entity received bond proceeds in YR 2, so cash should increase.
- The entity also made payments on debt, so cash should decrease.
- Capital outlay costs increased, so cash should decrease.

Investments increased substantially (136%) and cash increased 33%, so the financial forensic examiner must determine if the increase in the investments relates to transfers from cash. Here again, actual amounts are appropriate measurements to determine whether the increase in investments relates to transfers. Bond proceeds amounted to $6.5 million, while capital outlay expenses increased $.9 million and payments on existing debt amounted to $.6 million. Investments increased $3.8 million, while cash increased only $.7 million. Looking at the numbers, the financial forensic examiner should consider the increase in the investments as transfers from cash.

One other very important point relates to operating transfers in and out. In the governmental funds income statement, these transfers represent monies moving between the governmental funds and thus considered *inter-fund transfers*. The positive net effect of the transfers increased 69%. The use of Company 3 provides an excellent example to the financial forensic examiner of the need to understand the entity and the financial statement requirements to use these ratios and indices.

From YR 2 and YR 3

- Accounts receivable increased, so cash should decrease. Again, total revenues increased, with the majority of the increase related to intergovernmental revenues.
- Notes payable continued to decrease, so cash should increase.
- The primary government financial statements indicate that the due-to and due-from accounts eliminate properly.
- Inventory decreased, so cash should increase.
- Prepaid expenses increased, so cash should decrease.
- Accounts payable, accrued liabilities, and deferred revenues increased, so cash should increase. General and administrative expenses decreased while associated payroll expenses increased slightly.
- Capital outlay expenses increased, so cash should decrease.
- Debt payments increased, so cash should decrease.
- Both investments and cash decreased.

The decrease in both investments and cash appears reasonable considering the 43% increase in capital outlay costs. The government did not receive any additional funds related to new debt. Once more, the numbers provide the story, since capital outlay increased $2.6 million, investments decreased $1.5 million, and cash decreased $.9 million. This time, the net effect of the operating transfers decreased 28%.

From YR 3 to YR 4

- Accounts receivable increased while total revenues decreased, so cash should decrease.
- For the third time, notes payable decreased, so cash should increase.
- Once more, the due-to and due-from accounts are properly eliminated in the primary government financial statements. For the second time, the net effect of operating transfers decreased 16%.
- Inventory increased, so cash should decrease.
- Prepaid expenses decreased, so cash should increase.
- Accounts payable decreased, so cash should decrease.
- Both accrued liabilities and deferred revenues increased, so cash should increase.
- For the first time, capital outlay expenses decreased, so cash should increase.
- Debt payments increased, so cash should decrease. There were no new debt proceeds during this period as well that would increase cash.
- Both investments and cash decreased significantly, with investments decreasing 90% and cash decreasing 62%.

Based on these changes, the preliminary assessments indicate that cash should increase, not decrease. When looking at the dollar amounts, however, capital outlay expenses amounted to $7.6 million with investments decreasing $4.6 million and cash decreasing $1.3 million. When looking at the changes from this perspective, the decrease in cash appears reasonable and the decrease in investments relates to the transfer of funds to the operating account to assist in the capital outlay purchases.

From YR 4 to YR 5

- Accounts receivable increased, so cash should decrease. Total revenues increased, but the majority of the increase was related to inter-governmental revenues where a portion of these funds would increase cash.
- Notes receivable continued to decrease, so cash should increase.

- Both inventory and prepaid expenses increased, so cash should decrease.
- Accounts payable decreased, so cash should decrease.
- Both accrued liabilities and deferred revenues increased, so cash should increase.
- Debt payments increased, so cash should decrease. The company also received funds in the form of new debt, so cash should increase.
- Capital outlay expenses decreased, so cash should increase.
- When combined together, both general and administrative expenses and related payroll expenses increased slightly.

TABLE 2.9 Inter-Fund Analysis

	YR 1	YR 2	YR 3	YR 4	YR 5
Due from Other Funds	$ 3,288,257	$ 3,924,350	$ 4,719,495	$ 7,739,995	$ 9,472,608
Due to Other Funds	2,328,257	3,404,495	4,234,495	7,434,497	8,908,530
Difference	960,000	519,855	485,000	305,498	564,078
Operating Transfers In	6,350,000	7,815,000	7,341,000	5,935,000	6,479,000
Operating Transfers Out	4,753,000	5,120,000	5,406,000	4,310,000	4,009,000
Difference	1,597,000	2,695,000	1,935,000	1,625,000	2,470,000

Just like the last period, both cash and investments decreased. The capital outlay expenses continued to deplete both cash and investments, so these decreases seem reasonable. Again, the due-to and due-from accounts are properly recorded in the primary government financial statements, but the operating transfers in and out are troublesome since the financial statements do not explain the difference. Table 2.9 better illustrates this predicament. Since these facts pose questions for the financial forensic examiner, further analysis is required. Subsequent chapters analyze these differences in more detail.

Company 4

As a reminder, Company 4's financial statements meet the definition of "clean" financials since these financial statements meet the stringent rules of a publicly traded company; the various analytical tests and procedures within this book did not find any unexplained variations in the testing procedures. Figure 2.18 illustrates the balance sheet horizontal analysis while Figure 2.19 shows the income statement horizontal analysis.

(in thousands)	YR 1	YR 2		YR 3		YR 4		YR 5	
Assets									
Cash	$ 5,240	$ 2,812	-46.3%	$ 6,147	118.6%	$ 8,204	33.5%	$ 23,282	183.8%
Accounts Receivable	39,052	50,452	29.2%	67,626	34.0%	86,674	28.2%	68,675	-20.8%
Allowance for Bad Debts	(1,062)	(1,116)	5.1%	(1,834)	64.3%	(2,488)	35.7%	(1,640)	-34.1%
Inventory	26,715	34,994	31.0%	38,318	9.5%	43,155	12.6%	39,313	-8.9%
Prepaid Expenses	1,783	1,525	-14.5%	739	-51.5%	2,079	181.3%	1,775	-14.6%
Total Current Assets	71,728	88,667	23.6%	110,996	25.2%	137,624	24.0%	131,405	-4.5%
Other Assets	39,113	20,393	-47.9%	16,131	-20.9%	27,527	70.6%	23,830	-13.4%
Fixed Assets (net)	20,977	18,762	-10.6%	17,443	-7.0%	32,281	85.1%	33,807	4.7%
Total Assets	$ 131,818	$127,822	-3.0%	$144,570	13.1%	$197,432	36.6%	$189,042	-4.2%
Liabilities									
Accounts Payable	$ 34,164	$ 36,224	6.0%	$ 45,352	25.2%	$ 58,620	29.3%	$ 39,926	-31.9%
Other Liabilities	37,680	18,416	-51.1%	16,065	-12.8%	13,269	-17.4%	10,623	-19.9%
Current Portion of Debt	2,050	2,052	0.1%	1,595	-22.3%	1,623	1.8%	1,802	11.0%
Total Current Liabilities	73,894	56,692	-23.3%	63,012	11.1%	73,512	16.7%	52,351	-28.8%
Notes Payable	29,927	24,345	-18.7%	16,803	-31.0%	10,537	-37.3%	4,203	-60.1%
Total Liabilities	$ 103,821	$ 81,037	-21.9%	$ 79,815	-1.5%	$ 84,049	5.3%	$ 56,554	-32.7%
Shareholders Equity	27,997	46,785	67.1%	64,755	38.4%	113,383	75.1%	132,488	16.8%
Total Liabilities & SE	$ 131,818	$127,822	-3.0%	$144,570	13.1%	$197,432	36.6%	$189,042	-4.2%

FIGURE 2.18 Balance Sheet Horizontal Analysis for Company 4

(in thousands)	YR 1	YR 2		YR 3		YR 4		YR 5	
Revenues									
Sales	$205,996	$236,308	14.7%	$351,884	48.9%	$409,421	16.4%	$400,032	-2.3%
Less Cost of Goods Sold	179,008	205,021	14.5%	301,943	47.3%	349,639	15.8%	343,885	-1.6%
Gross Profit	26,988	31,287	15.9%	49,941	59.6%	59,782	19.7%	56,147	-6.1%
Expenses									
General & Admininstrative	13,841	15,812	14.2%	21,533	36.2%	24,229	12.5%	23,971	-1.1%
Depreciation	3,570	3,092	-13.4%	2,760	-10.7%	2,608	-5.5%	3,134	20.2%
Other Expense	6,291	4,657	-26.0%	4,012	-13.9%	3,518	-12.3%	3,392	-3.6%
Income Tax Expense	1,216	740	-39.1%	2,936	296.8%	2,454	-16.4%	9,319	279.7%
Total Expenses	24,918	24,301	-2.5%	31,241	28.6%	32,809	5.0%	39,816	21.4%
Misc Income	(16,223)	(1,511)	90.7%	(114)	92.5%	18,370	16214.0%	—	-100.0%
Net Profit (Loss)	$ (14,153)	$ 5,475	138.7%	$ 18,586	239.5%	$ 45,343	144.0%	$ 16,331	-64.0%

FIGURE 2.19 Income Statement Horizontal Analysis for Company 4

From YR 1 to YR 2

- Both accounts receivable and the allowance for bad debt increased, so cash should decrease.
- Inventory increased, so cash should decrease.
- Prepaid expenses decreased, so cash should increase.
- Other assets decreased, so cash should increase.
- Fixed assets decreased, so cash should increase.
- Accounts payable increased although total expenses decreased, so cash should increase.
- Other liabilities decreased, so cash should decrease.
- Notes payable decreased, so cash should decrease.
- Notice that both the changes in sales and the changes in the cost of goods sold do not fluctuate significantly.

Cash decreased 46% over the prior year. Considering the information in the horizontal analysis, the decrease appears reasonable. Inventory increased 31%, notes payable decreased 19%, net accounts receivable increased 30%, while sales increased 14% and accounts payable increased 6%. In this particular instance, sales increased only 15% while net accounts receivable increased 30%, so the likelihood of sales increasing cash is minimal.

From YR 2 to YR 3

- Net accounts receivable increased, so cash should decrease.
- Inventory increased, so cash should decrease.
- Prepaid expenses decreased, so cash should increase.
- Both other assets and fixed assets decreased, so cash should increase.
- Accounts payable increased, so cash should increase.
- Both other liabilities and notes payable decreased, so cash should decrease.
- Sales, cost of goods sold, and total expenses increased.

During this period, cash increased significantly (119%), whereas the changes in inventory, notes payable, other liabilities, and total expenses indicate that cash should decrease. Inventory increased 10%, other liabilities decreased 13%, and notes payable decreased 31% while current assets increased 25% and current liabilities increased 11%. One item missing that would explain the large increase in cash is the connection of the increases in accounts receivable and sales. Sales increased 49% while net accounts receivable increased only 33%, suggesting that some of the sales were cash sales.

When considering this aspect and the other changes that increase cash, the significant increase appears reasonable.

From YR 3 to YR 4

- Accounts receivable increased, so cash should decrease.
- Both inventory and prepaid expenses increased, so cash should decrease.
- Other assets increased, so cash should decrease.
- Fixed assets increased, so cash should decrease.
- Accounts payable increased, so cash should increase.
- Other liabilities and notes payable decreased, so cash should decrease.
- Sales, cost of goods sold, and total expenses increased as well.

From the information noted above, cash should decrease, but it increased 34% over the prior year, suggesting the possibility of disparity in the account relationships, so there are still missing pieces of information that should explain the difference. Sales increased 16% while net accounts receivable increased 30%, so any cash sales would be minimal at best. During YR 4, instead of paying off debt, management converted the debt to stock, so the 34% decrease in debt did not have an effect on cash. Knowing this information is good example of why a financial forensic examiner must research and understand the company's operations, since this knowledge is critical to understanding the changes in the account relationships that influence cash changes.

From YR 4 to YR 5

- Accounts receivable decreased, so cash should increase.
- Both inventory and prepaid expenses decreased, so cash should increase.
- Other assets decreased, so cash should increase.
- Fixed assets increased, so cash should decrease.
- Accounts payable decreased, so cash should increase.
- Other assets and notes payable decreased, so cash should decrease.
- Sales and cost of goods sold decreased slightly and, although total expenses increased, the increases were related to depreciation and estimated income tax expenses, which does not affect cash changes.

Cash increased significantly when compared to the prior-year increases. Since sales decreased only 2% while accounts receivable decreased 20%, it is more than likely that some of the cash increase relates to cash sales as well as receipts posted to accounts receivable. In addition, the change in fixed assets is minor compared to the change in accounts payable. This time, the decrease in the notes payable relates to a new line of credit that paid off the old debt, with the remaining cash used to increase production facilities at one of the plant locations. Knowing this information, the significant increase in cash appears reasonable.

So far, the liquidity ratios, the profitability ratios, and the use of horizontal analysis by themselves have not presented much insight into variations in the financial information that may represent possible fraudulent activity. Remember that Company 2 had several of these ratios applied in the company's annual compilations while fraud was occurring within the company. Yet, when combining the information and looking at the account relationships, a few unexplained variances surfaced, which explains the need for additional forensic analytical techniques. One such technique, vertical analysis, is not as commonly used as the other techniques already discussed. However vertical analysis is a better method of understanding account relationships and how they change over time.

VERTICAL ANALYSIS

From the discussions related to ratios and horizontal analysis, the financial forensic examiner understands the necessity in exploring financial information for possible anomalies that might indicate possible fraudulent activity. The vertical analysis actually investigates the relationship between the accounts listed in the financial statements. Vertical analysis, often called *common-sizing*, expresses the relationships to a specific base item. For example, in the balance sheet, total assets becomes the specific base number for analyzing all assets while total liabilities and stockholders' equity becomes the base for all of the liability and the stockholder accounts. As for the income statement, sales become the base for all other items listed in the income statement. Because a transaction in one account will have a known effect on other accounts, and a vertical analysis explores the operations of a company, the financial forensic examiner may discover anomalies in the financial statement information. In examining the vertical analysis of each of the four companies, the financial forensic examiner will build his or her knowledge concerning account relationships.

Company 1

Since Company 1's financial information varies so much in the earlier preliminary analytics, the vertical analysis should put those variances in perspective. Figure 2.20 illustrates the vertical analysis for the balance sheet and Figure 2.21 presents it for the income statement.

	YR 1		YR 2		YR 3		YR 4		YR 5	
Assets										
Cash	$ 13,478	9%	$ 1,195	0%	$ 3,519	2%	$ 330	0%	$ (5,299)	−4%
Accounts Receivable	18,011	12%	24,345	17%	29,994	20%	33,807	23%	28,138	20%
Total Current Assets	31,489	21%	25,540	17%	33,513	22%	34,137	23%	22,839	17%
Fixed Assets (net)	122,019	79%	121,058	83%	116,855	78%	113,473	77%	114,437	83%
Total Assets	$153,508	100%	$146,598	100%	$150,368	100%	$147,610	100%	$137,276	100%
Liabilities										
Accounts Payable	$ 12,545	8%	$ 10,612	7%	$ 5,447	3%	$ 7,642	5%	$ 10,441	8%
Total Current Liabilities	12,545		10,612		5,447		7,642		10,441	
Notes Payable	—		17,641	12%	31,192	21%	30,554	21%	32,862	24%
Total Liabilities	$ 12,545		$ 28,253	19%	$ 36,639	24%	$ 38,196	26%	$ 43,303	32%
Shareholders Equity	140,963	92%	118,345	81%	113,729	76%	109,414	74%	93,973	68%
Total Liabilities & SE	$153,508	100%	$146,598	100%	$150,368	100%	$147,610	100%	$137,276	100%

FIGURE 2.20 Balance Sheet Vertical Analysis for Company 1

	YR 1		YR 2		YR 3		YR 4		YR 5	
Sales	$145,246	100%	$121,842	100%	$130,859	100%	$128,344	100%	$138,443	100%
Less Purchases	9,017	6%	12,249	10%	17,248	13%	5,752	4%	5,820	4%
Less Labor Costs	4,542	3%	8,143	7%	6,115	5%	10,292	8%	2,988	2%
Gross Profit	131,687	91%	101,450	83%	107,496	82%	112,300	87%	129,635	94%
Expenses										
Selling Expenses	$ 1,712	1%	$ 2,657	2%	$ 2,001	2%	$ 8,939	7%	$ 12,730	9%
General & Administrative	41,946	29%	38,122	31%	36,668	28%	40,829	32%	30,378	22%
Salaries	9,820	7%	15,592	13%	8,266	6%	4,234	3%	43,490	31%
Repairs & Maintenance	5,842	4%	6,453	5%	1,132	1%	6,243	5%	3,603	3%
Bad Debt	—	0%	—	0%	—	0%	—	0%	4,280	3%
Rent	2,976	2%	2,000	2%	5,000	4%	7,504	6%	1,615	1%
Taxes & Licenses	5,937	4%	10,312	8%	5,791	4%	6,149	5%	8,284	6%
Insurance	2,570	2%	7,072	6%	4,883	4%	5,371	4%	5,242	4%
Utilities	15,782	11%	16,487	14%	16,823	13%	18,131	14%	17,177	12%
Supplies	4,590	3%	7,190	6%	8,368	6%	4,956	4%	4,066	3%
Depreciation	4,863	3%	4,664	4%	10,805	8%	5,882	5%	6,831	5%
Accounting Fees	1,050	1%	2,036	2%	1,320	1%	1,470	1%	1,110	1%
Vehicle Expense	2,291	2%	4,929	4%	—	0%	—	0%	—	0%
Civic Donations	580	0%	1,070	1%	770	1%	520	0%	130	0%
Legal Fees	709	0%	—	0%	—	0%	—	0%	—	0%

Internet Fees	161	0%	21	0%	—	0%	—	0%
Office Expenses	689	0%	—	0%	—	0%	—	0%
Freight	78	0%	—	0%	22	0%	—	0%
Postage	209	0%	244	0%	403	0%	386	0%
Lodging & Travel	—	0%	—	0%	300	0%	625	0%
Commissions	522	0%	54	0%	380	0%	870	1%
Total General Expenses	100,615	69%	100,145	77%	102,394	80%	128,087	93%
Total Expenses	102,327	70%	102,146	78%	111,333	87%	140,817	102%
Interest Income	949	1%	752	1%	374	0%	—	0%
Interest Expenses	5,360	4%	5,083	4%	5,656	4%	4,259	3%
Net Profit	$ 24,949	17%	$ 1,019	1%	$ (4,315)	−3%	$ (15,441)	−11%

FIGURE 2.21 Income Statement Vertical Analysis for Company 1

The vertical analysis of the balance sheet establishes several interesting points. After YR 1, accounts receivable remains comparatively stable, while fixed assets increase in YR 2 and YR 5 only. After YR 1, a new line item called *notes payable* appears, indicating that the company received additional funds. Accounts payable also remains comparatively stable. All of these items indicate that cash should also remain comparatively stable, but cash decreases every year. The vertical analysis clearly indicates inconsistency in the items' relationship to cash, although this difference was not as apparent in the horizontal analysis.

The vertical analysis of the income statement also contains many variances within the expense items from year to year. For example, salaries change from year to year even though there are no changes in the number of personnel within the company. Probably the most important item to note is the inconsistency in the total expenses: increasing, decreasing, and then increasing again in YR 5 over 100%. Is this truly bad bookkeeping, or a ruse to increase costs by having the company pay for personal items? The financial forensic examiner must answer this question with further studies.

Company 2

Figure 2.22 shows the balance sheet vertical analysis for Company 2 and Figure 2.23 illustrates the income statement vertical analysis for Company 2.

Compared to Company 1, accounts receivable is not stable at all, fluctuating from 19 to 32% of total assets. In fact, the only two asset accounts that are comparatively stable are prepaid expenses and the allowance for bad debts. As for the liability accounts, the only account that appears to be comparatively stable is other liabilities. Fixed assets decrease every year except for Y3. With so many fluctuations, it is difficult for the financial forensic examiner to determine if the account relationships are reasonable. For example, in YR 2 accounts receivable increases, inventory increases, fixed assets decrease, accounts payable increases, and yet cash also increases.

The vertical analysis for the income statement actually shows more consistency, with depreciation, income tax expenses, and miscellaneous income comparatively stable. After YR 1, general and administrative expenses are relatively stable. Even though cost of goods sold increased in YR 2, the rest of the years are comparable and gross profits follow the same trend. Yet compare the cost of goods sold vertical analysis with Company 4's income statement vertical analysis in Figure 2.29; the financial forensic examiner will see more consistency in the trends compared to Company 2, especially in YR 2.

	YR 1		YR 2		YR 3		YR 4		YR 5	
Assets										
Cash	$ 6,037	0%	$ 219,408	2%	$ 409,620	4%	$ 1,615,708	16%	$ 866,801	7%
Accounts Receivable	1,388,977	26%	2,905,601	32%	2,282,772	27%	2,158,034	21%	2,275,985	19%
Allowance for Bad Debts	(1,000)	0%	(60,000)	-1%	(37,172)	0%	(100,000)	-1%	(100,000)	-1%
Refundable Income Taxes	—	0%	—	0%	21,205	0%	47,000	0%	40,000	0%
Inventory	1,866,785	35%	3,904,040	41%	3,282,898	38%	3,887,568	38%	5,159,037	45%
Prepaid Expenses	256,677	5%	309,566	3%	176,110	2%	73,826	1%	75,412	1%
Total Current Assets	3,517,476	66%	7,278,615	77%	6,135,433	71%	7,682,136	75%	8,317,235	71%
Other Assets	—		—		—		—		963,459	8%
Fixed Assets (net)	1,786,908	34%	2,210,753	23%	2,472,082	29%	2,501,071	25%	2,421,222	21%
Total Assets	$5,304,384	100%	$9,489,368	100%	$8,607,515	100%	$10,183,207	100%	$11,701,916	100%
Liabilities										
Accounts Payable	$1,186,293	22%	$2,987,894	32%	$1,902,907	22%	$ 1,951,605	19%	$ 1,352,480	12%
Deferred Income Taxes	—	0%	—	0%	—	0%	30,000	0%	—	0%
Other Liabilities	26,150	1%	124,856	1%	64,452	1%	86,796	1%	461,000	4%
Total Current Liabilities	1,212,443	23%	3,112,750	33%	1,967,359	23%	2,068,401	20%	1,813,480	16%
Deferred Income Taxes	488,762	9%	873,317	9%	1,270,317	15%	424,317	4%	604,000	5%
Notes Payable	619,508	12%	1,719,098	18%	—	0%	—	0%	—	0%
Total Liabilities	2,320,713	44%	5,705,165	60%	3,237,676	38%	2,492,718	24%	2,417,480	21%
Stockholders Equity	2,984,671	56%	3,784,203	40%	5,369,839	62%	7,690,489	76%	9,284,436	79%
Total Liabilities & SE	$5,305,384	100%	$9,489,368	100%	$8,607,515	100%	$10,183,207	100%	$11,701,916	100%

FIGURE 2.22 Balance Sheet Vertical Analysis for Company 2

71

	YR 1		YR 2		YR 3		YR 4		YR 5	
Sales	$10,950,180	100%	$28,188,122	100%	$40,214,834	100%	$38,780,333	100%	$30,397,677	100%
Less Cost of Goods Sold	8,737,104	80%	23,312,675	83%	33,082,011	82%	31,270,725	81%	24,613,108	81%
Gross Profit	2,213,076	20%	4,875,447	17%	7,132,823	18%	7,509,608	19%	5,784,569	19%
Expenses										
General & Administrative	1,764,716	16%	3,534,123	13%	4,555,539	11%	3,722,301	10%	3,358,667	11%
Depreciation	203,295	2%	240,233	1%	306,697	1%	339,156	1%	375,978	1%
Income Tax Expense	162,287	1%	523,542	2%	950,439	2%	1,313,500	3%	890,000	3%
Total Expenses	2,130,298	19%	4,297,898	15%	5,812,675	14%	5,374,957	14%	4,624,645	15%
Misc Income	117,305	1%	221,983	1%	265,491	1%	185,999	0%	434,023	1%
Net Profit	$ 200,083	2%	$ 799,532	3%	$ 1,585,639	4%	$ 2,320,650	6%	$ 1,593,947	5%

FIGURE 2.23 Income Statement Vertical Analysis for Company 2

To the untrained eye, slight variances may go unnoticed, but the financial forensic examiner would realize that a 3% difference would be significant, especially if the company's trends indicate either stability or larger increases in its gross profit margins.

Company 3

The calculations for Company 3 include both the primary government financial statements and the governmental funds financial statements. Figure 2.24 illustrates the vertical analysis of the primary government balance sheets and Figure 2.25 shows it for the primary government income statements.

When looking at the vertical analysis for the primary government financial statements, there are very few accounts that differ from year to year: investments, fixed assets, and long-term liabilities. Cash and investments decrease each year, while fixed assets and debt swing between increases and decreases. The concern is whether the decreases in cash and investments offset the increases in fixed assets. Prior information and testing suggested that the decrease in investments merely represented a transfer to the cash operating account and that the increases in long-term debt provided a source of cash for funding additions to fixed assets, so the financial forensic examiner would need to focus on these relationships, should they contradict each other. In the case of Company 3, the relationships are comparable when including grants and contributions as a source of funding.

The vertical analysis shows the unpredictability of grant revenues just as in the horizontal analysis, and the financial forensic examiner knows that grant revenues in governments are not consistent. However, tax revenues tend to be comparable from year to year and the vertical analysis shows just the opposite. Although the transfer from the private trust fund is only 1% of total revenues, it is not a routine account normally found in primary government financial statements. General and administrative expenses, especially in YR 2, is significant, since the amount is 76% of total revenues and the amounts are not reasonably consistent.

Figure 2.26 shows the vertical analysis for the governmental funds balance sheets and Figure 2.27 shows it for the governmental funds income statements. Most of the accounts will follow the same patterns already discussed in the primary government analysis, so the focus of this analysis relates to the fund accounts that are not included in the primary government financial statements.

For the balance sheet items, the due-from-other-funds and the due-to-other-funds balances increase every year, with the exception of YR 2.

	YR 1		YR 2		YR 3		YR 4		YR 5	
Assets										
Cash	$ 7,127,424	8%	$ 5,829,038	7%	$ 3,503,752	4%	$ 1,282,307	1%	$ 1,299,373	1%
Investments	3,026,409	4%	6,883,554	8%	5,376,081	6%	802,697	1%	550,593	1%
Accounts Receivable	6,193,387	7%	5,675,948	6%	5,770,644	6%	6,221,333	7%	7,481,059	7%
Allowance for Bad Debts	(2,500)	0%	(2,500)	0%	(2,500)	0%	(52,500)	0%	(77,500)	0%
Inventory	176,657	0%	181,274	0%	140,525	0%	148,483	0%	183,381	0%
Prepaid Expenses	172,006	0%	181,279	0%	222,326	0%	103,951	0%	104,732	0%
Total Current Assets	16,693,383	20%	18,748,593	21%	15,010,828	16%	8,506,271	9%	9,541,638	9%
Restricted Cash	166,608	0%	192,647	0%	209,721	0%	287,989	0%	289,919	0%
Notes Receivable	67,528	0%	38,837	0%	33,202	0%	10,368	0%	7,726	0%
Restricted Investments	222,359	0%	225,587	0%	227,670	0%	163,779	0%	170,170	0%
Fixed Assets (net)	67,637,960	80%	69,924,748	78%	79,045,344	84%	85,833,195	91%	91,983,964	90%
Total Assets	$84,787,838	100%	$89,130,412	100%	$94,526,765	100%	$94,801,602	100%	$101,993,417	100%
Liabilities										
Accounts Payable	$ 563,946	1%	$ 761,336	1%	$ 1,332,591	1%	$ 643,130	1%	$ 1,422,480	1%
Accrued Liabilities	664,625	1%	664,470	1%	750,486	1%	858,797	1%	944,611	1%
Due to Pension Fund	—	0%	—	0%	—	0%	—	0%	264,032	0%

Long Term Due in 1 Year	1,579,370	2%	2,861,106	3%	2,350,037	2%	2,580,092	3%	6,454,289	6%
Total Current Liabilties	2,807,941	3%	4,286,912	5%	4,433,114	5%	4,082,019	4%	9,085,412	9%
Deferred Revenues	4,651,080	5%	4,020,322	5%	4,109,313	4%	4,169,035	4%	4,324,932	4%
Long Term Liabilities	24,126,024	28%	28,850,525	32%	32,039,458	34%	30,943,153	33%	29,059,876	28%
Total Liabilities	31,585,045	37%	37,157,759	42%	40,581,885	43%	39,194,207	41%	42,470,220	42%
Net Assets	53,202,793	63%	51,972,653	58%	53,944,880	57%	55,607,395	59%	59,523,197	58%
Total Liabilities & Net Assets	$84,787,838	100%	$89,130,412	100%	$94,526,765	100%	$94,801,602	100%	$101,993,417	100%

FIGURE 2.24 Primary Government Balance Sheet Vertical Analysis for Company 3

	YR 1		YR 2		YR 3		YR 4		YR 5	
Revenues										
Charges for Services	$ 6,084,880	36%	$ 5,704,315	33%	$ 6,139,777	31%	$ 5,828,204	31%	$ 6,923,015	32%
Taxes	9,129,602	55%	10,461,415	61%	10,500,843	53%	10,073,437	54%	10,603,535	49%
Interest Income	577,099	3%	410,530	2%	370,676	2%	149,676	1%	86,778	0%
Other Revenues	869,006	5%	403,249	2%	494,776	2%	1,347,473	7%	700,999	3%
Transfer from Private Trust Fund	—	0%	—	0%	—	0%	—	0%	200,000	1%
Grants & Contributions	30,421	0%	69,478	0%	2,463,413	12%	1,183,513	6%	3,341,682	15%
Total Revenues	16,691,008	100%	17,048,987	100%	19,969,485	100%	18,582,303	100%	21,856,009	100%
Expenses										
General & Administrative	10,488,090	63%	13,021,732	76%	13,080,004	65%	11,560,648	62%	12,360,554	57%
Depreciation E	3,702,017	22%	3,966,022	23%	4,333,368	22%	4,810,923	26%	5,303,901	24%
Interest Expense	93,559	1%	410,930	2%	583,886	3%	548,217	3%	275,752	1%
Total Expenses	14,283,666	86%	17,398,684	102%	17,997,258	90%	16,919,788	91%	17,940,207	82%
Change in Net Assets	$ 2,407,342	14%	$ (349,697)	−2%	$ 1,972,227	10%	$ 1,662,515	9%	$ 3,915,802	18%

FIGURE 2.25 Primary Government Income Statement Vertical Analysis for Company 3

	YR 1		YR 2		YR 3		YR 4		YR 5	
Assets										
Cash	$ 2,305,503	17%	$ 3,073,334	16%	$ 2,134,862	12%	$ 816,508	6%	$ 594,169	4%
Investments	2,839,407	22%	6,688,938	35%	5,174,742	30%	532,041	4%	284,067	2%
Accounts Receivable	4,514,877	34%	4,966,972	26%	5,060,185	29%	5,373,058	37%	5,679,331	35%
Due from Other Funds	3,288,257	25%	3,924,350	21%	4,719,495	27%	7,739,995	53%	9,472,608	59%
Inventory	23,331	0%	38,520	0%	20,316	0%	48,458	0%	60,221	0%
Prepaid Expenses	140,855	1%	146,444	1%	166,472	1%	53,949	0%	57,488	0%
Total Current Assets	13,112,230	99%	18,838,558	100%	17,276,072	100%	14,564,009	100%	16,147,884	100%
Notes Receivable	67,528	1%	38,837	0%	33,202	0%	10,368	0%	7,726	0%
Total Assets	$13,179,758	100%	$18,877,395	100%	$17,309,274	100%	$14,574,377	100%	$16,155,610	100%
Liabilities										
Accounts Payable	$ 298,718	2%	$ 297,522	2%	$ 899,478	5%	$ 450,921	3%	$ 295,905	2%
Accrued Liabilities	323,311	2%	377,450	2%	404,528	2%	522,458	4%	597,552	4%
Due to Other Funds	2,328,257	18%	3,404,495	18%	4,234,495	24%	7,434,497	51%	8,908,530	55%
Total Current Liabilities	2,950,286	22%	4,079,467	22%	5,538,501	32%	8,407,876	58%	9,801,987	61%
Deferred Revenues	3,359,531	25%	3,659,683	19%	3,732,514	22%	3,777,793	26%	3,926,262	24%
Total Liabilities	6,309,817	48%	7,739,150	41%	9,271,015	54%	12,185,669	84%	13,728,249	85%
Total Fund Balances	6,869,941	52%	11,138,245	59%	8,038,259	46%	2,388,708	16%	2,427,361	15%
Total Liabilities & Fund Balances	$13,179,758	100%	$18,877,395	100%	$17,309,274	100%	$14,574,377	100%	$16,155,610	100%

FIGURE 2.26 Governmental Funds Balance Sheet Vertical Analysis for Company 3

	YR 1		YR 2		YR 3		YR 4		YR 5	
Revenues										
Charges for Services	$ 431,025	4%	$ 453,688	4%	$ 446,319	3%	$ 453,633	4%	$ 428,142	3%
Taxes	3,137,291	28%	3,339,281	28%	3,524,222	24%	3,716,189	30%	3,756,412	28%
Licenses, Permits, Fees	283,344	3%	281,260	2%	266,924	2%	270,910	2%	282,192	2%
Fines and Penalities	159,788	1%	181,919	2%	148,360	1%	159,894	1%	129,461	1%
Other Revenues	620,379	6%	537,394	4%	667,642	5%	1,306,048	11%	614,931	5%
Intergovernmental Revenues	6,493,027	58%	7,191,612	60%	9,440,034	65%	6,507,210	52%	8,333,667	62%
Total Revenues	11,124,854	100%	11,985,154	100%	14,493,501	100%	12,413,884	100%	13,544,805	100%
Expenses										
General & Administrative	7,398,658	67%	9,123,875	76%	8,625,966	60%	9,738,780	78%	9,736,115	72%
Pension & SS Payments	970,971	9%	1,012,097	8%	1,042,311	7%	1,109,795	9%	1,123,927	8%
Capital Outlay	5,171,038	46%	6,032,238	50%	8,645,654	60%	7,634,565	62%	5,376,412	40%
Debt Service	623,000	6%	397,000	3%	691,000	5%	647,000	5%	1,154,666	9%
Interest Expense	375,710	3%	346,640	3%	523,556	4%	558,295	4%	264,032	2%
Total Expenses	14,539,377	131%	16,911,850	141%	19,528,487	135%	19,688,435	159%	17,655,152	130%
Excess (Deficiency)	(3,414,523)	-31%	(4,926,696)	-41%	(5,034,986)	-35%	(7,274,551)	-59%	(4,110,347)	-30%
Operating Transfers In	6,350,000	57%	7,815,000	65%	7,341,000	51%	5,935,000	48%	6,479,000	48%
Bond Proceeds	—	0%	6,500,000	54%	—	0%	—	0%	1,679,000	12%
Operating Transfers Out	4,753,000	43%	5,120,000	43%	5,406,000	37%	4,310,000	35%	4,009,000	30%
Changes in Fund Balance	$(1,817,523)	-16%	$4,268,304	36%	$(3,099,986)	-21%	$(5,649,551)	-46%	$ 38,653	0%

FIGURE 2.27 Governmental Funds Income Statement Vertical Analysis for Company 3

Strangely, both accounts receivable and deferred revenues are comparatively stable in the primary government balance sheets, but the governmental funds balance sheet illustrates the opposite. Since the differences in these statements relate to additional accruals, the disparity requires further investigation, especially the accrual entries.

Looking at tax revenues on the governmental funds income statement, the revenues are comparatively stable, but in the primary government financial income statements, the tax revenues are more diverse. Again, the accruals required in the primary government income statements create this inconsistency. As mentioned before, the operating transfers in and the operating transfers out should be consistent and, in the case of governmental funds income statements, should wash out.

Company 4

Figure 2.28 illustrates the balance sheet vertical analysis for Company 4 and Figure 2.29 illustrates the income statement vertical analysis for Company 4. Vertical analysis, like the other analytics already performed, demonstrates the specific items noted in Chapter 1.

The vertical analysis for the balance sheet shows some variations with the accounts, such as accounts receivable, inventory, fixed assets, and accounts payable. The changes in both other assets and other liabilities are comparable. More importantly, the vertical analysis demonstrates management's intentions to improve the financial stability of the company, with total current assets increasing through YR 3 and then becoming stable in both YR 4 and YR 5, while total current liabilities decrease every year. The decrease in fixed assets in YR 3 is reasonable, knowing that the company was finally able to close out the bankrupt subsidiary. Notice the consistency not only in cost of goods sold but in the other expense accounts as well. Gross profit is also comparatively stable. This stability is not found in the other three companies.

 SUMMARY

Although this chapter features calculations for each of the four companies from basic ratios generally renowned in the accounting arena, the financial forensic examiner now knows that these basic ratios at best provide only remote hints to anomalies in financial information. Yet these tests may provide glimpses of

(in thousands)	YR 1		YR 2		YR 3		YR 4		YR 5	
Assets										
Cash	$ 5,240	4%	$ 2,812	2%	$ 6,147	4%	$ 8,204	4%	$ 23,282	12%
Accounts Receivable	39,052	30%	50,452	39%	67,626	47%	86,674	44%	68,675	36%
Allowance for Bad Debts	(1,062)	–1%	(1,116)	–1%	(1,834)	–1%	(2,488)	–1%	(1,640)	–1%
Inventory	26,715	20%	34,994	27%	38,318	27%	43,155	22%	39,313	21%
Prepaid Expenses	1,783	1%	1,525	1%	739	1%	2,079	1%	1,775	1%
Total Current Assets	71,728	54%	88,667	69%	110,996	77%	137,624	70%	131,405	70%
Other Assets	39,113	30%	20,393	16%	16,131	11%	27,527	14%	23,830	13%
Fixed Assets (net)	20,977	16%	18,762	15%	17,443	12%	32,281	16%	33,807	18%
	$131,818	100%	$127,822	100%	$144,570	100%	$197,432	100%	$189,042	100%
Liabilities										
Accounts Payable	$ 34,164	26%	$ 36,224	28%	$ 45,352	31%	$ 58,620	30%	$ 39,926	21%
Other Liabilities	37,680	29%	18,416	14%	16,065	11%	13,269	7%	10,623	6%
Current Portion of Debt	2,050	2%	2,052	2%	1,595	1%	1,623	1%	1,802	1%
Total Current Liabilities	73,894	56%	56,692	44%	63,012	44%	73,512	37%	52,351	28%
Notes Payable	29,927	23%	24,345	19%	16,803	12%	10,537	5%	4,203	2%
Total Liabilities	$103,821	79%	$ 81,037	63%	$ 79,815	55%	$ 84,049	43%	$ 56,554	30%
Shareholders' Equity	27,997	21%	46,785	37%	64,755	45%	113,383	57%	132,488	70%
Total Liabilities & SE	$131,818	100%	$127,822	100%	$144,570	100%	$197,432	100%	$189,042	100%

FIGURE 2.28 Balance Sheet Vertical Analysis for Company 4

(in thousands)	YR 1		YR 2		YR 3		YR 4		YR 5	
Revenues										
Sales	$205,996	100%	$236,308	100%	$351,884	100%	$409,421	100%	$400,032	100%
Less Cost of Goods Sold	179,008	87%	205,021	87%	301,943	86%	349,639	85%	343,885	86%
Gross Profit	26,988	13%	31,287	13%	49,941	14%	59,782	15%	56,147	14%
Expenses										
General & Admininstrative	13,841	7%	15,812	7%	21,533	6%	24,229	6%	23,971	6%
Depreciation	3,570	2%	3,092	1%	2,760	1%	2,608	1%	3,134	1%
Other Expense	6,291	3%	4,657	2%	4,012	1%	3,518	1%	3,392	1%
Income Tax Expense	1,216	1%	740	0%	2,936	1%	2,454	1%	9,319	2%
Total Expenses	24,918	12%	24,301	10%	31,241	9%	32,809	8%	39,816	10%
Misc Income	(16,223)	–8%	(1,511)	–1%	(114)	0%	18,370	4%	—	
Net Profit (Loss)	$ (14,153)	–7%	$ (5,475)	2%	$ 18,586	5%	$ 45,343	11%	$ 16,331	4%

FIGURE 2.29 Income Statement Vertical Analysis for Company 4

possible inconsistencies in the financial information. These tests do provide the financial forensic examiner an overall picture of the company operations.

As an example, the working capital index is a means of measuring the change of current assets and current liabilities from year to year. Significant increases in the working capital turnover calculations could be a symptom of revenue-related fraud. The stock sales ratio is a means of determining a company's efficiency in maintaining its inventory and increases indicate that inventory is growing more rapidly than sales. The financial forensic examiner also knows that if management is running the company efficiently and effectively, gross profit margins will change very little over time, and any significant change warrants further investigation to determine the cause.

Horizontal analysis presents changes year over year, developing trends relating to the company's financial statements, and demonstrates that a more appropriate method of determining the changes is to calculate the percentage of the change year over year for each line item in the financial statements. Horizontal analysis also allows comparison of current and past performance and provides a broader picture of account relationships. However, this analysis does not provide the financial forensic examiner sufficient detection of smaller inconsistencies in the financial statements.

Where horizontal analysis provides a broad picture of account relationships, vertical analysis actually investigates the relationships between the accounts in the financial statements, which makes it a very useful tool for the financial forensic examiner. By using vertical analysis, the financial forensic examiner builds knowledge concerning account relationships and the interaction between individual transactions and the internal operations of the company. The studies of the horizontal analyses and the vertical analyses of the four companies in this chapter offer the financial forensic examiner the basic skills for understanding account relationships that will be essential in the next chapter.

CHAPTER THREE

The Importance of Cash Flows and Cash Flow Statements

CCORDING TO the background information for each of the four companies, cash flow statements were not part of the financial statements for Company 2 and not even prepared for Company 1. Cash flow statements are not required for governmental funds, only for the proprietary and business-type governmental entities. When these statements are missing, important information relating to a company's operations is also missing. More notably, these statements provide invaluable information to the financial forensic examiner, including the discovery of possible incentives to commit fraud, either in desperate attempts to conceal losses or in hiding possible theft of company funds. Either motive requires the manipulation of the cash flow statement.

Statement of Cash Flows, Topic AU 230 of the Codification of Financial Accounting Standards from the Financial Accounting Standards Board (FASB), provides guidance relating to cash flow statements and the prerequisites for the information required in the statement. Fundamentally, the cash flow statement is a "sources and uses" report of the company's cash, since the income statement includes accruals that obscure cash transactions unless the financial statements are prepared on a cash basis, which is not normally found in a company's prepared financial statements. For the financial forensic examiner, it is important to understand the mechanics of the statement and the relevance in its analysis.

There are three sections to the cash flow statement and two different methods to choose from in preparing it. Both methods include *cash from operations, cash from investing activities,* and *cash from financing activities,* which when added together equal the change in cash over the prior year. The two methods include the *direct method* and the *indirect method.* The direct method lists both the sources and uses of cash from operations and the difference between the two reported as cash flow from operations. The indirect method reconciles net income from the income statement and then adjusts the net income amount for non-cash revenues and expenses to arrive at cash flow for operations. The horizontal analysis discussion in Chapter 2 for each of the four companies touched on the basic concept of adjusting net income.

Cash flows associated with investing activities include cash transactions related to fixed assets, investments, or intangible assets. Transactions relating to fixed assets may be either purchases or sales of fixed assets while transactions for investments may include either purchases or sales of various types of investments, such as investments in securities and the stocks and bonds of other companies. From the financial forensic examiner's perspective, the underlying origins for these transactions are the important factors for possible deceptive financial transactions.

Cash flows associated with financing activities include cash transactions related to debt and equity securities. Transactions relating to debt may include issuing bonds, acquiring a loan, or repaying debt. Equity transactions may include the selling of company stock, the repurchase of company stock (treasury stock), or paying cash dividends to company shareholders. Again, the underlying reasons for these transactions should be the focus of the financial forensic examiner.

Last and most important are the cash flows associated with operations, for these transactions show the information from a company's normal routine business operations. The cash flows from operations segment of the cash flow statement is where net income from operations recorded on an accrual basis converts to actual cash transactions, so it is very important that the financial forensic examiner understand the concepts of these adjustments as presented in Chapter 2.

▪ Increases in accounts receivable decrease cash because the accrued revenues are higher than cash revenues, whereas decreases in accounts receivable occur when cash revenues are higher than accrued revenues increasing cash.

■ Increases in inventory decrease cash since purchased inventory exceeds the inventory sold and is consequently deferred to a subsequent period. When inventory decreased, the purchased inventory was not sufficient and deferred inventory had to be used, thereby increasing cash.

■ Decreases in prepaid expenses increase cash because the actual cash expense occurred in a prior period relating to costs occurring in the following period. These reductions become an expense against the current period's income, although the company does not pay any cash for these transactions. As prepaid expenses increase, cash decreases, because the actual cash payment is for the next period's costs and must be amortized and charged against the next period's income.

■ Increases in accounts payable and accrued liabilities increase cash because the company purchased goods or incurred costs but has not paid for these goods or costs during the current period. Conversely, when decreases occur in accounts payable and accrued liabilities, cash decreases, since the company made payments for prior purchases or prior costs incurred.

■ Decreases in income tax payable also decrease cash, since cash payments exceed the expenses included in the accrual. On the other hand, increases in income tax payable increase cash, since cash payments are less than the expenses included in the accrual.

By understanding these key concepts, the financial forensic examiner is able to build a simple cash flow analysis using the indirect method and focus on the sources and uses of cash in the financial statements. In addition, the financial forensic examiner is able to compare cash flows and financial statement information with other analytical tests, such as comparing cash flow from operations and net income from operations, cash flow and net income ratio, and the operating performance ratios included in this chapter.

CASH FLOWS AND NET INCOME

Many times a financial forensic examiner may not have prepared cash flow statements completed by a company and must prepare an analysis of sources and uses of cash in order to follow the cash transactions. This is a rather easy task once the financial forensic examiner understands how changes in account relationships affect cash flows. For most companies, it is only a matter of adjusting net income for the accruals included in the net income amount. Using the indirect method approach, cash flow statements may be prepared from the balance sheets and income statements of a company, or tax returns, knowing that adjustments on the M-1 schedule must be included. When the calculations are complete, and the financial forensic examiner finds differences between the calculated cash and the cash presented on the financial statements, more than likely the financial statements, especially the income statements, are hiding the results of fraudulent activity.

Fraudulent transactions may occur anywhere on the financial statements but the results of the fraudulent activity generally flow to the income statement, especially embezzlement schemes such as skimming and theft of inventory. *Skimming*, often known as an *off-book fraud*, leaves no audit trail since cash is misappropriated prior to recording the receipts in the company's financial records. While this particular scheme is difficult to detect, the results of this activity will flow through to the income statement, generally in the area of costs of sales (cost of goods sold) or other various revenue or expense accounts. Stealing inventory is another prime example of where the results of the fraudulent activity will flow through to the income statement, especially since cash is not directly involved in the transaction. Even with attempts to hide these types of fraudulent activity, signs are still in the financial statements. These examples alone justify a comparison of net income and operating cash flows.

One of the most effective ways to analyze net operating income in the financial statements is to compare net operating income with cash flows from operations, sometimes referred to as the *cash realization ratio*:

$$CRO = \text{Operating Cash Flow divided by Net Income}$$

Although variances differ greatly by industry, the result of the CRO equation should be less than 1 when considering that net income includes depreciation, amortization, and other non-cash items added back to net income when calculating cash flows. A company's CRO index should remain rather consistent over time and, with a bit of luck, increase over time. Operating cash flow tells much about a company, including a company's ability to continue. If the company is not generating cash, it cannot survive. While it may be easier to manipulate financial statements to show profitability, it is more difficult to manipulate cash flows. Although it is not impossible to stage-manage a cash flow statement, there are ways a company may temporarily boost cash flows, such as extending payables and reversing expenses made in prior quarters.

For the financial forensic examiner, reductions in net income and increases in cash flows create inconsistencies in how a company operates. For example, increased profitability increases cash flows, while decreases in profitability decrease cash flows, so the two processes parallel each other. Decreases in net income and increases in cash flows are a warning to the financial forensic examiner to search further. While this divergence is not common, it may surface as it does in Company 4 and not represent fraudulent activity.

In the following studies of the four companies, the financial forensic examiner learns the importance of cash flow statements and the comparison of operating cash flow and net income.

Company 1

Figure 3.1 shows a simplified version of the cash flow statements for Company 1, prepared from the tax returns of the company since the company did not prepare financial statements. The financial information includes the adjustments noted in Schedule M-1 of the tax return.

The financial information found in the tax returns of the company supplies sufficient information to develop financial statements, including information associated with cash flows. By YR 5, the differences between the cash reported in the financial statements and the cash calculated based on the financial information do not differ significantly.

- ■ In YR 2, the cash balance on the financial statements equals the calculated cash balance.
- ■ In YR 3, the cash balance on the financial statements is slightly higher than the calculated cash balance.
- ■ In YR 4, the cash balance on the financial statements equals the calculated cash.
- ■ In YR 5, the cash balance on the financial statements is slightly higher than the calculated cash.

Based on the differences between the cash balance on the financial statements and the calculated cash balance from analyzing the cash flows, the financial forensic examiner now understands how simple cash flow statements may or may not indicate possible fraudulent transactions in the financial statements. If misappropriations of cash are the basis of the fraudulent activity, the statement of cash flows may not indicate that fraud is occurring, especially if the cash is missing in the financial records and stashed away in an off-book bank account for future removal.

	YR 2	YR 3	YR 4	YR 5
Beginning Cash	$ 13,478	$ 1,195	$ 3,519	$ 330
Net Income	(22,618)	1,019	(4,315)	(15,441)
Depreciation	4,664	10,805	5,882	6,831
Prior Year A/R	18,011	24,345	29,994	33,807
Current Year A/R	(24,345)	(29,994)	(33,807)	(28,138)
Prior Year A/P	(12,545)	(10,612)	(5,447)	(7,642)
Current Year A/P	10,612	5,447	7,642	10,411
Cash from Operating Activities	(26,221)	1,010	(51)	(172)
Equipment Additions	(3,703)	(12,403)	(2,500)	(7,795)
Cash from Investing Activities	(3,703)	(12,403)	(2,500)	(7,795)
Current Year N/P	17,641	31,192	30,554	32,862
Prior Year N/P	—	(17,641)	(31,192)	(30,554)
Cash from Financing Activities	17,641	13,551	(638)	2,308
Net Change in Cash (Financial Statements)	(12,283)	2,324	(3,189)	(5,629)
Calculated Net Change in Cash	(12,283)	2,158	(3,189)	(5,659)
Difference	—	166	—	30
Ending Cash Calculated	$ 1,195	$ 3,353	$ 330	$ (5,329)
Per Books	$ 1,195	$ 3,519	$ 330	$ (5,299)

FIGURE 3.1 Cash Flows for Company 1

Table 3.1 shows the calculations for the cash realization ratio. Remember the calculations should be less than 1.

The calculations for the cash realized from operations indicate that YR 2 is outside the normal range of expectations while YR 3 would follow the general expectations of what the CRO calculations should be. However, YR 4 and YR 5 are both significantly lower than YR 3, and the difference between YR 3 and YR 4 is significant when compared to the difference between YR 3 and YR 2.

TABLE 3.1 CRO Calculations for Company 1

YR 2	YR 3	YR 4	YR 5
1.16	.99	.01	.01

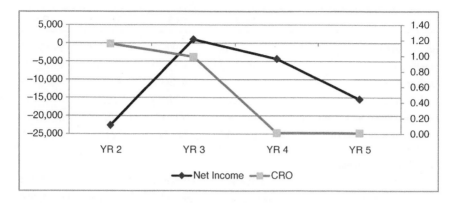

FIGURE 3.2 Cash Realized from Operations versus Net Income for Company 1

Perhaps a better technique to use for this test is a visual aid in the form of a dual-axis chart. Figure 3.2 shows the comparison of operating cash flows to net income.

- From YR 2 to YR 3, the chart definitely illustrates that operating cash flows do not match net income from operations, since net income is increasing while CRO is decreasing.
- From YR 3 to YR 4, operating cash flows decrease at an accelerated rate compared to net income.
- From YR 4 to YR 5, operating cash flows stabilize while net income continues to decrease.

From the financial forensic examiner's outlook, the CRO and net income relationship is not parallel and requires further study and examination.

Company 2

Using the same approach, Figure 3.3 illustrates the cash flows for Company 2, given that some of the financial statements did not include cash flow statements.

Unlike Company 1, Company 2's cash reported in the financial statements does not equal the calculated ending cash for every year except YR 5. Management discovered the fraud in the third quarter of YR 5 and corrected the financial statements prior to the end of the year. Since statements of cash flows were not part of the financial statements, management did not recognize

	YR 2	YR 3	YR 4	YR 5
Beginning Cash	6,037	219,408	409,620	1,615,708
Net Income	799,532	1,585,639	2,320,650	1,593,947
Depreciation	240,233	306,697	339,156	375,978
Bad Debt Expense	59,000	(22,828)	62,927	—
Prior Year Deferred Income Taxes	(488,762)	(873,317)	(1,270,317)	(424,317)
Current Year Deferred Income Taxes	873,317	1,270,317	424,317	604,000
Non-Cash Gain on Sale	—	—	—	(284,970)
Prior Year A/R	1,388,977	2,905,601	2,282,772	2,158,034
Current Year A/R	(2,905,601)	(2,282,772)	(2,158,034)	(2,275,985)
Prior Year Inventory	1,866,785	3,904,040	3,282,898	3,887,568
Current Year Inventory	(3,904,040)	(3,282,898)	(3,887,568)	(5,159,037)
Prior Year Prepaid Expenses	256,677	309,566	176,110	73,826
Current Year Prepaid Expenses	(309,566)	(176,110)	(73,826)	(75,412)
Prior Year Refundable Taxes	—	—	21,205	47,000
Current Year Refundable Taxes	—	(21,205)	(47,000)	(40,000)
Prior Year Other Liabilities	(26,150)	(124,856)	(64,452)	(116,796)
Current Year Other Liabilities	124,856	64,452	116,796	461,000
Current Year Other Assets	—	—	—	(963,459)
Non-Cash Addition to Other Assets				963,459
Prior Year A/P	(1,186,293)	(2,987,894)	(1,902,907)	(1,951,605)
Non-Cash Addition to A/P				116,773
Current Year A/P	2,987,894	1,902,907	1,951,605	1,352,480
Cash from Operating Activities	(223,141)	2,477,339	1,574,332	342,484
Equipment Additions	(435,186)	(483,393)	(332,822)	(1,091,391)
Cash from Investing Activities	(435,186)	(483,393)	(332,822)	(1,091,391)
Prior Year N/P	(619,508)	(1,719,098)	—	—
Current Year N/P	1,719,098	—	—	—
Cash from Financing Activities	1,099,590	(1,719,098)	—	—
Net Change in Cash (Financial Statements)	213,371	190,212	1,206,088	(748,907)
Calculated Net Change in Cash	441,263	274,848	1,241,510	(748,907)
Difference	(227,892)	(84,636)	(35,422)	—
Ending Cash Calculated	447,300	494,256	1,651,130	866,801
Per Books	219,408	409,620	1,615,708	866,801

FIGURE 3.3   Cash Flows for Company 2

the possibility of fraudulent activity occurring within the company. Figure 3.3 is a prime example of using cash flow statements in financial forensic analysis. When cash flow statements are not part of the financial statements, a financial forensic examiner needs to consider the absence of this statement and prepare a cash flow statement for analysis.

- In YR 2, the ending cash calculated amount is over 200% higher than the actual cash recorded on the books.
- In YR 3, the ending cash calculated amount is over 120% higher than the actual cash recorded on the books.
- In YR 4, the ending cash calculated amount is over 102% higher than the actual cash recorded on the books.
- In YR 5, the ending cash calculated amount equals the actual cash recorded on the books.

Similar to Company 1, though, the CRO calculations vary significantly. Table 3.2 illustrates the CRO calculations for Company 2.

TABLE 3.2   CRO Calculations for Company 2

YR 2	YR 3	YR 4	YR 5
−.28	1.56	.68	.21

Again, YR 3 poses the sticky situation for the financial forensic examiner with the calculation greater than 1. Other important factors include a change of 1.84 basis points from YR 2 to YR 3 and .88 basis points from YR 3 to YR 4. All of these departures are areas that the financial forensic examiner should investigate.

Using the dual-axis method for visual presentation, Figure 3.4 illustrates the comparison of net income to operating cash flows.

- From YR 2 to YR 3, operating cash flows increased at a greater rate than net income.
- From YR 3 to YR 4, operating cash flows decreased while net income continued to increase.
- From YR 4 to YR 5, the relationships between operating cash flows and net income become similar to each other as shown by the congruent lines in the graph, although net income decreased slightly more than operating cash flows.

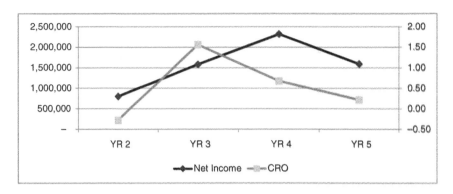

FIGURE 3.4   Cash Realized from Operations versus Net Income for Company 2

Obviously, from YR 3 to YR 4 poses the greatest concern for the financial forensic examiner, since the relationship between net income and operating cash flows is completely converse. The slight differences in the relationship for YR 5 relate to the additional non-cash adjustments shown in the cash flow statement rather than just the depreciation adjustment. There are no additional non-cash adjustments in the other years other than depreciation.

Company 3

Since governmental entities are only required to present statements of cash flows for the business-type entities, both the primary government and the governmental funds financial statements do not include cash flow statements, so the financial forensic examiner needs to prepare a simple version of these cash flow statements for analysis. Figure 3.5 shows a simplified cash flow statement for the primary government.

With the exception of YR 1, where there is a minor difference, the primary government cash flow statements that calculate ending cash also agree to the ending cash reported in the financial statements. Yet the CRO calculations in Table 3.3 pose some questions that the financial forensic examiner must research.

By remembering the formula for the cash realized from operations, the calculations of the primary government indicate that cash flows from operating activities definitely exceed net income in the subsequent years following YR 2, as well as the calculations in excess of 1, and pose questions for the financial forensic examiner. For the primary government, non-cash entries in the net income amount include not only depreciation but also losses on sales of fixed

	YR 2	YR 3	YR 4	YR 5
Beginning Cash	$ 7,294,032	$ 6,021,685	$ 3,713,473	$ 1,570,296
Net Income	(349,697)	1,972,227	1,662,515	3,915,802
Depreciation	3,966,022	4,333,368	4,810,923	5,303,901
Bad Debt Expense	—	—	50,000	25,000
Non-Cash Loss (Gain) on Sale of Fixed Assets	62,650	9,847	—	24,248
Prior Year Deferred Revenues	(4,651,080)	(4,020,322)	(4,109,313)	(4,169,035)
Current Year Deferred Revenues	4,020,322	4,109,313	4,169,035	4,324,932
Prior Year A/R	6,193,387	5,675,948	5,770,644	6,221,333
Current Year A/R	(5,675,948)	(5,770,644)	(6,221,333)	(7,481,059)
Prior Year Inventory	176,657	181,274	140,525	148,483
Current Year Inventory	(181,274)	(140,525)	(148,483)	(183,381)
Prior Year Prepaid Expenses	172,006	181,279	222,326	103,951
Current Year Prepaid Expenses	(181,279)	(222,326)	(103,951)	(104,732)
Prior Year Accrued Liabilities	(664,625)	(664,470)	(750,486)	(858,797)
Current Year Accrued Liabilities	664,470	750,486	858,797	944,611
Prior Year A/P	(563,946)	(761,336)	(1,332,591)	(643,130)
Current Year A/P	761,336	1,332,591	643,130	1,422,480
Cash from Operating Activities	3,749,001	6,966,710	5,661,738	8,994,607
Prior Year Investments	3,248,768	7,109,141	5,603,751	966,476
Current Year Investments	(7,109,141)	(5,603,751)	(966,476)	(720,763)
Equipment Additions	(7,196,204)	(13,463,811)	(11,598,774)	(11,478,918)
Cash from Investing Activities	(11,056,577)	(11,958,421)	(6,961,499)	(11,233,205)
Prior Year Long Term Debt	(25,705,394)	(31,711,631)	(34,389,495)	(33,523,245)
Current Year Long Term Debt	31,711,631	34,389,495	33,523,245	35,514,165
Prior Year Notes Receivable	67,528	38,837	33,202	10,368
Current Year Notes Receivable	(38,837)	(33,202)	(10,368)	(7,726)
Due to Pension Fund	—	—	—	264,032
Cash from Financing Activities	6,034,928	2,683,499	(843,416)	2,257,594
Net Change in Cash (Financial Statements)	(1,272,347)	(2,308,212)	(2,143,177)	18,996
Calculated Net Change in Cash	(1,272,648)	(2,308,212)	(2,143,177)	18,996
Difference	301	—	—	—
Ending Cash Calculated	$ 6,021,384	$ 3,713,473	$ 1,570,296	$ 1,589,292
Per Books	$ 6,021,685	$ 3,713,473	$ 1,570,296	$ 1,589,292

FIGURE 3.5 Primary Government Cash Flows

TABLE 3.3   CRO Calculations of the Primary Government for Company 3

YR 2	YR 3	YR 4	YR 5
−10.72	3.53	3.41	2.30

assets and bad debt expenses. While the change in the CRO calculations from YR 3 to YR 4 is only .12 basis points, the change from YR 2 to YR 3 is extreme at 14.25 basis points, and the change from YR 4 to YR 5 is 1.11 basis points.

To better analyze the differences, Figure 3.6 once again illustrates the usefulness of the dual-axis visual presentation to analyze net income and operating cash flows.

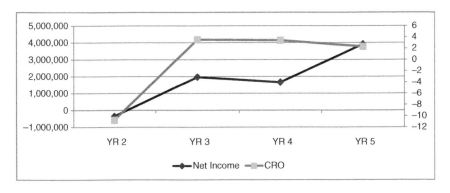

FIGURE 3.6   Cash Realized from Operations versus Net Income of the Primary Government for Company 3

The visual representation provides interesting variations for the financial forensic examiner. From YR 2 to YR 3, net income increases at a slower pace than CRO but they are both trending upward. From YR 3 to YR 4, both CRO and net income are relatively stable, with net income slightly trending downward, but from YR 4 to YR 5, CRO is decreasing while net income is increasing, creating a conflicting relationship. These trends definitely require further study by the financial forensic examiner.

Now, we look at the governmental funds analyses to see if similar trends are present. Figure 3.7 shows the simplified cash flow statement for the governmental funds.

Although the primary government cash flow statements indicate differences in the calculated ending cash and the stated cash for YR 2, the governmental funds cash flows have no discrepancies between the calculated

	YR 2	YR 3	YR 4	YR 5
Beginning Cash	$ 2,305,503	$ 3,073,334	$ 2,134,862	$ 816,508
Net Income	4,268,304	(3,099,986)	(5,649,551)	38,653
Prior Year Deferred Revenues	(3,359,531)	(3,659,683)	(3,732,514)	(3,777,793)
Current Year Deferred Revenues	3,659,683	3,732,514	3,777,793	3,926,262
Prior Year A/R	4,514,877	4,966,972	5,060,185	5,373,058
Current Year A/R	(4,966,972)	(5,060,185)	(5,373,058)	(5,679,331)
Prior Year Inventory	23,331	38,520	20,316	48,458
Current Year Inventory	(38,520)	(20,316)	(48,458)	(60,221)
Prior Year Prepaid Expenses	140,855	146,444	166,472	53,949
Current Year Prepaid Expenses	(146,444)	(166,472)	(53,949)	(57,488)
Prior Year Accrued Liabilities	(323,311)	(377,450)	(404,528)	(522,458)
Current Year Accrued Liabilities	377,450	404,528	522,458	597,552
Prior Year A/P	(298,718)	(297,522)	(899,478)	(450,921)
Current Year A/P	297,522	899,478	450,921	295,905
Cash from Operating Activities	4,148,526	(2,493,158)	(6,163,391)	(214,375)
Prior Year Investments	2,839,407	6,688,938	5,174,742	532,041
Current Year Investments	(6,688,938)	(5,174,742)	(532,041)	(284,067)
Cash from Investing Activities	(3,849,531)	1,514,196	4,642,701	247,974
Prior Year Due from Other Funds	3,288,257	3,924,350	4,719,495	7,739,995
Current Year Due from Other Funds	(3,924,350)	(4,719,495)	(7,739,995)	(9,472,608)
Prior Year Notes Receivable	67,528	38,837	33,202	10,368
Current Year Notes Receivable	(38,837)	(33,202)	(10,368)	(7,726)
Prior Year Due to Other Funds	(2,328,257)	(3,404,495)	(4,234,495)	(7,434,497)
Current Year Due to Other Funds	3,404,495	4,234,495	7,434,497	8,908,530
Cash from Financing Activities	468,836	40,490	202,336	(255,938)
Net Change in Cash (Financial Statements)	767,831	(938,472)	(1,318,354)	(222,339)
Calculated Net Change in Cash	767,831	(938,472)	(1,318,354)	(222,339)
Difference	—	—	—	—
Ending Cash Calculated	$ 3,073,334	$ 2,134,862	$ 816,508	$ 594,169
Per Books	$ 3,073,334	$ 2,134,862	$ 816,508	$ 594,169

FIGURE 3.7 Governmental Funds Cash Flow Statements for Company 3

ending cash and the cash recorded on the books. As demonstrated in the analyses of the primary government, the lack of discrepancies in the cash flow statements does not necessarily indicate the lack of any variation in the financial information.

Table 3.4 displays the CRO calculations of the governmental funds for Company 3.

TABLE 3.4   CRO Calculations of the Governmental Funds for Company 3

YR 2	YR 3	YR 4	YR 5
.97	.80	1.09	−5.5

Contrary to the primary government CRO calculations, in which the most significant change occurred between YR 2 and YR 3, the most significant variance for the governmental funds CRO calculations occurs from YR 4 to YR 5, where the change amounts to 6.59 basis points. YR 4 also suggests that operating cash flows were higher than net income, since the calculation exceeds 1. Once again, the financial forensic examiner needs to understand the reasons for these variances.

Figure 3.8 illustrates the comparison of the CRO to net income, optimistically providing a better analysis of CRO and net income.

The visual comparison of the CRO and net income shows that while the cash flow statements appear correct, the relationship between the CRO and net income totally contradict each other for all years presented. From YR 2 through YR 4, whereas CRO remained relatively stable, with a slight increase

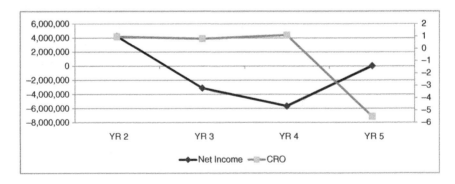

FIGURE 3.8   Cash Realized from Operations versus Net Income of the Governmental Funds for Company 3

from YR 3 to YR 4, net income continually decreased for all periods except YR 5. Even more of a quandary occurs from YR 4 to YR 5, when CRO decreases significantly while net income increases.

Thus, for both the primary government and the governmental funds, there are significant variances between the CRO calculations for some of the years, although different years for each, and contrasting relationships between CRO and net income. The financial forensic examiner should understand the reasons for variances of these trends to determine whether these trends have reasonable explanations from unusual operational events or are related to possible fraudulent activity.

Company 4

Figure 3.9 illustrates the cash flow statements for Company 4. Even at first glance, the financial forensic examiner will realize that the simplified version of cash flow statements used in the previous companies is not the way Figure 3.9 presents the cash flow statements for Company 4.

While the simplified method of calculating cash flows works for the majority of companies, it will not work for companies that have consolidated financial statements with foreign subsidiaries in the consolidation. In the consolidation process, when the foreign subsidiaries must adjust their financial statements to the functional currency, the balance sheet requires one method of calculating the exchange rate while the income statement requires another method. The consolidation requires the foreign subsidiary to use the exchange rate at the ending date of presentation for the balance sheet, whereas the exchange rate used for consolidating the income statement is an average of all the exchange rates over the period of presentation. For example, if the balance sheet date is as of December 31, XXX1, the exchange rate would be the exchange rate on the day of December 31, XXX1 and the income statement exchange rate would be the average of exchange rates from January 1, XXX1 through December 31, XXX1.

The cash flow statement includes calculations from three different exchange rates: beginning cash adjusted at one exchange rate, changes within the cash flow at a different rate, and the ending cash at yet another exchange rate. For this reason, simple addition and/or subtraction between balances will not be accurate. That does not prevent the financial forensic examiner from analyzing the cash flow statements, but the examiner must rely on other types of analyses, such as the CRO and the comparison of the CRO and net income.

Table 3.5 illustrates the CRO calculations for Company 4.

(in thousands)	YR 2	YR 3	YR 4	YR 5
Beginning Cash	$ 5,240	$ 2,812	$ 6,147	$ 8,204
Net Income	5,475	18,586	45,343	16,331
Depreciation	3,092	2,760	2,608	3,134
Amortization	938	480	236	123
(Gain) Loss from Discontinued Operations	1,511	114	(126)	—
Tax Benefit from Discontinued Operations	—	—	(18,244)	—
Deferred Tax Provision (Benefit)	—	—	(1,331)	7,716
Issuance of Non-Employee Director Shares	329	75	75	75
Bad Debt Provision	567	827	1,065	312
Stock-Based Compensation	—	—	308	308
Loss (Gain) on Sale of Equipment	10	—	—	(109)
Changes in A/R	(11,199)	(17,667)	(18,898)	17,305
Changes in Inventory	(7,288)	(4,579)	(3,496)	5,156
Changes in Prepaid Expenses	285	839	(1,390)	343
Changes in Other Assets and Other	(864)	(12)	(16)	46
Changes in Accounts Payable	1,271	9,952	12,090	(19,673)
Changes in Accrued Liabilities and Other	1,501	4,210	(343)	(2,497)
Net Cash from Operating Activities	(4,372)	15,585	17,881	28,570
Net Cash Used from Discontinued Operations	(1,341)	(2,225)	247	—
Net Cash Used in Operating Activities	(5,713)	13,360	18,128	28,570
Payments Received on Notes Receivable	122	227	604	482
Proceeds from Sale of Equipment	15	—	98	148
Equipment Additions	(695)	(1,425)	(12,564)	(8,718)
Cash from Investing Activities	(558)	(1,198)	(11,862)	(8,088)
Net Cash Provided from Discontinued Operations	4,454	1,421	25	—
Net Cash from Investing Activities	3,896	223	(11,837)	(8,088)
Proceeds from Issuance of Common Stock	4,235	—	—	—
Proceeds from Exercise of Stock Ooptions	27	720	1,325	616
Termination of Interest Rate Swap	96	57	—	—
Additions to Deferred Financing Costs	(522)	(389)	(5)	(42)

FIGURE 3.9   Cash Flows for Company 4

(in thousands)	YR 2	YR 3	YR 4	YR 5
Payments on Debt	(3,542)	(20,126)	(6,603)	(6,803)
Borrowings	5,132	12,007	329	—
Cash from Financing Activities	5,426	(7,731)	(4,954)	(6,229)
Net Cash Used in Discontinued Operations	(7,910)	(2,511)	—	—
Net Cash Used in Financing Activities	(2,484)	(10,242)	(4,954)	(6,229)
Effect of Exchange Rate Changes on Cash	293	(557)	697	825
Calculated Net Change in Cash	(4,008)	2,784	2,034	15,078
Change in Discontinued Operations	1,580	551	23	—
Ending Cash Calculated	$2,812	$ 6,147	$8,204	$23,282
Per Books	$2,812	$ 6,147	$8,204	$23,282

FIGURE 3.9 (Continued)

The CRO variance between YR 2 and YR 3 is 1.76 basis points, while the change from YR 3 to YR 4 is not very significant. However, between YR 4 and YR 5, the difference again is higher than 1 basis point, amounting to 1.35 basis points, and CRO is greater than net income. YR 5 also poses another problem since the calculation exceeds 1.

Figure 3.10 displays the visual comparison of CRO to net income for Company 4.

The comparison easily identifies the corresponding relationship between CRO and net income from YR 2 to YR 3, but this relationship diverges from YR 3 through YR 5. Since the relationship changes in these years, the financial forensic examiner again must study these changes and determine if there is a reasonable explanation for the unusual trend in the CRO and net income relationship.

Based on the general information provided in Chapter 1 and a review of the cash flow statements, the financial forensic examiner should notice that the influences of the discontinuing operations play a major part in the variances.

TABLE 3.5 CRO Calculations for Company 4

YR 2	YR 3	YR 4	YR 5
−1.04	.72	.40	1.75

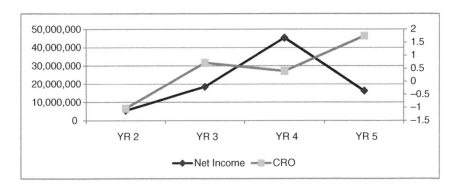

FIGURE 3.10 Cash Realized from Operations versus Net Income for Company 4

For example, in YR 4, the company has a rather large non-cash tax benefit and gain related to the liquidation and deconsolidation of the bankrupt subsidiary, and in YR 5 there is a significant increase in the deferred tax provision with the increase in tax rates. Both of these transactions are non-cash transactions influencing net income but not operating cash, and explain the divergence in the normal trend of the CRO and net income relationship.

By now, the financial forensic examiner should realize that a visual presentation comparing the CRO calculations to net income is an effective method of identifying anomalies in financial statement information and that these differences must be investigated further to determine if there are reasonable explanations for them, as in the case of Company 4. If the financial forensic examiner is unable to find reasonable explanations for the contrasting relationship between CRO and net income, the financial statements may be subject to manipulation and include fraudulent transactions.

Although not widely used in financial forensic analysis, several other useful ratios are effective in financial forensic analysis of financial statements. These include the operating cash flow ratio, the total debt coverage ratio, and, of course, common-sizing (vertical analysis) of cash flow statements. Its application to the four companies follows.

 OTHER CASH FLOW TECHNIQUES

In general, financial forensic examiners tend to associate vertical analysis, or *common-sizing*, with balance sheets and income statements, but this technique is quite useful in analyzing cash flow statements as well. As discussed in

Chapter 2, the technique for vertical analysis is to focus on parts of the financial information as a percentage of the whole. For cash flow statements, areas analyzed by vertical analysis include cash from operating activities, cash from investing activities, and cash from financing activities. The purpose of dividing the vertical analysis of the cash flow in this manner is to allow the financial forensic examiner to focus on the driving forces of changes in each section. A vertical analysis may also be prepared by using net change in cash to determine how each section affects the change of cash; for the purposes of forensic techniques, the presentation method applied in each of the four companies provides a better source of information relating to changes and possible inconsistencies.

While there are multiple types of cash flow ratios easily found in textbooks and other sources, these ratios, although seldom considered in forensic analysis, are very helpful in financial statement forensic analysis. Two such ratios include the *operating cash flow* and the *cash flow margin ratio*. The operating cash flow ratio measures a company's ability to pay current debt from the cash flows from the cash noted in the cash from operations section of the cash flow statement. The cash flow margin ratio measures a company's ability to turn sales into cash.

Operating Cash Flow Ratio = Cash Flow from Operations/Current Liabilities

Cash Flow Margin Ratio = Cash Flow from Operations/Net Sales

These ratios, along with the vertical analysis of each of the four companies' cash flow statements, supplement the financial forensic examiner's tools in examining financial statement information for possible inconsistencies. These techniques used in each of the four companies follow.

Company 1

Figure 3.11 illustrates the vertical cash flow analysis for Company 1.

In reviewing the vertical analysis for the cash from operating activities, the fluctuations in depreciation, although not a cash component, vary greatly from year to year. Even net income varies greatly from year to year, but this shows the end result of variations in the components that make up net income. For the financial forensic analysis, this poses questions related to these wide changes and the underlying transactions that require these extreme variances. In addition, both the changes in A/R and the changes in A/P, which do affect cash flow, exhibit the same characteristics. The changes in A/R vary so much

Figure 3.11 Vertical Analysis of Cash Flows for Company 1

	YR 2		YR 3		YR 4		YR 5	
Beginning Cash	$ 13,478		$ 1,195		$ 3,519		$ 330	
Net Income	(22,618)	86%	1,019	100%	(4,315)	8461%	(15,441)	8978%
Depreciation	4,664	–18%	10,805	1070%	5,882	–11533%	6,831	–3972%
Changes in A/R	(6,334)	24%	(5,649)	–559%	(3,813)	7476%	5,669	–3296%
Changes in A/P	(1,933)	8%	(5,165)	–511%	2,195	–4304%	2,769	–1610%
Cash from Operating Activities	(26,221)	100% 214%	1,010	100% 43%	(51)	100% 2%	(172)	100% 3%
Equipment Additions	(3,703)		(12,403)		(2,500)		(7,795)	
Cash from Investing Activities	(3,703)	100% 30%	(12,403)	100% –534%	(2,500)	100% 78%	(7,795)	100% 138%
Changes in N/P	17,641		13,551		(638)		2,308	
Cash from Financing Activities	17,641	100% –144%	13,551	100% 583%	(638)	100% 20%	2,308	100% –41%
Net Change in Cash (Financial Statements)	(12,283)		2,324		(3,189)		(5,629)	
Calculated Net Change in Cash	(12,283)		2,158		(3,189)		(5,659)	
Difference	—		166		—		30	
Ending Cash Calculated	$ 1,195		$ 3,353		$ 330		$ (5,329)	
Per Books	$ 1,195		$ 3,519		$ 330		$ (5,299)	

in the vertical analysis that this should alert the financial forensic examiner to perform further study in the A/R section. The same comment related to the changes in A/R is also applicable to the changes in A/P, so at this point the financial forensic examiner knows that further study must be performed in two areas, A/R and A/P, with the possibility of tampering with net income figures.

It is also appropriate to use vertical analysis to determine the percentage of each section that affects the net change in cash. In YR 2, cash from operating expenses amounts to 214% of the change in net cash, while cash from financing activities amounts to −144% of the change in net cash. In the subsequent years, the percentages of cash from operating expenses compared to net change in cash decrease and actually become an insignificant part of the net changes in cash. Even though these percentages are minor in total, it is still important to remember the comments about the individual changes each year between A/R, and A/P since the total cash from operating activities includes net income and the non-cash component depreciation.

Equipment additions represent only 30% of the change in net cash in YR 1. In the subsequent years, equipment additions and cash from investing activities become an integral part of the net change in cash, especially in YR 3, where the percentages in this section are less than 100% when using the net change in cash as recorded in the financial statements. Cash from financing activities also plays an important role in the net change in cash in YR 3 and again in YR 4. Since this section relates to a shareholder loan, the financial forensic examiner must study these changes closely and pursue other analysis.

Using the two additional cash flow ratios provides additional analysis relating to both changes in A/R and changes in A/P. Table 3.6 displays the calculations for both the operating cash flow ratio and the cash flow margin ratio. These ratios provide additional information relating to a company's ability to pay current debt and ability to generate cash from sales.

TABLE 3.6 Cash Flow Ratios for Company 1

	YR 2	YR 3	YR 4	YR 5
Operating Cash Flow Ratio	−2.09	.10	−.01	−.02
Cash Flow Margin Ratio	−.22	.01	−.0004	−.001

Both the operating cash flow ratio calculations and the cash flow margin ratio calculations confirm the same issues noted in the vertical cash analysis. The operating cash flow ratio calculations indicate that the company is not able to pay current debt, and the cash flow margin ratio indicates that the company is unable to generate cash from its sales. Now the financial forensic examiner has three separate analytical tests that indicate issues with changes in A/R, including sales, and changes in A/P, especially since A/P is the only current liability listed in the financial statements.

Company 2

Figure 3.12 illustrates the cash flow vertical analysis for Company 2.

In reviewing the vertical analysis for the cash flows of Company 2, the cash from operating activities includes several non-cash items, such as depreciation, gains on the sales of equipment and non-cash additions to other assets, and A/P related to the absorption of an additional facility in YR 5. However, when looking at the major players affecting cash from operating activities, changes in A/R is a significant amount in YR 2, while the change in inventory is a significant amount in YR 2 and YR 4. Also in YR 2 and YR 4, the change in A/P is a significant amount in cash from operating expenses. When reviewing the changes from year to year relating to these accounts, the financial forensic examiner recognizes that these accounts require further study.

When looking at the section totals and how these sections affect the net change in cash, cash flow from operating expenses becomes a significant amount of net change in cash, especially in YR 2. Notice that when calculating the percentages of each section relating to the net change in cash from the financial statements for YR 2, YR 3, and YR 4, the percentages do not equal 100%. This is an important clue for the financial forensic examiner, since it indicates that the net changes on the cash flow statements do not agree with the changes noted on the financial statements.

Cash from financing activities affects only YR 2 and YR 3. In YR 2 the change is positive, indicating the company received an additional source of cash, whereas in YR 3 the change is negative, indicating a use of cash. Even the cash from investing activities percentages to net change in cash remain similar for both YR 2 and YR 3, but this relationship changes in both YR 4 and YR 5 with a significant decrease in YR 4 and a significant increase in YR 5.

Table 3.7 shows the additional calculations relating to operating cash flow ratio and the cash flow margin ratio for the company.

The operating cash flow ratio indicates that in YR 3, the company has the ability to pay current debt from cash flows from operating activities, but for the same year, the cash flow margin ratio indicates that the company is not able to generate much cash flow from its sales. In fact, the cash flow margin ratios indicate that in any one year, the company is not able to generate much cash

	YR 2		YR 3		YR 4		YR 5	
Beginning Cash	$ 6,037		$ 219,408		$ 409,620		$1,615,708	
Net Income	799,532	−358%	1,585,639	65%	2,320,650	148%	1,593,947	465%
Depreciation	240,233	−108%	306,697	12%	339,156	22%	375,978	110%
Bad Debt Expense	59,000	−26%	(22,828)	−1%	62,927	4%	—	
Change in Deferred Income Taxes	384,555	−172%	397,000	16%	(846,000)	−54%	179,683	52%
Non-Cash Gain on Sale	—		—		—		(284,970)	−83%
Change in A/R	(1,516,624)	680%	622,829	25%	124,738	8%	(117,951)	−34%
Change in Inventory	(2,037,255)	912%	621,142	25%	(604,670)	−38%	(1,271,469)	−372%
Change in Prepaid Expenses	(52,889)	24%	133,456	5%	102,284	6%	(1,586)	0%
Change in Refundable Taxes	—		(21,205)	−1%	(25,795)	−2%	7,000	2%
Change in Other Liabilities	98,706	−44%	(60,404)	−2%	52,344	3%	344,204	101%
Current Year Other Assets	—		—		—		(963,459)	−281%
Non-Cash Addition to Other Assets							963,459	281%
Change in A/P	1,801,601	−808%	(1,084,987)	−44%	48,698	3%	(599,125)	−175%

(continued)

	YR 2			YR 3			YR 4			YR 5		
Non-Cash Addition to A/P										116,773		34%
Cash from Operating Activities	(223,141)	100%	−105%	2,477,339	100%	1302%	1,574,332	100%	131%	342,484	100%	−46%
Equipment Additions	(435,186)			(483,393)			(332,822)			(1,091,391)		
Cash from Investing Activities	(435,186)	100%	−204%	(483,393)	100%	−254%	(332,822)	100%	−28%	(1,091,391)	100%	146%
Prior Year N/P	(619,508)	−56%		(1,719,098)			—			—		
Current Year N/P	1,719,098	156%		—			—			—		
Cash from Financing Activities	1,099,590	100%	515%	(1,719,098)	100%	−904%	—		0%	—		0%
Net Change in Cash (Financial Statements)	213,371			190,212			1,206,088			(748,907)		
Calculated Net Change in Cash	441,263			274,848			1,241,510			(748,907)		
Difference	(227,892)			(84,636)			(35,422)			—		
Ending Cash Calculated	$ 447,300			$ 494,256			$1,651,130			$ 866,801		
Per Books	$ 219,408			$ 409,620			$1,615,708			$ 866,801		

FIGURE 3.12 Cash Flow Vertical Analysis for Company 2

TABLE 3.7 Cash Flow Ratios for Company 2

	YR 2	YR 3	YR 4	YR 5
Operating Cash Flow Ratio	−.07	1.26	.76	.19
Cash Flow Margin Ratio	−.01	.06	.04	.01

flow from sales. Thus, for the financial forensic examiner, the question becomes: What allows the company to pay current liabilities in YR 3 when the cash flow margin indicates otherwise?

For both YR 3 and YR 4, a significant part of cash from operating activities is net income, and it should generate cash for the company. Net income also varies greatly from year to year as part of the cash flows from operations and includes a significant number of non-cash adjustments in YR 5. For the other years, the ratios indicate that the company cannot pay its current debt from operating cash flows and is able to generate very little cash flow from sales. For these reasons, the financial forensic examiner needs to focus on the components of cash from operating activities and plan further study on those components with significant changes, which include A/R, A/P, and inventory, remembering that some fraudulent schemes only manifest themselves somewhere within the income statement, although the balance sheet accounts may contain the fraudulent transactions.

Company 3

Figure 3.13 shows the vertical analysis for the cash flows of the primary government for Company 3.

The cash from operating activities section of the vertical analysis of cash flows for the primary government does not really indicate any major changes other than net income, and depreciation, which is a non-cash element, and the changes in A/R. A/R changes vary from 14% to −14%, while A/P changes range from 5% to −11%. Looking at this analysis, the financial forensic examiner would see that inventory, accrued liabilities, and prepaid expenses change very little in terms of affecting overall cash from operating activities. Depreciation, although a non-cash item in the cash from operating activities, does provide a significant influence on the total cash from operating activities, because depreciation is a reduction of income and added back to get a true net income that should provide cash for the company.

Both the changes in investments and the equipment additions fluctuate from year to year. With the exception of YR 2, the equipment additions are the

	YR 2		YR 3		YR 4		YR 5	
Beginning Cash	$ 7,294,032		$ 6,021,685		$ 3,713,473		$ 1,570,296	
Net Income	(349,697)	-9%	1,972,227	29%	1,662,515	30%	3,915,802	44%
Depreciation	3,966,022	106%	4,333,368	62%	4,810,923	86%	5,303,901	58%
Bad Debt Expense	—		—		50,000	-2%	25,000	0%
Non-Cash Loss (Gain) on Sale of Fixed Assets	62,650	2%	9,847	0%	—	0%	24,248	0%
Change in Deferred Revenues	(630,758)	-18%	88,991	1%	59,722	1%	155,897	2%
Change in A/R	517,439	14%	(94,696)	-1%	(450,689)	-8%	(1,259,726)	-14%
Change in Inventory	(4,617)	0%	40,749	1%	(7,958)	0%	(34,898)	0%
Change in Prepaid Expenses	(9,273)	0%	(41,047)	-1%	118,375	2%	(781)	0%
Change in Accrued Liabilities	(155)	0%	86,016	1%	108,311	2%	85,814	1%
Change in A/P	197,390	5%	571,255	8%	(689,461)	-11%	779,350	9%
Cash from Operating Activities	3,749,001	100% -295%	6,966,710	100% -302%	5,661,738	100% -264%	8,994,607	100% 47350%
Change in Investments	(3,860,373)	35%	1,505,390	-13%	4,637,275	-67%	245,713	-2%
Equipment Additions	(7,196,204)	65%	(13,463,811)	113%	(11,598,774)	167%	(11,478,918)	102%

	Amount	%		Amount	%		Amount	%		Amount	%	
Cash from Investing Activities	(11,056,577)	100%	869%	(11,958,421)	100%	518%	(6,961,499)	100%	325%	(11,233,205)	100%	−59135%
Change in Long Term Debt	6,006,237	100%		2,677,864	100%		(866,250)	103%		1,990,920	88%	
Change in Notes Receivable	28,691	0%		5,635	0%		22,834	−3%		2,642	0%	
Due to Pension Fund	—			—	0%		—			264,032	12%	
Cash from Financing Activities	6,034,928	100%	−474%	2,683,499	100%	−116%	(843,416)	100%	39%	2,257,594	100%	11885%
Net Change in Cash (Financial Statements)	(1,272,347)			(2,308,212)			(2,143,177)			18,996		
Calculated Net Change in Cash	(1,272,648)			(2,308,212)			(2,143,177)			18,996		
Difference	301			—			—			—		
Ending Cash Calculated	$ 6,021,384			$ 3,713,473			$ 1,570,296			$ 1,589,292		
Per Books	$ 6,021,685			$ 3,713,473			$ 1,570,296			$ 1,589,292		

FIGURE 3.13 Vertical Analysis of Cash Flows of the Primary Government for Company 3

key components for the use of cash from investing activities, whereas, with the exception of YR 2, the changes in investments are negative, indicating that the changes in investments do not provide sufficient cash to fund the equipment additions, so another source of cash is cash from financing activities.

As the vertical analysis suggests, the major player in cash from financing activities is the change in long-term debt. The changes in notes receivable is minor and provides a minimal source of cash. With the exception of YR 5, the changes in long-term debt provide a source of cash for the company, but once again, they do not provide sufficient cash for the equipment additions. At this point, the vertical analysis does not indicate any inconsistency with the financial statements, so the financial forensic examiner should consider each section's contribution to the net change in cash. When looking at how each section contributes to the net change in cash, the financial forensic examiner should notice that with the exception of YR 5, the primary government is consuming cash reserves for equipment purchases. The calculations of the operating cash flow ratio and the cash flow margin ratio found in Table 3.8 should also confirm this trend.

TABLE 3.8 Cash Flow Ratios of the Primary Government for Company 3

	YR 2	YR 3	YR 4	YR 5
Operating Cash Flow Ratio	.87	1.57	1.39	.99
Cash Flow Margin Ratio	.22	.35	.30	.41

The operating cash flow ratio indicates that the primary government is generating enough cash from operating activities to pay its current liabilities, especially in both YR 3 and YR 4. Yet, the cash flow margin ratio indicates that the primary government is unable to generate much cash from its sales. These calculations tend to contradict each other, and the financial forensic examiner ought to perform additional studies relating to the underlying transactions noted in the cash flow statements.

Now that the financial forensic examiner knows to conduct further studies on the primary government, he or she also needs to review the vertical analysis of the governmental funds cash flows. Because the governmental funds cash flows represent the modified-accrual presentation for financial statements, removing most of the accrual amounts found in the primary government financial statements, the governmental funds financial statements may provide the financial forensic examiner with additional clues. Figure 3.14 illustrates the vertical analysis of the cash flows of the governmental funds for Company 3.

Line Item	YR 2			YR 3			YR 4			YR 5		
	Value	%	%	Value	%	%	Value	%	%	Value	%	%
Beginning Cash	$2,305,503			$3,073,334			$2,134,862			$816,508		
Net Income	4,268,304	103%		(3,099,986)	124%		(5,649,551)	93%		38,653	-18%	
Change in Deferred Revenues	300,152	7%		72,831	-3%		45,279	-1%		148,469	-69%	
Change in A/R	(452,095)	-11%		(93,213)	4%		(312,873)	5%		(306,273)	143%	
Change in Inventory	(15,189)	0%		18,204	-1%		(28,142)	0%		(11,763)	5%	
Change in Prepaid Expenses	(5,589)	0%		(20,028)	1%		112,523	-2%		(3,539)	2%	
Change in Accrued Liabilities	54,139	1%		27,078	-1%		117,930	-2%		75,094	-35%	
Change in A/P	(1,196)	0%		601,956	-24%		(448,557)	7%		(155,016)	72%	
Cash from Operating Activities	4,148,526		100%	(2,493,158)	540%	100%	(6,163,391)	266%	100%	(214,375)	468%	96%
Change in Investments	(3,849,531)			1,514,196			4,642,701			247,974		
Cash from Investing Activities	(3,849,531)		100%	1,514,196	-501%	100%	4,642,701	-162%	100%	247,974	-353%	-111%
Change in Due from Other Funds	(636,093)	-136%		(795,145)	-1964%		(3,020,500)	-1493%		(1,732,613)	677%	
Change in Notes Receivable	28,691	6%		5,635	14%		22,834	11%		2,642	-1%	

(continued)

	YR 2			YR 3			YR 4			YR 5	
Change in Due to Other Funds	1,076,238	230%		830,000	2050%		3,200,002	1582%		1,474,033	-576%
Cash from Financing Activities	468,836	100%	61%	40,490	100%	-4%	202,336	100%	-15%	(255,938)	100% / 115%
Net Change in Cash (Financial Statements)	767,831			(938,472)			(1,318,354)			(222,339)	
Calculated Net Change in Cash	767,831			(938,472)			(1,318,354)			(222,339)	
Difference	—			—			—			—	
Ending Cash Calculated	$3,073,334			$2,134,862			$ 816,508			$ 594,169	
Per Books	$3,073,334			$2,134,862			$ 816,508			$ 594,169	

FIGURE 3.14 Vertical Analysis of Cash Flows of the Governmental Funds for Company 3

Looking at the changes in the cash from operating activities, significant changes relate, to A/R with changes from −11% to 143%, changes in A/P from −24% to 72%, and changes in deferred revenues from 7% to −69%. Net income changes vary from 124% to −18%. Since non-cash entries, such as depreciation and non-cash gains and losses, are absent in the governmental funds cash flows, net income influences cash from operating activities more than any of the other components, meaning that net income should generate cash while net losses will use cash resources.

As for cash from investing activities and cash from financing activities, only one of these sections provides a significant clue for the financial forensic examiner. The only component of cash from investment activities relates to the changes noted in investments. The one component that provides a significant source of cash is the change in investments, with the exception of YR 2. However, there are two important components in cash from financing activities that vary significantly from year to year: changes in due from other funds and changes in due to other funds. Again, these two accounts provide challenges for the financial forensic examiner and require further study and analysis.

When comparing each section of the cash flows to the net change in cash, with the exception of YR 5, cash from financing activities provides only a minor source of cash for the company fund, and the majority of this cash source relates to the due from other funds and the due to other funds. The changes in notes receivable provides minor cash to the funds. Table 3.9 illustrates the calculations for the operating cash flow ratio and the cash flow margin ratio. These calculations should support the findings in the vertical analysis of the cash flows of the governmental funds.

Only in YR 2 does the operating cash flow ratio indicate that the governmental funds are able to cover the payments of current debt. Since the funds do not contain long-term debt, current liabilities include accounts payable, accrued liabilities, and the due to other funds. Since the governmental funds are unable to pay current liabilities, the financial statements cannot

TABLE 3.9 Cash Flow Ratios of the Governmental Funds for Company 3

	YR 2	YR 3	YR 4	YR 5
Operating Cash Flow Ratio	1.02	−.45	−.73	−.02
Cash Flow Margin Ratio	.35	−.17	−.50	−.02

portray the due to other funds as current liabilities, but rather as sources of cash from financing activities.

Additionally, the cash flow margin ratio indicates that the governmental funds are not able to generate a sufficient amount of cash from their sales, which agrees with the vertical analysis of the cash flow statement relating to the changes of the components in the cash from operating activities. Given that the cash flow margin tells the financial forensic examiner that operating activities do not provide sufficient cash for continued operations, the unusual changes in the component items from the cash from operating expenses need additional analysis, as well as net income. Since net income poses questions for the financial forensic examiner, additional analysis of these major sections should narrow the focus of additional study to more specific areas.

Company 4

Figure 3.15 presents the vertical analysis of cash flows for Company 4. When reviewing the vertical analysis, the financial forensic examiner should notice the significant items that are included in the cash used in operating activities that are non-cash transactions affecting net income. Moreover, YR 2, YR 3, and YR 4 provide unusual entries in a cash flow statement relating to cash used from discontinued operations. For these reasons, discourse relating to the vertical analysis will focus on those changes that directly affect cash.

Figure 3.15 displays the vertical analysis of cash flows for Company 4.

Major items affecting cash from operating activities include changes in A/R, changes in A/P, and changes in inventory. Changes in prepaid expenses and changes in other assets are minimal from year to year. Cash used from discontinued operations only slightly affects cash from operating activities, and any effect on all sections of the cash flow statements wash out in YR 4. The changes in A/R and A/P for YR 2, YR 3, and YR 4 also reflect items related to the discontinued operations, as well as a significant sales contract occurring in YR 3. In YR 5, the changes in A/R and A/P positively affect cash, indicating that in YR 5 the cash flow statements relate specifically to ongoing operations. As discussed earlier, the effect of exchange rate changes on cash affects net change in cash, so analysis of each section's influence over net change in cash is relevant only when excluding the effect of the exchange rate.

When reviewing net cash from investing activities and net cash from financing activities, equipment additions provide the greatest influence on investing activities while borrowings and payments on debt significantly influence financing activities. From a forensic perspective, borrowings and

(in thousands)	YR 2		YR 3		YR 4		YR 5	
Beginning Cash	$ 5,240		$ 2,812		$ 6,147		$ 8,204	
Net Income	5,475	-96%	18,586	139%	45,343	250%	16,331	57%
Depreciation	3,092	-54%	2,760	21%	2,608	14%	3,134	11%
Amortization	938	-16%	480	4%	236	1%	123	0%
(Gain) Loss from Discontinued Operations	1,511	-26%	114	1%	(126)	-1%	—	
Tax Benefit from Discontinued Operations	—		—		(18,244)	-101%	—	
Deferred Tax Provision (Benefit)	—		—		(1,331)	-7%	7,716	27%
Issuance of Non-Employee Director Shares	329	-6%	75	1%	75	1%	75	0%
Bad Debt Provision	567	-10%	827	6%	1,065	6%	312	1%
Stock-Based Compensation	—		—		308	2%	308	1%
Loss (Gain) on Sale of Equipment	10	0%	—		—		(109)	0%
Changes in A/R	(11,199)	196%	(17,667)	-132%	(18,898)	-104%	17,305	61%
Changes in Inventory	(7,288)	128%	(4,579)	-34%	(3,496)	-19%	5,156	18%
Changes in Prepaid Expenses	285	-5%	839	6%	(1,390)	-8%	343	1%
Changes in Other Assets and Other	(864)	15%	(12)	0%	(16)	0%	46	0%
Changes in Accounts Payable	1,271	-23%	9,952	74%	12,090	67%	(19,673)	-69%
Changes in Accrued Liabilities and Other	1,501	-26%	4,210	32%	(343)	-2%	(2,497)	-8%
Net Cash from Operating Activities	(4,372)		15,585		17,881		28,570	
Net Cash Used from Discontinued Operations	(1,341)	23%	(2,225)	-17%	247	1%	—	0%
Net Cash Used in Operating Activities	(5,713)	100%	13,360	100%	18,128	100%	28,570	100%
Payments Received on Notes Receivable	122	4%	227	102%	604	-5%	482	-6%

(continued)

(in thousands)	YR 2		YR 3		YR 4		YR 5	
Proceeds from Sale of Equipment	15	0%	—		98		148	-2%
Equipment Additions	(695)	-18%	(1,425)	-639%	(12,564)	106%	(8,718)	108%
Cash from Investing Activities	(558)		(1,198)		(11,862)		(8,088)	
Net Cash Provided from Discontinued Operations	4,454	114%	1,421	637%	25	0%	—	0%
Net Cash from Investing Activities	3,896	100%	223	100%	(11,837)	100%	(8,088)	100%
Proceeds from Issuance of Common Stock	4,235	-170%	—	0%	—	0%	—	0%
Proceeds from Exercise of Stock Options	27	-1%	720	-7%	1,325	-27%	616	-10%
Termination of Interest Rate Swap	96	-4%	57	-1%	—	0%	—	0%
Additions to Deferred Financing Costs	(522)	21%	(389)	4%	(5)	0%	(42)	1%
Payments on Debt	(3,542)	143%	(20,126)	196%	(6,603)	134%	(6,803)	109%
Borrowings	5,132	-207%	12,007	-117%	329	-7%	—	0%
Cash from Financing Activities	5,426		(7,731)		(4,954)		(6,229)	
Net Cash Used in Discontinued Operations	(7,910)	318%	(2,511)	25%	—	0%	—	0%
Net Cash Used in Financing Activities	(2,484)	100%	(10,242)	100%	(4,954)	100%	(6,229)	100%
Effect of Exchange Rate Changes on Cash	293		(557)		697		825	
Calculated Net Change in Cash	(4,008)		2,784		2,034		15,078	
Change in Discontinued Operations	1,580		551		23			
Ending Cash Calculated	$ 2,812		$ 6,147		$ 8,204		$23,282	
Per Books	$ 2,812		$ 6,147		$ 8,204		$23,282	

FIGURE 3.15 Vertical Analysis of Cash Flows for Company 4

payments on debt do not require further analysis other than confirming the transactions with the third party. Equipment additions require more analysis before the financial forensic examiner dives into a detailed investigation of every purchase. Although the vertical analyses of cash flows indicate signifi-cant changes, it is worth noting that these variances are explainable. It is on the unexplained variances that the financial forensic examiner must focus.

Table 3.10 shows the calculations for the operating cash flow ratio and the cash flow margin ratio. Knowing that YR 2, YR 3, and YR 4 include transactions related to the discontinued operations of the subsidiary, these should affect the calculations of each ratio.

TABLE 3.10 Cash Flow Ratios for Company 4

	YR 2	YR 3	YR 4	YR 5
Operating Cash Flow Ratio	−.10	.21	.25	.55
Cash Flow Margin Ratio	−.02	.04	.04	.07

The vertical analyses of the cash flow statements and the cash flow ratios all exhibit a company restructuring itself from losses. The operating cash flow ratio indicates that by YR 5 the company was able to pay at least one-half of its current debt from cash from operating activities and the sale of stock as payment on debt in order to maintain sufficient cash flows for operations. Again, the cash flow margin ratio also indicates that the cash flow margin is growing slowly and the company is starting to generate cash from its net sales. YR 5 is probably more important, since the cash flow statements no longer record the ins and outs of the discontinued operations and exhibit cash flows strictly from ongoing operations.

SUMMARY

In this chapter, the financial forensic examiner now has several tools and techniques in the toolbox to use when required, depending on the specific characteristics of the engagement. The cash flow statement is a wealth of information for the financial forensic examiner and a "must" in examining financial statement information. If a cash flow statement is not prepared as part of the financial statements, the potential for not detecting fraudulent activity is greater. While financial statements are easy to manipulate, the manipulation of the cash flow statement is more difficult, since the statement deals with just cash transactions and must balance. Yes, a cash flow statement may be "plugged" to balance, but if differences, other than rounding, occur, then there are non-cash transactions within the information not identified. If a cash flow statement is not present in the financial statements, the financial forensic examiner now knows how to analyze the changes in the accounts from year to year and how to build a simple cash flow statement for analysis. The financial forensic examiner also knows that there are limitations to the simple cash flow statements, such as consolidated financial statements that include subsidiaries of a different currency, and that the exchange rate variances affect the statement of cash flows.

Another technique, comparing cash realized from operations to net income, is an effective method for determining differences in the financial statements, thus requiring the financial forensic examiner to search for explainable reasons for these variances. The best method for comparing cash realized from operations to net income is in the form of a dual-axis chart in order to see if the relationships are matching or opposite. Normally, net income and CRO have corresponding relationships, but when these relationships move away from each other in opposite directions, the financial forensic examiner must take this as a warning and investigate further. Opposite relationships between CRO and net income provide evidence of variances in the financial information, but not necessarily possible fraud, so the variances require research and explanation. Any unexplained variance requires further investigation for possible fraudulent activity.

Additionally, using a vertical analysis technique in cash flow statements provide clues to anomalies in financial statement information. Vertical analysis shows inconsistencies in cash-related changes in each line item of the cash flow statement from year to year. Changes within each account from year to year actually remove the accruals in the financial statement so that the result is the actual cash activities for the year. The financial forensic examiner must understand these changes and determine if the changes are explainable—if not, then the variances may indicate possible fraudulent activity.

Furthermore, financial analysts use cash flow ratios relating to liquidity and earnings management, but some financial forensic examiners generally do not use these in financial forensic examination, even though they provide useful hints and pointers to variances in financial statement information. Two ratios used in this chapter, the operating cash flow ratio and the cash flow margin ratio, provide useful information to the financial forensic examiner by estimating a company's ability to pay its current debt from operating cash and whether the company is actually generating cash from its sales.

CHAPTER FOUR

The Beneish M-Score Model

T HE BENEISH M-Score model (the Model), developed in 1999 by Messod D. Beneish, Ph.D., professor of accounting in the Kelley School of Business at Indiana University—Bloomington, consists of eight indices capturing financial statement anomalies that can result from earnings manipulation or other types of fraudulent activity. Actual data in the financial statements builds the calculations of the indices that create the overall M-Score describing the degree of possible earnings manipulation or possible other fraudulent activity, such as concealing embezzlement activity. In his study, Beneish found that he could correctly identify 76% of the earnings manipulators and incorrectly identify 17.5% as non-manipulators.[1] In other words, Beneish found that 17.5% of the companies whose financial statements he thought were free from earnings manipulation re-filed financial statements later due to earnings manipulation. From the financial forensic examiner's perspective, the percentage of correct identification provides reassurance that the calculations deliver reliable information concerning the examination of the financial information, thus allowing the investigative work to be more effective and efficient.

Beneish also determined that if the calculation of the Model is greater than a negative (−) 2.22, the calculation suggests a higher probability of financial statement manipulation. To understand exactly which numbers are greater than a -2.22 requires the understanding of the movement of negative numbers (i.e., -2.21 is greater than -2.22 and -2.23 is less than -2.22). This calculation also works very well with the attempted disguise of embezzlement activities, as well as earnings manipulation, because the attempted coverup will generally distort the calculations of either or both of the overall M-Score and the eight indices.

The Model is an excellent tool for the financial forensic examiner, not only in that it provides an overall inspection of the financial statements, but each of the components in the Model provides its own specific scrutiny of the details of the financial statements by measuring changes that occur from period to period, whether it be monthly, quarterly, or yearly. Both the overall M-score calculations and the calculations of the component indices provide the financial forensic examiner with general benchmarks that can be used to predict variances within the financial statements. These indices provide a roadmap for the financial forensic examiner showing where to focus the investigation on successive levels of documentation. The formula for the Model is:

$$M = -4.84 + 0.92 \times \text{DSRI} + 0.528 \times \text{GMI} + 0.404 \times \text{AQI} + 0.892 \times \text{SGI} +$$
$$0.115 \times \text{DEPI} - 0.172 \times \text{SGAI} + 4.679 \times \text{TATA} - 0.327 \times \text{LVGI}^2$$

The formula is a weighted average of these components:

- DSRI—Days sales in receivable index
- GMI—Gross margin index
- AQI—Asset quality index
- SGI—Sales growth index
- DI or DEPI—Depreciation index
- SGAI or SGAEI—Selling, general and administrative expenses index
- TATA—Total accruals to total assets index
- LI or LVGI—Leverage index

The individual formulas[3] for each component of the Model follow:

$$\text{DSRI} = (\text{CY A/R/Sales})/(\text{PY A/R/Sales})$$

$$\text{GMI} = ((\text{PY Sales} - \text{PY COS})/\text{PY Sales})/(((\text{CY Sales} - \text{CY COS})/\text{CY Sales})$$

$$\text{AQI} = (1 - (\text{CY CA} + \text{CY Net FA})/\text{CY Total Assets}))/$$
$$(1 - (\text{PY CA} + \text{PY Net FA})/\text{PY TA}))$$

$$\text{SGI} = \text{CY Sales/PY Sales}$$

DI (DEPI) = (PY DE/(PY DE + PY Net PPE))/(CY DE/(CY DE + CY Net PPE))

SGAI (SGAEI) = (CY SGA/CY Sales)/(PY SGA/PY Sales)

LI (LVGI) = ((CY LTD + CY CL)/CY TA))/((PY LTD + PY CL)/PY TA))

TATA = ((CY WC − PY WC) − (CY Cash − PY Cash) + (CY Income Tax Payable − PY Income Tax Payable) + (CY Current LTD − PY Current LTD) − CY DE))/CY TA

Component Abbreviations

(CY = current year)
(PY = prior year)
(WC = working capital)
(COS = cost of sales)
(CA = current assets)
(FA = fixed assets)
(TA = total assets)
(DE = depreciation and amortization expense)
(PPE = property, plant, and equipment)
(SGA = selling, general and administrative expenses)
(LTD = long-term debt)
(CL = current liabilities)

Along with the formulas, Beneish provided general benchmarks for both the Model, noted earlier as −2.22, and the Model's indices. While Beneish noted that general benchmarks for the indices might vary from period to period, the variations should be minor and any major change is indicative of possible manipulation of the financial information. For example, the general benchmark of DSRI is 1, but if the calculations show a lopsided relationship, then there is the possibility of potential fraudulent activity, such as earnings manipulation, revenue recognition issues by overstating revenues, or an attempted coverup of embezzled funds.

The benchmark for the gross margin index is also 1. When the GMI is greater than 1, a company is experiencing decreases in its gross margins and is conveying a negative signal relating to the company's ability to continue operations long term. As gross margin deteriorates, the company may decide to cover up the deterioration by manipulating earnings. As in the case of Company 2, fraudulent transactions covering up the embezzlement also created decreases in its gross margins, influencing the GMI calculations. Exploitation in inventory or other production costs will also cause gross margins to either increase or decrease, depending on the circumstances of the exploitation. For example, if there is theft of inventory, then the gross margins will decrease; if there are fictitious figures inflating inventory, the gross margins will increase.

The benchmark for the asset quality index is also 1 and calculated amounts greater than 1 indicate possible discrepancies in the financial statements. In this instance, though, instead of increasing revenues, the discrepancies relate to deferring costs such as capitalizing costs instead of expensing them, not recording liabilities, or not recording costs in the correct period. All of these items affect the AQI calculations.

As with the other indices discussed so far, the sales growth index also has a general benchmark of 1. With SGI, there may be several factors increasing the index that are not fraudulent in nature, such as market-share growth or major acquisitions. However, growth spurts also create an additional problem for the company due to the company's lack of attention and concern over controls and reporting while focusing on additional growth potential. Once a company's growth slows down, stock prices decrease and investors or owners become concerned. The perception alone may entice a company to manipulate earnings. If both DSRI and SGI increase, the company may be recording fictitious revenues to prevent investor concerns over a slow-growth period after experiencing significant growth in the prior period.

The depreciation index is very specific as it calculates the rate of depreciation from the prior year to the current year. As with the other components of the Model, the general benchmark for DEPI is 1. When DEPI is greater than 1, there is the possibility that a company has revised the useful life estimates of its fixed assets, or the company has adopted a new depreciation method that increases income compared to the existing method. Either way, the company is increasing income by deferring costs. For example, if the company either changes the useful life estimates of its fixed assets or adopts a new depreciation method, and the company chooses not to disclose this information in the notes to the financial statements, then the financial statements are fraudulent because the company's management chose not to divulge this information to its shareholders. Omitting information in the notes to the financial statements misrepresents the company's earnings from year to year, thus manipulating earnings, and is just as fraudulent even if the numbers are correct. In addition, if the company elects to change methods of depreciation from year to year to more favorable income-producing methods, then the company is manipulating income from year to year.

The sales, general and administrative expenses index includes the same concept as the sales growth index when it comes to significant changes relating to acquisitions, increases in market share, and so on. Once again, the general benchmark for the SGAI is 1. Yet, in the case of SGAI, the calculations should remain reasonably stable, with little variance from period to period under normal operations. For the financial forensic examiner, an increase in SGAI may suggest possible coverups of fraudulent transactions related to expense reimbursement schemes, such as overstating expense reimbursements, fictitious or multiple expense reimbursements, and commission schemes.

The financial forensic examiner uses the leverage index to determine possible earnings manipulation related to debt covenants. The general benchmark for this index of the Model is also 1. An increase in leverage greater than 1 suggests either new debt or increases in existing debt by the company. Increases in debt may also call for debt covenants that a company must achieve to prevent the existing debt from requiring prompt payment. If a company is unable to meet its debt covenants, there is an increased possibility of the company manipulating earnings to prevent the debt from becoming current and reducing liquidity ratios, depending on the circumstances of the covenants.

The last component of the Model, the total accruals to total assets index (TATA), is relatively stable and has a general benchmark of zero. For the financial forensic examiner, accruals provide an opportunity to commit and conceal fraud. High levels of accruals compared to assets may be an indicator of financial statement manipulation, as shown in Company 3's governmental funds financial statements.

While the overall M-Score may have limitations in financial forensic examinations, the components of the Model are very valuable in providing insight into the company's financial statement information by segregating analysis to specific areas that may contain fraudulent transactions from various fraud schemes within the company, as well as a company's attempt to increase earnings. The components are actually measuring the changes from period to period, whereas most ratios compare information for only one period. Another facet of the Model is that some of the components of TATA also provide analysis for specific areas such as the following, listed by the authors of the March 2012 *United States Attorney Bulletin*[4]:

▪ TCATA—Total current assets to total assets

$$((\text{Total CY CA} - \text{CY cash})/\text{CY TA})/((\text{Total PY CA} - \text{PY Cash})/\text{PY TA})$$

- TARTA—Total accounts receivable to total assets

$$(CY\ A/R/CY\ TA)/(PY\ A/R/PY\ TA)$$

- TITA—Total inventory to total assets

$$(CY\ Inventory/CY\ TA)/(PY\ Inventory/PY\ TA)$$

- TCLTA—Total current liabilities to total assets

$$((Total\ CY\ CL - CY\ Current\ LTD - CY\ Income\ tax\ payable)/CY\ TA)/$$
$$((Total\ PY\ CL - PY\ Current\ LTD - PY\ Income\ tax\ payable)/PY\ TA)$$

- TAPTA—Total accounts payable to total assets

$$(CY\ A/P/TA)/(PY\ A/P/TA)$$

- DEPTA—Depreciation and amortization to total assets

$$(CY\ DE/CY\ TA)/(PY\ DE/PY\ TA)$$

Component Abbreviations

(A/R = accounts receivable)
(A/P = accounts payable)

These drill-down components should also become part of the financial forensic examiner's toolbox, for they are a very effective way of measuring specific relationships from period to period.

The forensic financial examiner will find that, as with any other type of toolbox, not every tool is necessary all of the time. The choice of what types of tools to use depends on the engagement, with the others stowed away for later use. For illustration purposes, all of these tools and techniques are included in the study for each of the four companies so that the financial forensic examiner may better understand each component's relevance to the individual engagement.

 ## COMPANY 1

To begin with, the first calculations for Company 1 are the totals of the Beneish M-Score model. There are several free Excel worksheets for the Model that can be downloaded from the Internet, but be careful, as the downloaded worksheet might not exactly follow the Model calculations and might require fine-tuning before using it; the financial forensic examiner may choose to create his or her own spreadsheet using Excel. Since the Model calculates changes from period to period, these calculations begin with YR 2. However, the greater the number of periods under review, the easier for the financial forensic examiner to fine-tune any minor changes within a company that occur from period to period. The financial forensic examiner must also consider the impact of negative numbers within the formulas and make modifications as required so that the calculations are correct.

Table 4.1 shows the overall M-Score calculations for Company 1.

TABLE 4.1 Beneish M-Score Calculations for Company 1

	YR 2	YR 3	YR 4	YR 5
Overall Score	−1.55	−3.49	−2.79	−3.50

When reviewing the overall scores, YR 2 is the only year where the totals are greater than −2.22, suggesting earnings manipulation. While the Model does assist the financial forensic examiner in a preliminary analysis, it is not perfect, especially since embezzlement activities occurred throughout all years under review. The financial forensic examiner gets a better picture of possible variations in the financial information when using the eight indices of the Model.

Table 4.2 illustrates the calculations for the eight indices for Company 1.

Since the calculations for the eight indices are now complete, the financial forensic examiner needs to focus on each variable to develop further insight into the relationships from period to period. Once again, using visual aids will

TABLE 4.2 Calculations of the Eight Indices for Company 1

Index	YR 2	YR 3	YR 4	YR 5
DSRI	1.611	1.147	1.149	0.772
GMI	1.089	1.014	0.939	0.934
AQI	0.000	0.000	0.000	0.000
SGI	0.839	1.074	0.981	1.079
DEPI	1.033	0.438	1.717	0.875
SGAI	1.381	0.802	1.111	1.173
TATA	0.108	−0.015	−0.007	−0.070
LVGI	0.936	3.187	1.062	1.219

help the financial forensic examiner to focus on details that may be vague or hidden when looking only at the numbers. Figure 4.1 illustrates the DSRI calculations for Company 1 and the comparison of the calculations to the general benchmark.

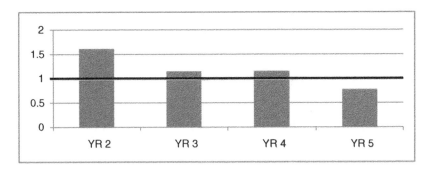

FIGURE 4.1   DSRI—Company 1

Using the number 1 as the general benchmark, the chart shows some rather significant swings between YR 2 and YR 3 and once again between YR 4 and YR 5, while YR 3 and YR 4 are relatively stable. Since the calculation of DSRI in YR 2 is definitely greater than the benchmark of 1, the financial forensic examiner should drill down to the underlying transactions in order to determine the reason for the significant increase. Explanations may determine that the change resulted from the effect of a natural, but unusual, event. If the change is unexplainable, then the financial forensic examiner needs to determine whether there is possible manipulation of earnings or a coverup from the misappropriations of assets.

One other issue that may concern the financial forensic examiner is the change in YR 5 that puts DSRI below the benchmark of 1. While the change may be strictly from an operational standpoint, the change is definitely not in line with YR 3 and YR 4 and should be uncovered. Remember from the discussion in Chapter 1 one purpose of the fraudulent financial transactions relates to reducing the net worth of the company, so significant changes may indicate possible fraudulent activity.

Figure 4.2 shows the GMI calculations for Company 1 and the comparison of the calculations to the general benchmark.

Once again, YR 2 is the red flag, since the GMI index is greater than 1. Remember that when the GMI is greater than 1, the company is experiencing decreases in its gross margins, suggesting the operations of the company are

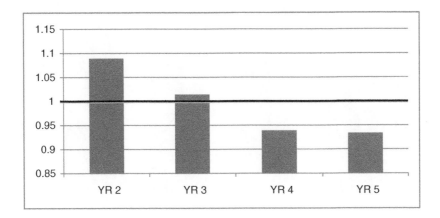

FIGURE 4.2 GMI—Company 1

deteriorating, thus reducing the net worth. YR 3 approximates the benchmark while YR 4 and YR 5 become relatively stable just below the benchmark. When comparing the GMI to the gross profit margins calculated in Table 2.6, the financial forensic examiner now has two separate analytical tests to compare. The table also substantiates a significant decrease in the gross profit margins from YR 1 to YR 2 and indicates increasing gross profit margins from YR 3 through YR 5. Figure 4.2 also indicates increasing gross margins, as the GMI falls below the general benchmark of 1.

Yet, in the case of this company, the GMI calculations are not very effective as a forensic tool, because the operations of the company relate to communication services and not manufacturing operations. GMI becomes quite relevant in analyzing manufacturing operations because of the impact of inventory turnover in the GMI calculations. However, since GMI includes the salaries of the individuals who perform the services for this company, the GMI calculations do suggest the possibility of fraudulent activity related to payroll operations and require further investigation.

Since the AQI calculates to zero each year and below the general benchmark of 1, a visual aid is not required. For the financial forensic examiner, the consistency indicates there has not been any change in asset realization from period to period. However, a visual aid of SGI to compare the calculations to the benchmark will be useful. Figure 4.3 illustrates the SGI calculations for Company 1 and the comparison of the calculations to the benchmark.

The SGI is reasonably consistent when compared to the benchmark, although the visual indicates somewhat of a cyclical trend every two years.

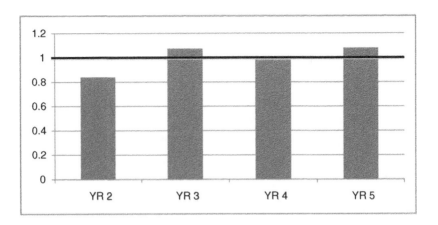

FIGURE 4.3 SGI—Company 1

Although the trend is over a four-year period, having more information for comparison would substantiate cyclic theories. The more information that the financial forensic examiner has, the more accurate the analysis will be. On the other hand, there is another possibility related to the cyclic nature of the SGI concerning revenue recognition. Could it be that the company is deferring revenues from one year to the next to better position the tax impact on its shareholders? Remember, this company is an S-corporation, and net income flows through to its shareholders. Information relating to shareholder 2's personal finances suggested this possibility, but since the company did not document or record minutes from shareholder meetings, there was no evidence to substantiate the theory. The financial forensic examiner must consider all possibilities when performing analytical techniques to find possible fraudulent activity.

DEPI presents an interesting challenge for the financial forensic examiner. Figure 4.4 shows the calculations of DEPI for Company 1 and the comparison of the calculations to the general benchmark.

Both YR 3 and YR 4 pose questions for the financial forensic examiner because of the significant variances from the benchmark. In YR 3, there is a significant decrease in DEPI, indicating that the rate of depreciation accelerated significantly, while YR 4 indicates a significant increase over the benchmark, indicating that the rate of depreciation slowed significantly. Not only does each change raise a red flag for the financial forensic examiner, but so does the fact that the changes occurred consecutively. Company 1 actually recorded the rental property on the corporation's books as an asset in YR 3 and removed the

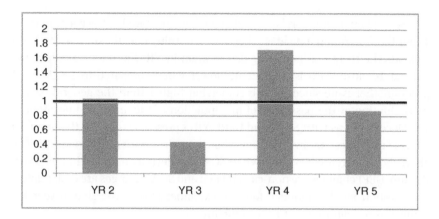

FIGURE 4.4 DEPI—Company 1

rental property in YR 4 for the sole purpose of increasing depreciation expense in YR 3 to offset net income.

As stated earlier in Chapter 1, inconsistent posting of similar expenses created problems when performing a detailed analysis of each account. To overcome this situation, computations of SGAI allow the financial forensic examiner to perform analysis at a higher level and still be able to determine if further detailed analysis is required.

Figure 4.5 illustrates the calculations of SGAI for Company 1 and the comparison of those calculations to the general benchmark noted by Beneish.

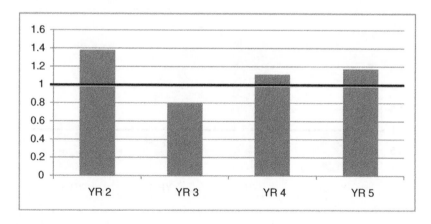

FIGURE 4.5 SGAI—Company 1

SGAI should remain relatively stable when compared to the benchmark of 1, but the illustration indicates otherwise. If nothing else, the decrease in YR 3 supports the theory of increasing depreciation in YR 3 in order to reduce net income, because SGAI is significantly lower when compared to YR 2. YR 2 poses another issue since SGAI is somewhat higher than the general benchmark, hinting at the possibility of manipulation of the financial information.

Once again as with SGAI and DEPI, YR 3 presents issues for the financial forensic examiner, not by itself, but when compared with SGAI and DEPI. The chart shows increased leverage when SGAI has decreased and DEPI increased. Because DEPI changes are non-cash related and SGAI changes are cash related, the question for the financial forensic examiner is why the shareholder felt compelled to loan money to the company.

For example, between YR 2 and YR 3, DSRI declined, but YR 2 was unusually high when compared to the benchmark, suggesting the possibility of earnings manipulation. Yet in YR 3, the GMI was relatively stable with the benchmark. SGI appeared to be somewhat cyclic in nature, but none of the calculations was highly unusual when compared to the benchmark. Obviously, the financial forensic examiner needs to determine the reasons for the notes payable to the shareholder when reviewing the results of the other indices.

The leverage index for Company 1 is important to the financial forensic examiner because it is measuring the changes in the notes payable to the shareholder, since that is the only debt on the books. Figure 4.6 shows the changes of LVGI compared to the general benchmark

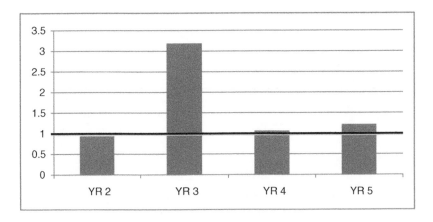

FIGURE 4.6   LVGI—Company 1

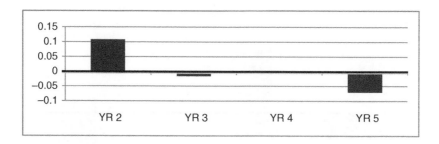

FIGURE 4.7 TATA—Company 1

TATA is the last variable of the Model that requires analysis. Figure 4.7 illustrates the calculations of TATA for Company 1 with comparisons to the general benchmark.

Usually the financial forensic examiner should expect to see TATA approximate zero, since that is the general benchmark, or less than zero. When the TATA calculation is positive, as in YR 2, the positive calculation suggests the possibility of earnings manipulation. Positive calculations represent high levels of accruals relative to total assets, thus reducing cash. Although the change between YR 3 and YR 4 is negative, the trend of the movement is positive, actually approaching the general benchmark of zero. The positive movement is also a red flag for the financial forensic examiner. Remember also that in Chapter 2, Company 1 already had fluctuations in its working capital calculations and the working capital index calculations from year to year as well. In addition, Table 2.4, illustrating the current ratio calculations, indicates that in YR 1 and YR 2, current liabilities were higher when compared to the following periods.

Since the calculations from the indices of the Beneish Model suggested possible irregularities in DSRI, DEPI, and SGAI, using some of the specific formulas for these areas is appropriate. Remember that these specific formulas also have a benchmark of 1, since they are parts of the eight indices from the Beneish M-Score model. Figure 4.8 illustrates the calculations of DEPTA or depreciation and amortization divided by total assets for Company 1.

In DEPI, the changes in the relationships consider the PY when compared to the CY, whereas in DEPTA, the changes in the relationships consider the CY amounts over the PY amounts. This is important for the financial forensic examiner to remember when reviewing the charts because now both the charts and two separate analytical tests are essentially telling the financial forensic examiner the same information: YR 3 suggests manipulation.

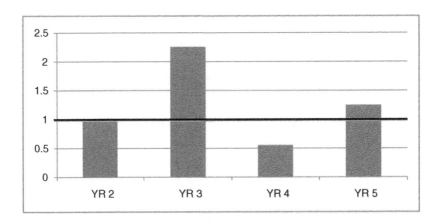

FIGURE 4.8 DEPTA—Company 1

One more specific index that the financial forensic examiner may use is TAPTA as a comparison with SGAI. Figure 4.9 displays the analysis of TAPTA for Company 1.

SGAI was significantly greater than the benchmark in YR 2 and then started creeping upward in YR 4 and YR 5. Although YR 4 and YR 5 were not significantly greater than the benchmark for SGAI, the same cannot hold true for TAPTA.

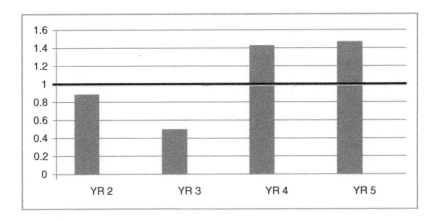

FIGURE 4.9 TAPTA—Company 1

For both YR 4 and YR 5, TAPTA is significantly greater than the benchmark. Since SGAI and A/P are interrelated, the financial forensic examiner now has two tests that indicate variations in the financial information that require further investigation. Using the specific indices from the Model provides the financial forensic examiner with two different analytical tools that will measure a set of financial information in two different ways, allowing verification of the first analytical test as shown in the examples with DEPTA and TAPTA for Company 1.

From the testing of the eight indices and the overall Model for Company 1, the financial forensic examiner now understands that the overall M-Score fluctuates, but only YR 2 suggests possible manipulation of the financial information, although every year contains fraudulent information. Therefore, the Model is not the only inclusive tool to use. The DSRI, GMI, DEPI, SGAI, LVGI, and TATA also hint to the financial forensic examiner that these areas need further investigative analysis. Using DEPTA and TAPTA as secondary analytical tools provides the financial forensic examiner with corroborative evidence for additional investigations related to DEPI and SGAI.

COMPANY 2

Before beginning the analysis of Company 2's financial statements, both the overall M-Score and the indices require computing. Table 4.3 illustrates the overall Beneish M-Score amounts for Company 2.

Unlike Company 1, the overall M-Scores for Company 2 indicate two years where there is the possibility of earnings manipulation: YR 2 and YR 5.

As discussed in Chapter 1, the cessation of the fraudulent activity occurs during YR 5, and the financial forensic examiner must consider the effects of correcting the financial statements in the calculations. Once again, these calculations need additional analysis by calculating the indices of the Model. Table 4.4 shows the calculations of the eight indices for Company 2.

Once more, the use of charts with the benchmark noted is the preferred method for analyzing the relationships from year to year.

TABLE 4.3 Beneish M-Score Calculations for Company 2

	YR 2	YR 3	YR 4	YR 5
M-Score	−.70	−2.73	−3.15	−1.53

TABLE 4.4 Calculations of the Eight Indices for Company 2

Index	YR 2	YR 3	YR 4	YR 5
DSRI	0.796	0.553	0.950	1.349
GMI	1.168	0.975	0.916	1.018
AQI	1.000	1.000	1.000	0.918
SGI	2.574	1.427	0.964	0.784
DEPI	1.042	0.888	0.924	0.888
SGAI	0.778	0.904	0.847	1.151
TATA	0.126	−0.080	−0.128	0.172
LVGI	1.474	0.495	0.889	0.763

Figure 4.10 displays the DSRI calculations for Company 2 compared to the benchmark of 1.

When reviewing the company information in Chapter 1, the DSRI calculations in the chart should not indicate any very unusual variations. The company had a very good relationship with its customers, with most of them paying timely or at the time of shipment, and the company had little, if any, bad debt. Yet, the illustrations of DSRI compared to the general benchmark indicate increases from YR 3, indicating the possibility that customers are not paying as timely as before. The financial forensic examiner might consider the changes from YR 3 to YR 5 suspect and might consider that they may include manipulation. However, once again, the fraud terminated in YR 5 with the

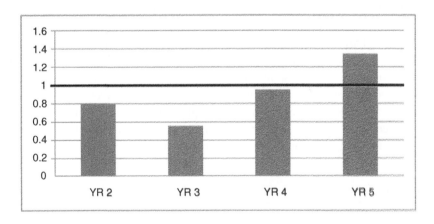

FIGURE 4.10 DSRI—Company 2

financial statements corrected, so the YR 5 calculation may include the effects of this change since DSRI is greater than the benchmark for this period.

Figure 4.11 displays the second index calculations, GMI, for Company 2, which may provide more clues for the financial forensic examiner.

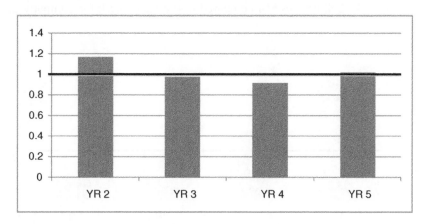

FIGURE 4.11   GMI—Company 2

The first item in this illustration that should alert the financial forensic examiner is the changes that occur from year to year. GMI should be reasonably consistent from year to year, unless management is absorbing increases in its cost of sales in order to maintain its market share. Additionally in Chapter 2, Table 2.6 indicates that the gross profit margins were not reasonably consistent. However, Company 2 produced highly specialized products for a specific market niche, so it is unlikely that the company would be willing to reduce its profit margins in order to maintain its market share. YR 2 suggests the possibility of earnings management, since it is significantly higher than the benchmark of 1.

Another facet for the financial forensic examiner is the continued decrease from YR 2 through YR 4 in the GMI. What happens if cost of sales expenses also includes fraudulent transactions covering up embezzlement? The declines, especially in YR 4, warrant further inspection by the financial forensic examiner simply to determine whether the cost of sales includes manipulation associated with embezzlement. From the company history in Chapter 1, cost of sales included fictitious invoices supposedly paid to various vendors providing raw materials used in the production process in an attempt to cover up the true theft of funds by the office manager.

Since there is little change from year to year for AQI and the calculations are comparable to the benchmark, the use of a chart is not necessary. Because AQI is so stable, the financial forensic examiner may determine that further investigative work is unnecessary and move forward to analyzing SGI.

Figure 4.12 illustrates SGI compared to the benchmark for Company 2.

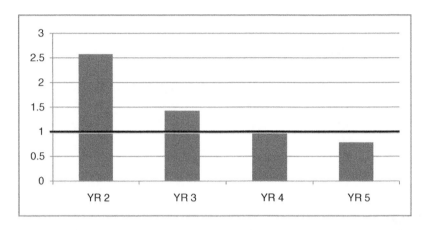

FIGURE 4.12   SGI—Company 2

When comparing SGI to the benchmark, both YR 2 and YR 3 pose questions for the financial forensic examiner, since the calculations for these years are significantly higher than the general benchmark of 1, especially YR 2. Both of these years suggest faster growth rates for the company and significant variances may suggest possible earnings manipulation. Yet, in embezzlement schemes, recording fictitious revenues is an attempt to hide a company's inability to generate cash flow or conceal declining gross profits. In either case, the financial forensic examiner needs to investigate these variations.

Since depreciation is an area where a company may manipulate earnings, the financial forensic examiner needs to calculate this index. Remember also that increasing expenses is another method of reducing income for tax purposes. Figure 4.13 displays the calculations for DEPI and their comparisons to the benchmark of 1.

Unlike Company 1, the calculations for DEPI do not suggest that the rate of depreciation has decreased during the years under review, although DEPI for YR 1 is higher than the general benchmark. When looking at the vertical axis parameters, the differences are very slight between YR 3, YR 4, and YR 5, and YR 3 and YR 5 are comparatively stable. The financial forensic examiner

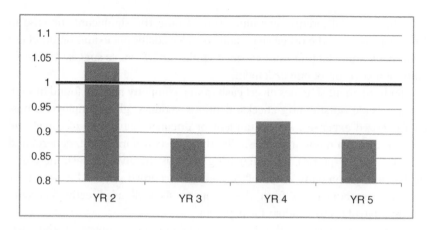

FIGURE 4.13 DEPI—Company 2

should investigate the change between YR 2 and YR 3 by examining the underlying documentation for these years.

Because the index SGAI should remain relatively stable, the financial forensic examiner should review these calculations for possible variations that may suggest possible fraudulent activity indicative of embezzlement. Figure 4.14 shows the calculations for the SGAI for Company 2 and their comparisons to the general benchmark.

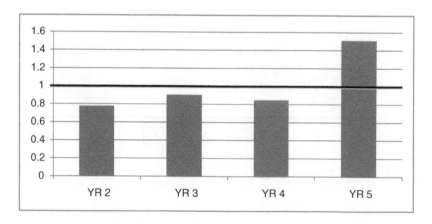

FIGURE 4.14 SGAI—Company 2

The financial forensic examiner should note the significant increase in YR 5 compared to the other years and consider additional examination of the underlying financial information, since significant increases suggest the possibility of a coverup of embezzlement.

Embezzlement schemes divert cash from a company and are found in such items as stale outstanding checks, fictitious vendors, ghost employees, mischaracterized expenses, and fraudulent or duplicate payments of travel and expenses, just to name a few. Usually, these costs are in selling, general and administrative expenses, thus increasing SGAI as the diverted cash increases. In the case of Company 2, the office manager recorded personal expenses for personal reimbursement from the company as well as directly recording personal payables to vendors for payment.

Figure 4.15 displays the TATA calculations for Company 2 and their comparison to the benchmark of zero. Remember that higher positive ratings mean less cash.

From reading the chart, the financial forensic examiner determines that both YR 2 and YR 5 represent less available cash and higher levels of accruals. Higher levels of accruals may indicate possible financial statement manipulation. In addition, TATA should remain relatively stable, and the chart indicates significant changes from YR 2 to YR 3 and again from YR 4 to YR 5. In the case of Company 2, YR 5 shows the greatest strain on cash from the embezzlement activities, since the company was falling behind in its payments to its suppliers. Table 2.2 in Chapter 2 also shows a significant decrease in the working capital index from YR 4 to YR 5. Many times embezzlement cases go unnoticed until

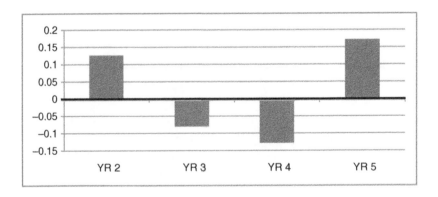

FIGURE 4.15 TATA—Company 2

the company develops a severe cash flow problem, and TATA is one method used to analyze increasing accruals and, therefore, less cash.

The purpose of LVGI is to determine the extent of new or increased debt and the potential of earnings manipulation related to debt covenants. In the case of Company 1, YR 2 is the only measurement indicative of new or increased debt and already noted in the financial statements. The financial statements also indicate that in YR 3 the company paid all debt. The only other component of long-term debt relates to deferred income taxes that do not relate to debt covenants, so for Company 2, the LVGI calculations are not relevant.

So far, the indices indicate variances in DSRI, SGI, GMI, SGAI, and TATA, requiring further analysis. Using the drill-down components in TATA, the financial forensic examiner can further assess these variances. The TARTA calculation is a useful tool to address both DSRI and SGI variances. Figure 4.16 illustrates the TARTA calculations.

The analysis for DSRI indicates a significant change in YR 5 that is greater than the benchmark and TARTA supports the increase from YR 4. Therefore, the financial forensic examiner should question the change in DSRI for YR 5. However, both the TARTA analysis and SGI analysis indicate significant changes in YR 2, but the change in DSRI is inconsistent and should cause concerns for the financial forensic examiner. Since DSRI does not follow the same pattern as TARTA and SGI in YR 2, inspection of documents is necessary to determine whether documentation such as excessive credit memos or fictitious customers hides potential fraudulent activity or financial statement earnings manipulation.

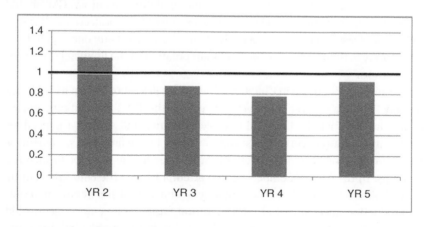

FIGURE 4.16   TARTA—Company 2

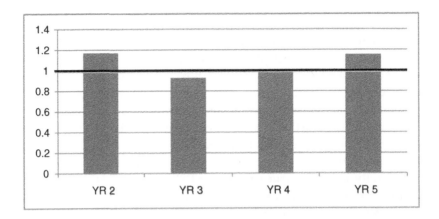

FIGURE 4.17 TITA—Company 2

Since the GMI index indicates issues with the changing relationships of the gross margins, another subset of the analytical procedure that measures inventory to total assets (TITA) is necessary to determine if changes in inventory is part of the variances of changes with GMI. Figure 4.17 displays the TITA calculation for Company 2.

TITA provides some interesting information for the financial forensic examiner since YR 4 indicates an interesting anomaly to study further. In YR 4, GMI continues to decrease, yet TITA shows an increase in inventory to total assets for the same period. Changes in inventories affect cost of sales, which is a component of GMI, so if one is manipulating inventory, GMI should increase, not decrease, and TITA should also increase, not decrease. Because TITA has excessive changes, especially from YR 2 to YR 3 and once again from YR 4 to YR 5, there is the possibility of manipulation in the financial statement information.

As already discussed in Chapter 2, the stock sales ratios shown in Table 2.7 literally "bounce around" from year to year, so the TITA calculations provide additional clues for the financial forensic examiner and support the need for further investigative work. Increasing inventory in the financial statements is the usual method to reduce overall cost of sales in the attempt to increase earnings. In the case of Company 2, the attempt to hide the embezzlement by using fictitious invoices from the company's vendors that supply raw materials for production affected cost of sales such that falsifying inventory records hid the embezzlement from the company by attempting to manipulate the gross profit margins.

In the attempt to determine if there are issues with SGAI, the TAPTA calculations are a means of measuring the changes in accounts payable to total assets to determine if the omission of payables is a method used to manipulate the financial statement information. Figure 4.18 shows the TAPTA calculations for Company 2.

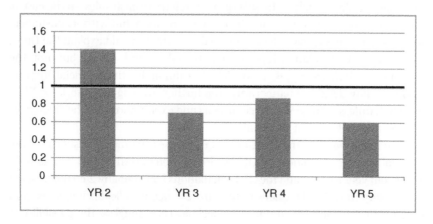

FIGURE 4.18 TAPTA—Company 2

TAPTA appears to be reasonably stable for YR 3 through YR 5, although YR 4 does show a slight increase from YR 3 to YR 4. YR 2 is high when comparing the calculation to the index and the other years, and creates a variance that the financial forensic examiner needs to question. More important to the financial forensic examiner is the relationship between TAPTA and SGAI. Normally, if SGAI increases, TAPTA should also increase, as the payables will also increase unless the company pays invoices within 30 days to take advantage of significant discounts offered by its vendors. For example, in YR 3, TAPTA decreases and SGAI increases, whereas in YR 4, TAPTA increases and SGAI decreases, but the changes are relatively stable. More crucial to the financial forensic examiner is the relationship between SGAI and TAPTA in YR 5. Since SGAI increases significantly and TAPTA decreases in YR 5, TAPTA does not provide any additional insight into the underlying causes that made SGAI increase significantly in YR 5. Therefore, for the financial forensic examiner, the change in YR 5 for SGAI, without a significant corresponding change in TAPTA, warrants further investigative procedures.

In summarizing the eight variable indices analysis for Company 2, even though DRSI indicates possible manipulation in YR 5, the TARTA calculation in YR 5 may support the same hypothesis due to TARTA's increase from YR 4, although the increase is below the general benchmark. Yet, the TARTA and DSRI calculations also do not support the SGI changes, leaving the financial forensic examiner with a couple of puzzling variances that need further investigative work. Typically, sales growth also means increases in accounts receivables, unless much of the sales growth relates to cash sales. In the case of Company 2, the company maintained a good relationship with its customers and most customers paid in less than 30 days, which would explain the DRSI, SGI, and TARTA relationships from both YR 2 and YR 3, but not the relationship changes in YR 4 and YR 5. Ultimately, the financial forensic examiner may decide to temporarily stop further investigative work for YR 2 and YR 3, unless management's comments and explanations for the differences in DRSI and SGI are not reasonable.

The one area from the eight indices that poses the most questions for the financial forensic examiner is GMI. As already noted, GMI should be relatively stable from year to year, and the GMI calculations for Company 2 do not indicate any stability in GMI. TITA adds to the puzzle, since it indicates increases from YR 3 to YR 4 while GMI continues to decline. TITA suggests the possibility of inventory manipulation in both YR 2 and YR 5, but TAPTA does not support the possibility for YR 2 since payables also increased, assuming the increase in the payables relates to increased purchases from inventoried items.

Yet, overall, the big issue for the financial forensic examiner is the instability in GMI. To assist the financial forensic examiner further, an analysis comparing GMI to SGI points directly to anomalies in the financial information. Figure 4.19 illustrates the comparison of SGI and GMI for Company 2.

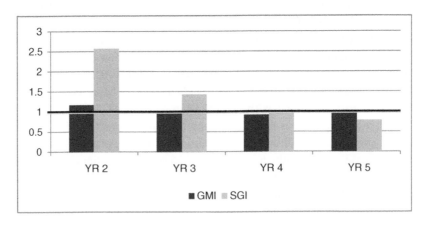

FIGURE 4.19 GMI and SGI—Company 2

The illustration in Figure 4.19 provides the financial forensic examiner with sufficient information to use drill-down investigative techniques for further examination. As sales growth declines, gross margins should remain comparatively stable but GMI declines slightly until YR 4 where it also approximates SGI. More importantly, in YR 5, gross margin changes increase to the point where the changes are greater than the changes in sales growth.

The analysis for Company 2 also indicates that the changes in SGAI for YR 5 require further inspection or, at the very least, a validated explanation for the significant change. In the case of this company, the increase in SGAI in YR 5 related directly to the bad debt expense from the embezzlement, but this may be only part of the reason for the change, since some embezzlement occurred during the same time.

 ## COMPANY 3

Further inspection of the Model and the eight indices continues with Company 3. For this company's presentation, the overall Model and the eight indices are comparisons of both the primary government and the governmental funds at the same time. When analyzing the governmental funds financial statements, the due-from-other-funds accounts are noted as part of other current assets while the due-to-other-funds accounts are noted as current long-term debt for the explicit purpose of determining just how these accounts relate to the financial statements. Remember that in Chapter 1, the due-from-other-funds and the due-to-other-funds should amount to zero in the consolidated governmental funds, and the significance of these funds relates to amounts embezzled through an off-book bank account. Any amounts due to or amounts due from another type of fund, such as a fiduciary fund, are normally accounted for as "other receivables."

Taking into consideration that Company 3 includes both primary government financial statements and governmental funds financial statements, Table 4.5 illustrates the overall M-Scores for both sets of financial statements.

TABLE 4.5 Overall Beneish M-Scores for the Primary Government and the Governmental Funds Financial Statements

	YR 2	YR 3	YR 4	YR 5
Primary Government	−2.63	−2.64	−2.70	−2.54
Governmental Funds	−1.48	−2.79	−2.71	−1.92

TABLE 4.6 Calculations for Seven of the Eight Indices for the Primary Government of Company 3

Index	YR 2	YR 3	YR 4	YR 5
DSRI	0.897	0.868	1.149	1.020
AQI	1.000	1.000	1.000	1.000
SGI	1.021	1.171	0.931	1.176
DEPI	0.967	1.033	0.979	0.974
SGAI	1.216	0.858	0.950	0.909
TATA	0.005	−0.044	−0.068	−0.053
LVGI	1.170	1.038	0.958	1.012

The overall Beneish M-Scores for the primary government financial statements suggest that they are free from manipulation. Yet, the governmental funds financial statements suggest the possibility of manipulation, especially in YR 2 and YR 5, since the scores are greater than −2.22. However, since the primary government financial statements consist of the governmental fund amounts plus the required accruals for GAAP presentation as well as the business activities, the possibility of manipulation exists also in the primary government financial statements, although the score calculations do not suggest manipulation.

Table 4.6 displays the indices' calculations for the primary government financial statements. Since it is in the primary government financial statements where property, plant, and equipment, depreciation, and long-term debt transactions are accounted for, seven of the eight indices apply to the financial statements. GMI is not applicable because manufacturing is not part of a government's activities and, therefore, no cost of sales is recorded. Modifications of gross margin calculations are useful in other types of analysis, but not for the Beneish M-Score model studied here.

Table 4.7 displays the indices' calculations for the governmental funds. Since the governmental funds do not record depreciation as well as having no cost of sales, both DEPI and GMI are not applicable. As stated earlier, for the expressed purpose of analyzing the due-to-other-funds impact on the financial statements, the analysis considers these as current long-term liabilities as in the financial statements. The LVGI calculations highlight the effect of these funds in the financial information. There is no other debt recorded in the governmental funds.

TABLE 4.7 Calculations for Six of the Eight Indices for the Governmental Funds of Company 3

Index	YR 2	YR 3	YR 4	YR 5
DSRI	1.021	0.842	1.240	0.969
AQI	1.003	1.000	1.001	1.000
SGI	1.077	1.209	0.857	1.091
SGAI	1.080	0.955	1.177	0.822
TATA	0.219	−0.018	0.018	0.131
LVGI	0.965	1.481	1.803	1.052

Indices of the Primary Government

Once more, the preferred method of analyzing the eight indices of the Beneish M-Score model is to use graphics for comparing the calculations to the standard benchmarks. Figure 4.20 displays the DSRI for the primary government financial statements, comparing the DSRI to the general benchmark of 1.

The chart for the primary government indicates that the DSRI calculations for both YR 2 and YR 3 are comparatively stable, while there is a significant change from YR 3 to YR 4. Even though YR 4 is higher than the benchmark of 1, both YR 4 and YR 5 are once again comparatively stable, similar to YR 2 and YR 3. Thus, for the financial forensic examiner, the significant change between

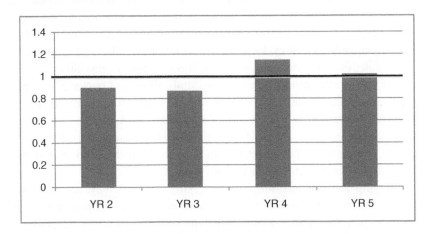

FIGURE 4.20 DSRI for the Primary Government of Company 3

YR 3 and YR 4 requires further study and explanation, especially since the horizontal analysis indicated increasing A/R from YR 3 through YR 5 and conflicting relationships between CRO and net income from YR 4 through YR 5.

Since the AQI calculations are quite comparable to the benchmark of the Model, the financial forensic examiner may find it more prudent to move to the next index, SGI. Figure 4.21 illustrates SGI for the primary government financial statements, comparing the SGI to the general benchmark of 1.

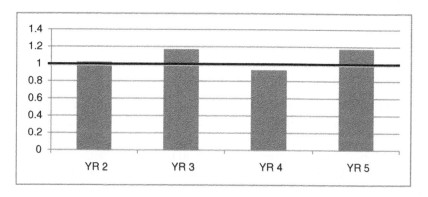

FIGURE 4.21 SGI for the Primary Government of Company 3

The SGI chart indicates that in both YR 3 and YR 5, the calculated changes are in excess of the general benchmark, with both of these years comparable to each other, while in YR 4, SGI decreases but is comparable to the benchmark in YR 2. The chart suggests possible cycles in sales growth but, with the limited number of periods under examination, confirming this theory is not possible although sales growth cycles are not common in governmental entities. In Chapter 2, the gross margins were comparable in YR 1, YR 4, and YR 5, with these years having the higher calculations, and both YR 2 and YR 3 with lower gross margin calculations. Yet, once again, especially in YR 5, the comparison of net income and CRO noted in Chapter 3 suggests conflicting relationships, so the financial forensic examiner must consider the possibility of further investigative work.

Studying the relationships between DSRI and SGI may provide some additional information in assisting the financial forensic examiner's determination to perform further investigative procedures. Figure 4.22 shows a comparison of DSRI and SGI, along with the benchmark for the primary government's financial statements.

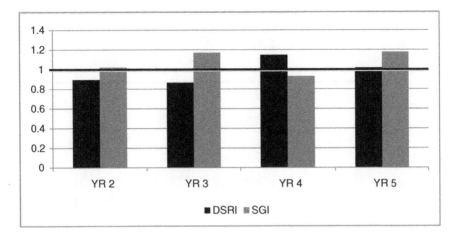

FIGURE 4.22 DSRI and SGI Comparison for the Primary Government of Company 3

In this instance, the chart tells the financial forensic examiner that when SGI increases, DSRI decreases, and when SGI decreases, DSRI increases. It is more intuitive to expect to see a possible increase in DSRI when SGI decreases, since the financial forensic examiner would consider the possibility of customers paying their bills later than normal; but would it be normal for both SGI and DSRI to increase? In the case of the primary government, SGI and DSRI calculations include both the governmental activities and the business activities, so the financial forensic examiner will want to perform this analysis at both component levels. The governmental funds follow later in the chapter.

Since the financial statements of the primary government include depreciation expenses, Figure 4.23 depicts the DEPI calculations and their comparisons to the general benchmark of 1.

The most obvious DEPI calculation that appears unusual is YR 3, because it is significantly higher than the benchmark. Remember that when DEPI is greater than the benchmark of 1, the calculation indicates the possibility that the rate of depreciation has slowed from the previous year and implies the possibility of a change in the useful lives of the assets in order to manipulate earnings, or that the company changed to a method of depreciation that is more "income producing." It is important to the financial forensic examiner to determine whether this occurred.

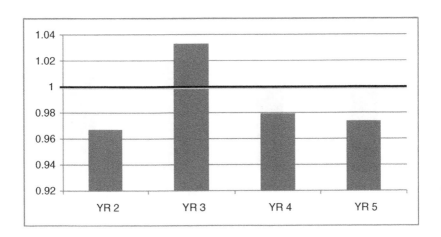

FIGURE 4.23 DEPI for the Primary Government of Company 3

The notes to the financial statements did not disclose any change in accounting methodology relating to the computation of depreciation expense for any of the years under review, so the financial forensic examiner should perform further investigative procedures relating to YR 3. More importantly, the horizontal analysis of the balance sheets in Chapter 2 indicates increases in fixed assets from year to year, so the financial forensic examiner should expect to see increases in depreciation as well, indicating decreasing DEPI from year to year as seen in both YR 4 and YR 5, which makes YR 3 more questionable. Remember that part of the coverup scheme to hide the embezzled funds included the recording of fictitious assets. So that changes in net fixed assets would appear normal, recording of additional depreciation expense was also necessary.

Figure 4.24 displays the SGAI calculations and their comparisons to the benchmark of 1 for the primary government of Company 3.

SGAI should remain reasonably stable from period to period, although there may be minor fluctuations when compared to the benchmark. The SGAI calculations for the primary government remain reasonably stable from year to year. Although YR 2 is somewhat higher than the general benchmark, the financial forensic examiner may want to continue to the next index unless other information becomes apparent that warrants further inspection.

Figure 4.25 shows the TATA calculations for the primary government of Company 3.

Since a positive calculation may suggest possible manipulation of financial statement information, the YR 2 calculation of TATA may be susceptible to

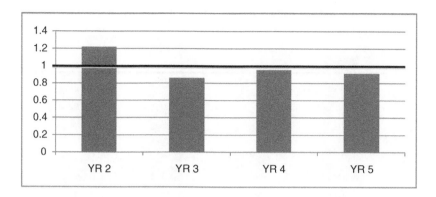

FIGURE 4.24 SGAI for the Primary Government of Company 3

manipulation, although the calculation is reasonably stable to the benchmark. Higher levels of accruals, and therefore less cash, are areas where earnings manipulation may occur and create the positive variance. This positive variance suggests the possibility of not properly recording all of the accruals in the financial statements or only partially recording the accruals. The other periods are comparatively stable to the index benchmark, but also remember that in Chapter 2, both the working capital calculations and the working capital index fluctuated from year to year. For the financial forensic examiner, YR 2 may require further study and analysis.

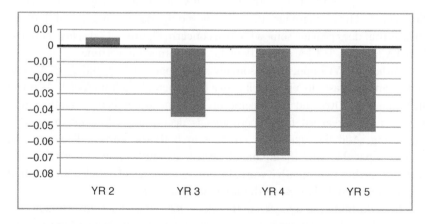

FIGURE 4.25 TATA for the Primary Government of Company 3

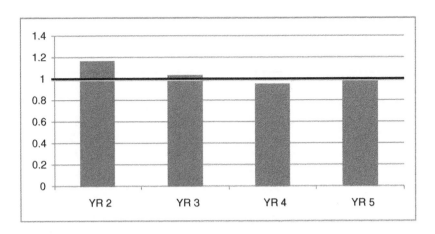

FIGURE 4.26 LVGI for the Primary Government of Company 3

Figure 4.26 depicts LVGI, the final index to calculate for the primary government of Company 3.

By remembering that LVGI greater than 1 describes increased leverage, the calculation for LVGI in YR 2 suggests increasing debt or the addition of new debt, while YR 3 and YR 4 indicates lower debt. Debt increases again in YR 5 but falls short of the general benchmark. However, the changes from year to year are reasonable, so the financial forensic examiner may not need to perform any detailed additional investigative work at this time.

Although the LVGI does not indicate any variances that should concern a financial forensic examiner, there is one comparison using the drill-down indices that does provide somewhat of a concern. Figure 4.27 displays both the TAPTA and the TCLTA calculations for the primary government.

Although LVGI appears reasonably stable, both TCLTA and TAPTA show significant increases in YR 5, well above the general benchmark of 1. As noted in Chapter 3, CRO and net income in YR 5 have conflicting relationships, whereas cash realized from operations is decreasing while net income is increasing. Add the significant changes in both the current liabilities and accounts payable, and the financial forensic examiner now understands the need for further investigative work, including a review of detailed information supporting these balances on the financial statements.

In performing the analyses of the Model for the primary government, the financial forensic examiner now must determine whether the variances relate to the governmental activities or the business activities. Accordingly, the next

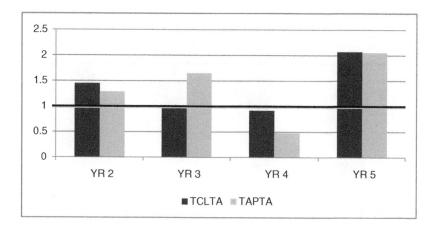

FIGURE 4.27 TCLTA and TAPTA for the Primary Government for Company 3

logical step would be to perform the same computations for both the governmental activities and the business activities. In the case of Company 3, the governmental funds, whose amounts are included in the governmental activities and the primary government financial statements, provide the clues necessary to unearth the embezzlement. Therefore, for the rationale of studying Company 3, the next section relates to the calculations of the indices for the governmental funds.

Indices of the Governmental Funds

Since the governmental funds' financial statement information is a component of the primary government's financial statements, the indices of the funds calculations are also part of the primary government's indices, but may or may not follow along the same trends. Also, remember that the current assets include the "due from other funds" while the current liabilities include the "due to other funds" for these calculations, since these were areas covering up the embezzlement of funds and the current portion of long-term debt is not part of the governmental fund's financial statements. The detailed analysis begins with the first index, DSRI.

Figure 4.28 depicts the DSRI calculations for the governmental funds of Company 3.

YR 2 and YR 4 both indicate a disproportionate relationship between sales and receivables, since the DSRI calculations are greater than 1, even though YR 1 is only slightly higher than the benchmark. More importantly, YR 2 is

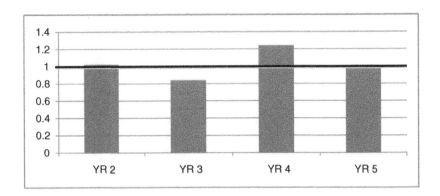

FIGURE 4.28 DSRI for the Governmental Funds of Company 3

also identified as a year of potential earnings manipulation based on the overall M-Score calculations greater than −2.22. Two other factors to consider relate to the change between YR 3 and YR 4 and then to YR 4, itself, since DSRI is greater than the general benchmark. Another interesting factor is that the DSRI of the primary government in YR 4 is also above the general benchmark and the same significant change occurs from YR 3 to YR 4 even though the primary government's financial information includes both the governmental entities and the business entities. Some similarities in the index calculations should take place between the different sets of financial statements.

From the financial forensic examiner's perspective, the DSRI calculations indicate that further investigative work is required for both sales and receivables. Significant changes and DSRI calculations that significantly exceed the general benchmark, such as in YR4, indicate the potential to manipulate earnings through sales and receivables. For the embezzler, though, this type of manipulation hides excessive losses from management or, in the case of Company 3, the town's officials.

Once again, GMI is not applicable to the governmental funds, so the financial forensic examiner does not need to spend time performing these calculations. In performing these tests, the financial forensic examiner begins to understand that calculating the individual indices provides both an efficient and effective method of determining where to focus the investigative work.

Although the AQI calculations are comparable to the general benchmark of 1 for the primary government, the AQI calculations are a little bit different for the governmental funds. Figure 4.29 illustrates the AQI for the governmental funds.

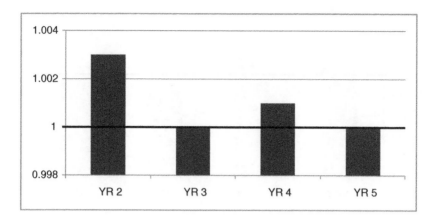

FIGURE 4.29 AQI for the Governmental Funds for Company 3

Once again, YR 2 stands out from the other years in that the calculations of AQI are greater than the general benchmark of 1, and YR 2 indicates possible earnings manipulation for the governmental funds from the overall Beneish M-Score calculations. The importance of AQI related to the governmental funds actually correlates to the due-from-other funds classified as current assets. As AQI increases and becomes greater than 1, the financial statement information may possibly contain "cost deferral" transactions, such as capitalizing costs instead of expensing them, similar to recording fictitious assets in the primary government. In the case of Company 3, the due-from-other funds offset the due-to-other funds, which were actually part of the embezzled funds, deferring the costs of the embezzlement since most of the cover-up transactions did not influence net income.

Figure 4.30 displays the SGI calculations for the governmental funds. Once again, the governmental SGI calculations have similarities to the SGI calculations of the primary government.

In general, SGI calculations that are greater than the general benchmark of 1 indicate growth, which is not necessarily bad for a company, or in this case, for a local government, but growth does put pressure on capital needs and the stress of maintaining the growth from year to year. Both YR 3 and YR 5 indicate growth for the governmental funds plus a significant decrease from YR 3 to YR 4 that may be troublesome for the local officials. The same pattern is also visible in the calculations of SGI for the primary government, even though these calculations include both the governmental and business entities, once

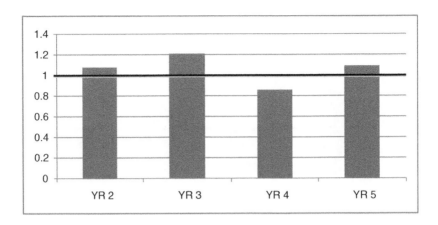

FIGURE 4.30 SGI for the Governmental Funds for Company 3

again demonstrating the effect of the governmental funds on the primary government's financial statements.

The SGI calculations include grant revenues that may fluctuate from year to year, so the changes are not as dramatic to the governmental funds as they would be to a private or public entity. However, from the financial forensic examiner's point of view, grant revenues may provide a playground for earnings manipulation by recording earnings and receivables prior to earning the grant funds or by noncompliance with the terms of the grants, so further work may be necessary. Remember that grant revenues are separate in the primary government's financial statements, but combined with other inter-governmental revenues in the governmental funds' financial statements. However, the horizontal analysis and the vertical analysis of the primary government financial statements in Chapter 2 indicate significant swings in grant revenues in both YR 3 and YR 5, consistent with the SGI findings for both the governmental funds and the primary government.

The next index for the governmental funds is SGAI. Figure 4.31 shows the SGAI calculations for the governmental funds. SGAI should remain relatively stable from year to year.

Although SGAI should remain relatively stable, the calculations of SGAI for the governmental funds do not portray such stability, especially in YR 4 and YR 5. In addition, unlike some of the other indices, SGAI of the primary government does not portray similar patterns. For the governmental funds, the change between YR 3 and YR 4 is significantly larger than the change between

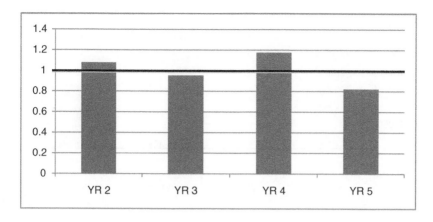

FIGURE 4.31 SGAI for the Governmental Funds for Company 3

YR 2 and YR 3, but smaller than the change from YR 4 to YR 5. Expenses related to grant revenues are also part of SGAI, but the calculations should follow the same trends as the grant revenues. In the case of YR 5, although grant revenues increased, the decrease in expenses decreased dramatically compared to the SGI increase. The financial forensic examiner should review YR 5 for possible earnings manipulation since the change is more significant compared to the other years.

Once again, the embezzler used several approaches to hide the missing funds—a strategy used by many fraudsters—so YR 4 also presents another issue for the financial forensic examiner, since the SGAI index for that year is above the general benchmark. Thus, the financial forensic examiner should review expenses by category to determine if any anomalies exist. By using vertical analysis, the financial forensic examiner can drill down to the specific expense accounts that have unusual changes from year to year for further investigative work.

The next index, TATA, should remain relatively stable to the general benchmark of zero. Figure 4.32 depicts the TATA calculations for the governmental funds.

In general, the financial forensic examiner should expect to see these calculations around zero or less than zero. A positive calculation may indicate possible earnings manipulation of the financial statements. The TATA calculations in YR 2 and again in YR 5 coincide with the overall M-Scores, indicating possible manipulation. Now the financial forensic examiner has two different analytical tests that indicate manipulation in the governmental funds of the

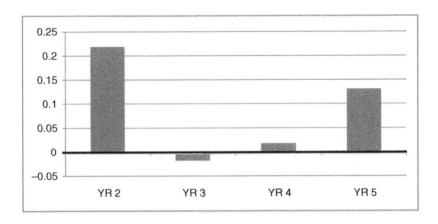

FIGURE 4.32 TATA for the Governmental Funds for Company 3

financial statements, while the overall M-score calculations and the TATA calculations of the primary government did not indicate any potential earnings manipulation.

The last index of the Beneish M-Score model for the governmental funds is LVGI. Figure 4.33 shows the LVGI calculations and their comparisons to the general benchmark of 1.

Normally, LVGI would not be required for governmental funds because the income statements document any transactions related to debt—not the balance sheets. However, in the case of Company 3, the due-to-other funds

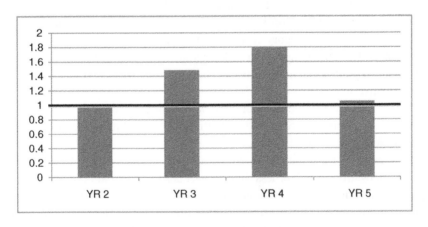

FIGURE 4.33 LVGI for the Governmental Funds for Company 3

in the governmental funds financial statements represent current liabilities, which need to be measured because the interfund transactions do not net to zero. The LVGI for YR 4 is significantly higher than the benchmark, indicating a significant increase in debt or, as indicated in the horizontal analysis in Chapter 2, a significant increase in the due-to-other-funds amounts and correlates to the cost deferral aspects of the AQI calculations in YR 4. The financial forensic examiner should expect a similar response in the current assets related to the due-from-other funds. When comparing the two accounts in the vertical analysis of the balance sheet, both accounts increased significantly in both YR 4 and YR 5.

Since the due-from-other funds and the due-to-other funds accounts are significant to current assets and current liabilities, two of the drill-down components of TATA, TCATA and TCLTA, will enable the financial forensic examiner to view the changes in these accounts. A very useful approach for the financial forensic examiner to use is a comparison of these calculations combined into one chart. Figure 4.34 demonstrates the combination of these calculations.

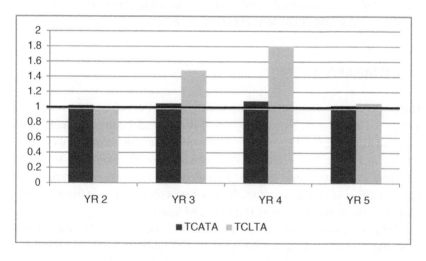

FIGURE 4.34 TCATA versus TCLTA for the Governmental Funds for Company 3

From the comparison, the financial forensic examiner finds that both YR 2 and YR 5 are comparable, but in both YR 3 and YR 4, TCLTA is definitely greater than TCATA and significantly higher than the benchmark of 1. Remember that one of the ploys to hide the embezzled funds included fabricated transactions posted to the due-to-other-funds accounts of the various governmental fund financial statements while the funds were diverted to an off-book bank account and withdrawn for personal use.

For Company 3, the financial forensic examiner faces multiple issues because the primary government financial statements do not exhibit the variations in the financial statements as much as the governmental fund financial statements—a quandary, since the primary government financial statements contain the elements of the governmental fund financial statements. The overall Beneish M-Scores disagree between the two types of financial statements, with the governmental funds indicating possible earnings manipulation for both YR 2 and YR 5. Although some of the indices are comparable, the other ones provide more information for the financial forensic examiner and indicate further investigative work.

Although the calculations of the indices of the Model separate the primary government and the governmental funds, calculations in total from Chapter 2 also provide evidence for the financial forensic examiner. For example, working capital index calculations in Table 2.1 vary greatly from year to year, and the current ratio calculations decrease every year, which supports the LVGI and TCLTA calculations of the governmental funds.

COMPANY 4

The last company to analyze using the Beneish M-Score model and its eight indices is Company 4. Since Company 4 is the model company with correct financial information untouched by earnings manipulation and embezzlement activity, it is very important for the financial forensic examiner to use this company as a comparison in order to understand the differences noted in the previous three companies, whose financial statements include inconsistencies related to the manipulation of the financial information.

Table 4.8 provides the calculations for the Beneish M-Score model and the comparison of the -2.22 that suggests manipulation of financial information.

Once more, Company 4's calculations suggest possible earnings manipulation for YR 2, YR 3, and YR 4 while YR 5 falls within the guidelines of the

TABLE 4.8 Overall Beneish M-Score Calculations for Company 4

	YR 2	YR 3	YR 4	YR 5
Overall M-Score	−0.73	−1.88	−1.90	−2.98

Model. Again, it is important for the financial forensic examiner to remember that the calculations are merely suggestive of possible fraudulent activity, and a thorough understanding of the company's operations provides basic information that requires validation. For Company 4, information in the notes to the financial statements provides specific information related to the unusual transactions. Upon completion of the unusual events related to the subsidiary's bankruptcy in YR 4 and the deconsolidation of the subsidiary from the financial statements, the following YR 5 returns to overall scores that fall within the guidelines of the Beneish model.

Next follows the calculations of the indices of the Model. Since Company 4 produces products for sale, Table 4.9 depicts the calculations for all eight indices.

TABLE 4.9 Calculations of the Eight Indices for Company 4

Index	YR 2	YR 3	YR 4	YR 5
DSRI	1.132	0.896	1.100	0.815
GMI	0.990	0.933	0.972	1.040
AQI	1.203	1.057	0.969	1.016
SGI	1.147	1.489	1.164	0.977
DEPI	1.028	1.036	1.584	1.02
SGAI	0.886	0.838	0.934	.881
TATA	0.286	0.042	0.048	−0.096
LVGI	0.805	0.871	0.771	0.703

Along with the other companies, the indices are in graphical form and analyzed individually, beginning with DSRI.

Figure 4.35 depicts the DSRI calculations for Company 4, comparing the calculations to the general benchmark of 1. Once more, a disproportionate increase may indicate manipulation by increasing revenues.

For Company 4, the DSRI calculations are comparatively stable, although there is somewhat of a decline in YR 5, indicating that year over year the relationships between sales and accounts receivable remain steady, unlike the changes noted in Company 1 and Company 2. By using Company 4 as a comparison, the financial forensic examiner begins to train the eye to see subtle changes that normally would not be identifiable.

Figure 4.36 illustrates the GMI calculations and their comparisons to the benchmark for Company 4.

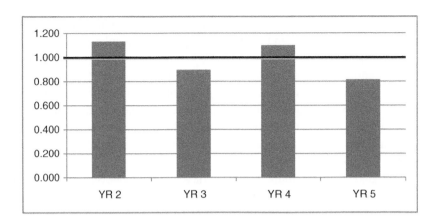

FIGURE 4.35 DSRI—Company 4

From the graphical depiction of the GMI calculations, the financial forensic examiner is able to determine that from YR 2 to YR 3, the company may have declining profits and definitely a negative signal about the firm's future prospects and the burden on the firm from the deteriorating subsidiary. However, when looking at the scale of the change, the amounts differ very little from year to year. It does become intuitively obvious in YR 3 that the subsidiary is no longer functioning as GMI starts to increase in YR 4, upon the final dissolution of the subsidiary. In YR 5, the firm is continuing to grow once

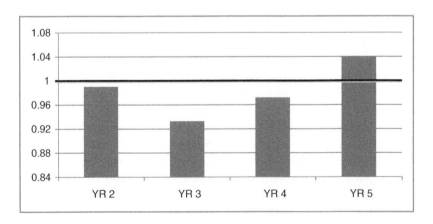

FIGURE 4.36 GMI—Company 4

more. Although these signals are present and readily detectable in the chart, it is also important to note that even these issues are not changing GMI that dramatically based on the scale of change, thus confirming that GMI should remain relatively stable from period to period under normal operations. Remember also that in Table 2.6 in Chapter 2, the gross profit margin calculations are comparatively stable.

As stated earlier, GMI should remain relatively stable year over year, and declining GMI is a concern for the financial forensic examiner, indicating possible pressure to increase earnings by manipulation. To better view variability in GMI, Figure 4.37 compares the GMI of Company 2 to the GMI of Company 4.

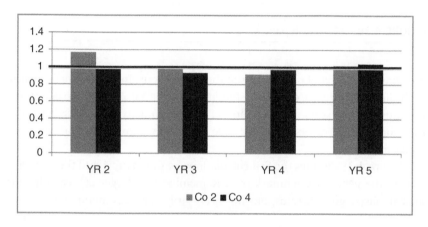

FIGURE 4.37   GMI Comparisons of Company 2 and Company 4

When comparing the GMI of Company 2 to the GMI of Company 4, the financial forensic examiner can easily see the differences where Company 2's GMI fluctuates instead of remaining relatively stable like in Company 4. So now, the financial forensic examiner begins to understand that the indices of the Beneish M-Score model provide an excellent roadmap for further investigative work by pointing out variances in the financial information that are unusual and not within the standard operation of the business.

The next index to review for Company 4 is AQI. Figure 4.38 shows the AQI calculations for Company 4 and their comparisons to the general benchmark of 1.

The AQI of YR 2 and YR 3 are the only calculations that are in excess of the benchmark, yet all calculations are moderately stable. Remember that calculations in excess of 1 indicate the possibility of cost deferral but every company

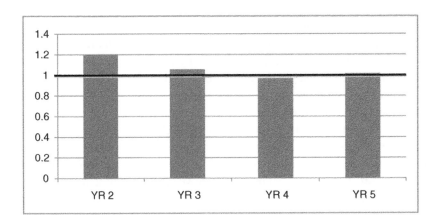

FIGURE 4.38 AQI—Company 4

may have a little bit of unevenness in the calculations. In the case of Company 4, the financial forensic examiner should review the YR 2 activity to determine the cause of the excess greater than 1. For this company, the excess relates to the non-current assets held for sale from the subsidiary that filed for bankruptcy.

Figure 4.39 displays the SGI calculations for Company 4 and the comparisons to the general benchmark of 1. Remember that larger SGI calculations indicate faster growth rates, but not necessarily earnings manipulation.

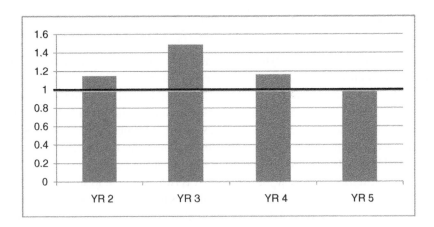

FIGURE 4.39 SGI—Company 4

SGI for YR 3 represents significant growth for Company 4 when compared to the other calculations. While growth alone does not indicate manipulation, financial forensic examiners should remain skeptical and consider potential earnings manipulation, since accelerated growth puts pressure on a company to continue to perform and meet earnings targets. In YR 3, Company 4 received several special orders during the year that created the growth spurt. The company did not receive any special orders in both YR 4 and YR 5, and the SGI returned to normal operational levels with a slight decrease in YR 5 associated with economic conditions of the period. It is common for Company 4 to receive special orders at various times, creating unusual swings in the sales growth index. This type of information is valuable to the financial forensic examiner in the interpretation of testing results and generally documented in discussions with company's management over the company's general operations.

Figure 4.40 depicts the next index, DEPI, for Company 4 and comparisons to the general benchmark.

YR 4 signifies an issue for the financial forensic examiner because DEPI is significantly greater than the benchmark of 1 and definitely not consistent with the other calculations. Thus, the question is whether the company deliberately changed the useful lives of its assets or changed depreciation methods in order to manipulate earnings for this period. The unusual DEPI calculation for YR 4 describes the deconsolidation of the subsidiary upon the final report from the trustee and the liquidation of its assets. For the financial forensic examiner, it is important to remember that unusual events may occur within a company and

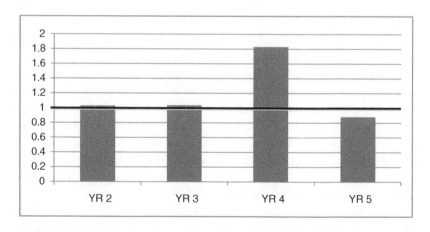

FIGURE 4.40   DEPI—Company 4

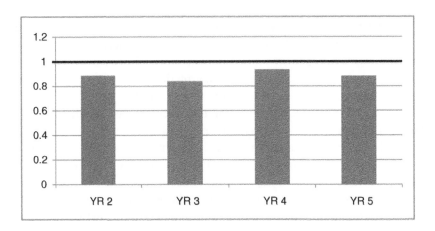

FIGURE 4.41　SGAI—Company 4

no fraud occur. However, only additional investigative work will substantiate the true reasons for any unusual variations found from the analytical process.

Figure 4.41 depicts the SGAI calculations for Company 4, along with their comparisons to the general benchmark of 1.

The SGAI calculations for Company 4 actually illustrate stability, since these calculations vary little from period to period, especially when compared to Company 1. From the financial forensic examiner's point of view, SGAI does not have any unusual variations suggestive of manipulation, and further analysis is not required.

Figure 4.42 shows the TATA calculations for Company 4 and their comparisons to the general benchmark of zero.

Even though YR 2, YR 3, and YR 4 have positive calculations, suggesting the possibility of manipulation because of instability in the financial statement relationships, high levels of accruals during this period link the instability to the subsidiary that files for bankruptcy. The financial forensic examiner is able to determine that once the bankruptcy allowed dissolution of the subsidiary, the relationships become more stable as shown by the negative calculation in YR 5.

Figure 4.43 depicts the final index, LVGI, for Company 4 along with the comparisons to the general benchmark of 1.

Since the LVGI calculations are below the benchmark for all years reviewed, apparently Company 4 does not have the increasing debt that may provide incentives for earnings manipulation in order to meet debt

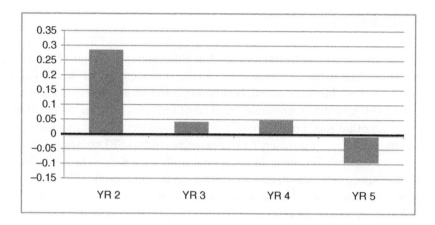

FIGURE 4.42   TATA—Company 4

covenants. This would make sense to the financial forensic examiner, since one of the company's subsidiaries was in financial trouble and filing for bankruptcy. Therefore, the financial forensic examiner may determine that further investigative work is not necessary. In fact, none of the calculations of any of the indices indicates any unexplained unusual variances, so the drill-down calculations from TATA are not necessary for Company 4.

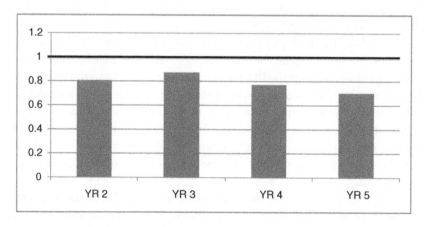

FIGURE 4.43   LVGI—Company 4

SUMMARY

First, a synopsis of the techniques used in this chapter for each of the four companies defines the requirements of further investigative work. For Company 1, the first clue is the overall benchmark being greater than -2.22 in YR 2. Next, the graphical representation of DSRI indicates unusual swings from year to year that need further study, but YR 2 poses the greatest quandary for the financial forensic examiner. TATA also supports the DSRI irregularity in YR 2 and provides reinforcement for additional study for YR 2. As for GMI, these calculations are representative of salaries and, once more, YR 2 is the abnormality. SGAI also has questionable calculations in YR 2, as well as in YR 4 and YR 5 since these are greater than the general benchmark. Additionally, SGAI should remain relatively stable, and SGAI for Company 1 is definitely not stable. Because all of these analytic techniques point to YR 2, the financial forensic examiner now knows that YR 2 is going to require additional study and further investigative work, requiring drill-down techniques in receivables, salaries, sales, and specific general administrative expenses identified in a vertical analysis of the detailed accounts.

The other questionable area for Company 1 involves YR 3. Both DEPI and DEPTA have unusual calculations. In YR 3, DEPI decreases significantly in YR 2 while DEPTA increases in YR 3, indicating a significant increase in depreciation expense from the prior year. One would think that such an increase in depreciation would indicate significant purchases in fixed assets, and the cash flow statement in Chapter 3 prepared for Company 1 supports this theory. However, the vertical analysis of the balance sheet indicates little change in net fixed assets from the prior year, suggesting that depreciation accelerated for the new purchases that year. In contrast, YR 4 also poses questions for the financial forensic examiner because depreciation slowed down significantly, since the DEPI is significantly higher than the benchmark for that year. So just from the techniques of the Beneish M-Score model, the financial forensic examiner knows that in YR 3 and YR 4, fixed assets and depreciation expense require further investigation. However, more importantly, finding unusual variations among the different indices over different periods indicates the possibility of some type of manipulation occurring in each period.

As for Company 2, the most important clue for the financial forensic examiner is GMI. GMI should be consistent from year to year, the GMI calculations do not show this consistency, and YR 4 indicates the greatest variation of the GMI calculations. This instability of GMI is more apparent when compared with the GMI of Company 4, and the financial forensic examiner must learn to train the eye to see when these changes indicate unusual deviations in the financial information. Interestingly, TITA also shows the same variation in YR 4, but increasing while GMI is decreasing, supporting the need for further investigative work associated with both cost of sales and inventory.

Furthermore, comparing GMI and SGI also supports the instability of GMI. The change from YR 2 to YR 3 indicates a significant decrease in sales growth but only a slight decrease in the gross margin. Notably in YR 4, sales growth shows a greater decrease than the decrease in GMI. Finally, in YR 5, GMI increases while SGI decreases, such that the changes in the cost of sales exceed the changes in sales.

YR 5 is the period of unusual relationships for DSRI, and since the change is significant, sales and receivables require further study. YR 5 also poses challenges related to SGAI, since the SGAI calculations are substantially higher than the general benchmark. Once more, YR 5 also indicates unusual variations in TATA because the positive nature of the calculations indicates higher accruals, similar to YR 2. Additionally, the overall M-Scores for Company 2 indicate possible manipulation of the financial information for both YR 2 and YR 5. Once again, like Company 1, finding unusual variations of the different indices in different years suggests the possibility of some type of manipulation in every period.

The governmental funds financial statements of Company 3 provide more interest to the financial forensic examiner compared to the primary government financial statements, especially LVGI and TATA. Both of these indices illustrate the importance of the due-from-other funds and due-to-other funds and their relevance in these calculations. LVGI shows that both the YR 3 and YR 4 governmental funds are highly leveraged, while LVGI for the primary government actually indicates decreases and falls within the expectations of the general benchmark. The TATA calculations for the governmental funds are all positive, indicating a high level of accruals and, therefore, less cash, which becomes important in the investigation of embezzlement. Comparing TCATA to TCLTA also confirms the high level of accruals. Thus, in this instance, two separate analytical techniques confirm the possibility of manipulation.

As for the primary government, DEPI in YR 3 indicate that depreciation has slowed considerably compared to the other years, including the following YR 4, indicating a significant change over YR 3. Yet the vertical analysis in Chapter 2 indicates that depreciation expense remained consistent between YR 2 and YR 3 but showed an increase in YR 4. DEPI also illustrates that the change from YR 4 to YR 5 is somewhat consistent and meets the expectations of the general benchmark.

The important point for the financial forensic examiner to remember relating to the comparison of DSRI and SGI is that if both DSRI increases and SGI increases, there is the possibility that the financial information includes fictitious sales, thus manipulating the earnings. Although DSRI increases significantly from YR 3 to YR 4, SGI decreases, implying that customers are not paying timely. The TARTA calculations support the increase of receivables in YR 4 as well.

Although TATA and LVGI of the primary government do not support the same conclusions of the governmental funds, both TAPTA and TCLTA do support the increases in the current liabilities as shown in the government funds TATA calculations. In both YR 3 and YR 5, TAPTA is significantly higher than the general benchmark of 1, and when comparing the two, TAPTA is a significant portion of total current assets in both of these years. Once again, using more than one analytical technique and computing similar results provides the financial forensic examiner with sufficient evidence to proceed with further investigative work.

One motive for using Company 4 as a comparison to the other companies is that where some of the techniques used throughout this book suggest possible fraudulent activity, the financial forensic examiner is able to validate the reasons for the possible anomalies. For example, the SGI calculations indicate significant growth that may put pressure on management to manipulate earnings for investor relations. Yet, most of the sales growth is related to special orders the company received during YR 3. DEPI is another example where YR 4 indicates a significant slow-down in depreciation, usually related to changes in methods or useful lives that manipulate earnings. However, for Company 4, the change in YR 4 relates to the deconsolidation of the bankrupt subsidiary and the liquidation of all of its assets.

Another reason is for the financial forensic examiner to see the differences from what is normal versus what is not normal. The comparison of GMI between Company 2 and Company 4 is an excellent example of this concept. The DSRI calculations for Company 4 illustrate more stability in their relationships to the general benchmark compared to the other companies. Furthermore, the SGAI calculations also depict stability in relationship to the general benchmark, and all calculations were below 1.

By using enhanced analytical techniques for the four companies' financial information, this chapter provides the financial forensic examiner with a copious amount of analytical techniques that assist in pinning down areas of financial information that include unusual variations or anomalies that require further investigative work. These techniques also allow the financial forensic examiner to dismiss areas of the financial information that do not include anomalies, which allows the financial forensic examiner to work more efficiently and effectively without using the hunt-and-peck practice that makes the investigation both ineffective and inefficient.

The Beneish M-Score model allows the financial forensic examiner to determine whether overall the financial statements suggest manipulation, either by earnings manipulation or attempted coverups of embezzled funds, by using the general benchmark of -2.22. Based on Beneish's scientific approach in developing the Model, the financial forensic examiner is able to rely on the Model and its components' calculations to determine the path of the investigation of the financial information. By breaking the Beneish M-Score model into its components, the financial forensic examiner has the ability to calculate the indices of the eight components of the Model.

The eight indices cover specific areas of the financial information, such as the changes in days sales in receivable, changes in the gross margin, changes in asset quality, changes in sales growth, changes in depreciation, changes in sales and general administrative expenses, changes in total debt to total assets, and changes in total accruals to total assets. These calculations may be from month to month, quarter to quarter, or year to year and still be reliable. Beneish also provided general benchmarks for each of the eight indices that allow the financial forensic examiner to compare each calculation to the benchmark of each index. This permits the financial forensic examiner to determine whether each calculation may contain unusual variances or anomalies that require further investigative work, in order to conclude whether the variances relate to possible fraudulent activity or, if reasonable, validated explanations exist for the variances.

The authors of the March 2012 *United States Attorney Bulletin* provide additional drill-down techniques from the TATA index for further analysis in specific areas. These areas include changes in working capital to total assets, changes in depreciation and amortization to total assets, changes in current assets to total assets, changes in current liabilities to total assets, changes in accounts receivable to total assets, changes in inventory to total assets, changes in accounts payable to total assets, and income taxes payable to total assets.

By applying these techniques to each of the four companies, the financial forensic examiner learns that not all techniques are required for each investigation, and that the drill-down techniques are not always required, yet these techniques are applicable to all types of companies, regardless of whether the company is a public one or a private one. This also includes a manufacturing entity, a governmental entity, a nonprofit entity, or a financial institution. The financial forensic examiner also knows that slight variations are common, depending on the individual characteristics of the company, and that calculations made over multiple periods will identify these slight variances.

This chapter provides the financial forensic examiner with specific analytical techniques that point to unusual variations in financial information that require further investigative work. In addition, the financial forensic examiner is able to combine various calculations or use drill-down techniques to support the original test showing unusual variations in the financial information. The financial forensic examiner now has a methodical process that permits a more effective and efficient investigation.

NOTES

1. Messod D. Beneish, "The Detection of Earnings Manipulation," *Financial Analyst Journal*, 55, No. 5 (September–October 1999) 17.
2. Ibid., Table 3.
3. Ibid., Table 3.
4. Darrell Dorrell, Gregory A. Gadawaski, Heidi Bowen, and Janet F. Hunt, "Financial Intelligence: People and Money Techniques to Prosecute Fraud, Corruption, and Earnings Manipulation," *United States Attorney Bulletin*, 60, No. 2 (March 2012) 46.

CHAPTER FIVE

The Accruals

G ENERALLY, when reviewing accruals in financial statements, one considers accounts such as accounts payable, accrued expenses, and future tax liabilities. Yet, accruals also include non-cash assets such as accounts receivable, accrued interest receivable, deferred tax assets, and intangibles and goodwill, not to mention accruals subject to estimations by management, such as allowance for uncollectible accounts and reserves for warranty expenses and inventory. Accruals provide information linking business activities unrelated to cash transactions, such as revenues based on credit, or future costs incurred by the company, such as accrued payroll and accrued payroll taxes. From the financial forensic examiner's viewpoint, accruals provide a playing field for potential financial manipulation and earnings management. Many of the accruals are skewed toward management's assumptions and estimates and, accordingly, create possible bias from management in accounting for these items. This chapter provides three different perspectives in analyzing accruals, hence adding three different analytical techniques to the financial forensic examiner's toolbox.

Remember that in the previous chapter the TATA index measures the ratio of total accruals to total assets for each year, and the indexes should remain rather stable. Also noted in that chapter is that when TATA is positive, there are high levels of accruals relative to assets, indicating a possibility of earnings manipulation. Since TATA is just one method of measuring accruals, the financial forensic examiner should use other analytical techniques to measure accruals to either support the conclusions reached from TATA calculations, or perform separate analytical tests for accruals in the financial statement information for further study. Techniques covered in this chapter not only provide additional insight into the TATA calculations, they also provide different methods of tackling the locations of possible manipulation in financial information so that the financial forensic examiner does not have to rely totally on reviewing all detailed information or upon professional judgment alone when using any particular analytical technique. These techniques also locate areas within financial information containing unusual relationships requiring additional forensic procedures.

There have been multiple research papers analyzing accruals and their relationship to net income. Many argue that accruals, especially discretionary accruals, allow management to control earnings from period to period, which is known as *income smoothing* or managing earnings, especially for public companies where investors are willing to purchase stock at premium prices from companies that have predictable, steady earnings from period to period. While income smoothing does not rely on "creative" accounting or misstatements that would constitute fraud, the practice is the result of various interpretations of GAAP but does not necessarily provide thoroughly accurate financial information within the period of reporting. Investors are generally unaware of this practice and its relationship to net income when reviewing financial statements of companies. These techniques not only point to areas within the financial statements that do contain fraudulent transactions, but also point to areas of possible income smoothing in financial statements. As with all other techniques discussed in this book, having more periods under study allows the financial forensic examiner to determine the small variations that occur over multiple periods related to the normal operations of the company.

The three techniques discussed in this chapter include the Dechow–Dichev Accrual Quality, the Jones Nondiscretionary Accruals, and Sloan's Accruals. Each method provides a forensic approach for determining if accrual information in the financial statements includes unusual variations and inconsistencies representing the possibility of fraud or earnings management. The *Dechow–Dichev Accrual Quality* equation measures the change in working capital and cash flows, *Sloan's Accruals* equation measures not only the implied cash component of earnings but also the accrual component of earnings, and the *Jones Nondiscretionary Accruals* equation indirectly measures discretionary accruals that Jones believes provide more opportunity for manipulation compared to nondiscretionary accruals. This chapter focuses on each technique and its application to the four companies as a forensic tool for measuring both possibilities of fraudulent activity in financial statement information and earnings management.

DECHOW–DICHEV ACCRUAL QUALITY

The model developed by professors Patricia Dechow and Ilia Dichev in their paper, "The Quality of Accruals and Earnings: The Role of Accrual Estimation Errors" (2001), measures the quality of accruals based on the extent of realized cash flow from the accruals and earnings outcome. The key concept of their research indicates that firms with low accrual quality have more accruals that are unrelated to actual cash flows compared to firms with higher accrual quality. For the financial forensic examiner, low accrual quality also represents the possibility of fraudulent transactions influencing the financial statements. These calculations apply to all types of business entities, including private and publicly held corporations, governments, nonprofits, and financial institutions.

One important item for the financial forensic examiner to remember is that the model only points to anomalies that need further examination, since the calculations cannot determine whether the accrual manipulation is intentional or just an error. However, Dechow and Dichev do convey in their research that precise estimates do imply future cash flows and stable relationships within the accrual quality, while ill-defined or imprecise estimates will not likely produce future cash flows and produce instability in the accrual quality. They also identify certain behaviors from their research relating to the accrual quality, including the following listing based on their research:

- A longer operating cycle decreases accrual quality in contrast to a smaller operating cycle increasing accrual quality.
- The size of the firm affects accrual quality, with smaller firms having lower accrual quality.
- Instability in sales decreases accrual quality.
- Unpredictable cash flow decreases accrual quality.
- Unstable accruals lower accrual quality.
- Continued losses lower accrual quality.
- More accruals lower accrual quality.

The Dechow–Dichev Accrual Quality measurement combines the change in working capital and cash flow from operations for the current year compared to the average of total assets for both the current and prior year:

$$(cy \text{ Operating Cash Flow } + \Delta\, cy \text{ WC}) \div (cy \text{ TA } + py \text{ TA})^{1}$$

Component Abbreviations

$(cy = \text{current year})$
$(py = \text{prior year})$
$(\Delta = \text{change from prior year})$
$(\text{WC} = \text{working capital})$
$(\text{TA} = \text{total assets})$

The most effective method for the financial forensic examiner to use with this calculation is to compare the accrual quality calculations with net income. Thus, in reviewing the four companies and calculating the accrual quality in this model, the use of a dual-axis chart will compare the accrual quality calculations to net income. Besides calculating the entire formula, Dechow and Dichev also noted in the same paper an easy method for calculating earnings that will compare net income to the Dechow–Dichev earnings, described as *earnings after short-term accruals but before long-term accruals*, and is actually part of the accrual quality formula:

$$cy \text{ Operating Cash Flow } + \Delta\, cy \text{ WC} = \text{ Earnings}^{2}$$

This method will also assist in determining low accrual quality by comparing net income to the Dechow–Dichev earnings, using a chart for visualizing the comparison. The analyses for the four companies will include both methods.

Since the calculations for the Dechow–Dichev model rely on changes in working capital from the previous year, the analysis begins with YR 2 and continues through YR 5. Company 3's calculations separate the primary government and the governmental funds since the due-to-other funds represent current liabilities that require analysis for the influence of these accounts in both the primary government and the governmental funds financial statements. Table 5.1 illustrates the calculations of the Dechow–Dichev Accrual Quality for all four companies, while Table 5.2 illustrates the calculations of earnings.

Now that the fundamental calculations are complete, the financial forensic examiner is able to follow the analyses of the four companies using the Dechow–Dichev Accrual Quality method.

The Four Companies: Dechow–Dichev Model

Beginning with the complete equation of the Dechow–Dichev Accrual Quality, Figure 5.1 depicts the analysis of the calculations to net income using a dual-axis chart.

TABLE 5.1   Dechow–Dichev Accrual Quality for the Four Companies

	YR 2	YR 3	YR 4	YR 5
Company 1	−0.06	0.04	0.01	−0.03
Company 2	0.09	0.13	0.10	0.09
Primary Gov't	0.03	0.03	0.01	0.03
Gov't Funds	0.25	−0.13	−0.33	0.01
Company 4	0.06	0.05	0.09	0.07

TABLE 5.2   Dechow–Dichev Implied Cash Earnings Compared to Net Income for the Four Companies

	YR 2	YR 3	YR 4	YR 5
Company 1	−17,954	11,824	1,567	−8,640
Company 2	1,424,030	2,289,336	1,813,905	1,981,411
Primary Gov't	5,597,587	5,390,955	1,651,453	5,007,585
Gov't Funds	7,977,842	−4,576,206	−10,426,475	197,728
Company 4	15,444,000	12,687,360	32,199,000	28,434,000

In reviewing the chart, Company 1 had a significant change in accrual quality in YR 3, while the Dechow–Dichev earnings compared to net income in Figure 5.2 follow the same trend as net income. For the financial forensic examiner, the significance of the change in YR 3 also indicates instability in the accrual quality. Considering that Company 1 is a smaller company, the financial forensic examiner expects to see lower accrual quality compared to larger companies, suggesting that the change in YR 3 is somewhat unusual. Based on the horizontal analysis of the income statement, Company 1 did have some unevenness in sales from year to year, suggesting decreased accrual quality. Negative earnings also suggest decreased accrual quality, but even with these events, accrual quality should be stable. Instability in the accrual

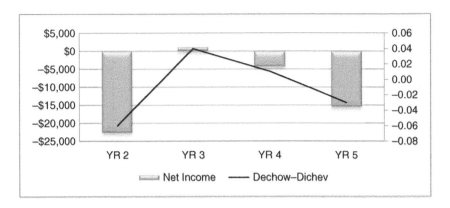

FIGURE 5.1 Dechow–Dichev Accrual Quality for Company 1 and Net Income

quality from year to year increases the possibility that the company's accruals are not precise and the lack of future cash flows questions whether the accruals contain errors or possible manipulation.

Figure 5.2 illustrates Dechow–Dichev's earnings calculations compared to net income, as a comparison to Figure 5.1.

The financial forensic examiner can readily determine that using the earnings formula as a comparison to net income provides an interesting

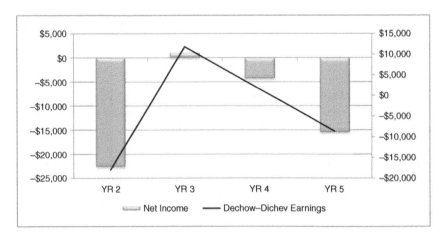

FIGURE 5.2 Dechow–Dichev Earnings to Net Income for Company 1

analysis between actual net income and the calculations of the Dechow–Dichev earnings. Once again, YR 3 shows the greatest effect of accruals to net income, while YR 2 shows marginal effects of the accruals to net income. In YR 4, the effects of the accrual quality influencing net income show that income should be positive, although the company's financial statements show a loss. In YR 5, once again, accruals tend to impact net income more than in YR 2 and YR 3.

The financial forensic examiner generally should expect to see a comparative relationship between earnings and net income or a rather stable relationship in the Dechow–Dichev accruals and net income. In other words, if income increases, then earnings should follow a similar trend. In Figure 5.2, the relationships between net income and earnings follow similar patterns, lessening the possibility of manipulation in the financial statements, while in Figure 5.1, the accruals are not that stable, suggesting the possibility of earnings manipulation. Since the two methods do not provide substantive evidence of manipulation, the financial forensic examiner must use other techniques to determine if manipulation actually exists. Of particular interest to the financial forensic examiner is that in all of the years, the accruals negatively influence net income, so the financial forensic examiner must ask what possible explanations provide reasons as to why a company would continually want to decrease earnings.

Company 2 provides a different comparison of the two equations compared to Company 1. Figure 5.3 shows the comparison of the Dechow–Dichev

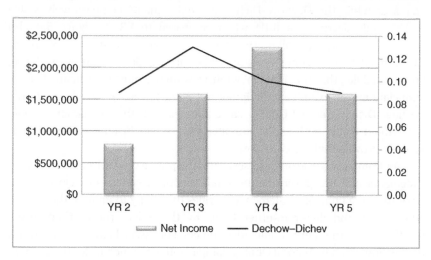

FIGURE 5.3 Dechow–Dichev Accrual Quality and Net Income for Company 2

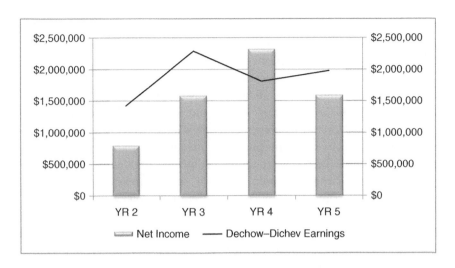

FIGURE 5.4 Dechow–Dichev Earnings and Net Income for Company 2

Accrual Quality calculations to net income, while Figure 5.4 shows the comparison of earnings before long-term accruals to net income.

Overall, Figure 5.3 indicates a comparatively stable relationship for the years under investigation, suggesting that accruals recorded in the financial statements relate to realized cash flows. However, in YR 4, net income increases while the Dechow–Dichev accrual remains comparatively stable and actually decreases a little when compared to YR 3. Figure 5.4 also confirms that earnings follow the same trends with net income, except for YR 4. In YR 4, net income increases while earnings decrease, thus exhibiting another red flag that the financial forensic examiner must investigate. For the financial forensic examiner, the important point to remember relating to the Dechow–Dichev Accrual Quality calculations is that the calculations should not remain stable with significant increases in net income if the accruals actually provide realized cash flows.

For Company 3, the analysis separates the primary government's financial statements and the governmental funds' financial statements. Once again, separating the financial statements provides the ability to analyze the due-to-other funds and due-from-other funds by themselves rather than mixed together with other current liabilities and current assets. Figure 5.5 illustrates the Dechow–Dichev Accrual Quality comparison to net income for the primary government, and Figure 5.6 illustrates the Dechow–Dichev earnings comparison to net income.

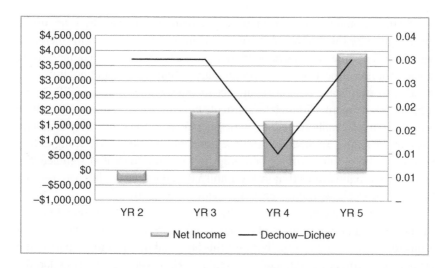

FIGURE 5.5 Dechow–Dichev Accrual Quality and Net Income for the Primary Government of Company 3

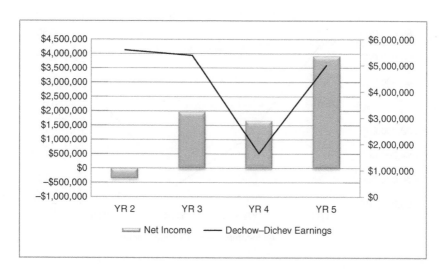

FIGURE 5.6 Dechow–Dichev Earnings and Net Income for the Primary Government of Company 3

Figure 5.5 indicates a reasonably stable relationship over the years under investigation for the primary government. However, in YR 3, income increases significantly, while the Dechow–Dichev Accrual Quantity is comparatively stable. Another aspect of the accrual quality is that the accrual quality is the same with significant differences in net income. For example, in YR 2, the primary government's financial statements indicate a loss, while in YR 3 there is more than a $2 million increase in net income with the same accrual quality calculation. Figure 5.6 also confirms the unusual variation in YR 3, suggesting very little change in earnings, although net income increased significantly. Figure 5.6 also illustrates that in YR 4 and YR 5, the relationship between net income and Dechow–Dichev earnings follows similar trends.

Before the financial forensic examiner can reach any conclusion relating to the possibility of manipulation of the financial information, the governmental funds require analytic testing, because this financial information is part of the primary government's financial information. However, the analysis for the primary government does show unusual relationships in the accrual quality for both YR 2 and YR 3 and is confirmed once again in Figure 5.6, comparing net income to the Dechow–Dichev earnings.

Figure 5.7 demonstrates the Dechow–Dichev Accrual Quality and net income for the governmental funds of Company 3 and Figure 5.8 demonstrates

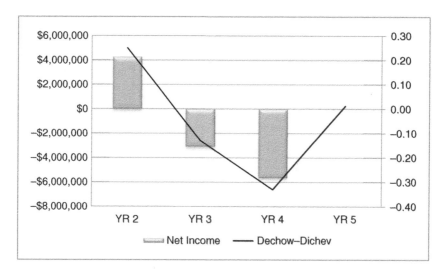

FIGURE 5.7   Dechow–Dichev Accrual Quality and Net Income for the Govern-mental Funds of Company 3

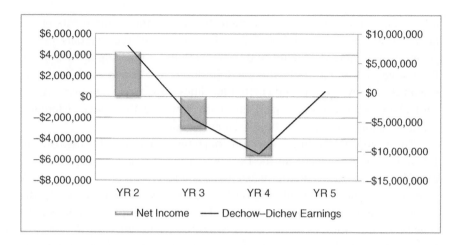

FIGURE 5.8 Dechow–Dichev Earnings and Net Income for the Governmental Funds of Company 3

the Dechow–Dichev earnings compared to net income. Comparing these to the primary government gives the financial forensic examiner additional information before deciding about a supposition centered on the Dechow–Dichev testing.

In reviewing Figure 5.7, the Dechow–Dichev Accrual Quality does not appear to be comparatively stable, with changes in the calculations varying 58 basis points between YR 2 and YR 4. Yet, when reviewing the changes in net income, the financial forensic examiner expects to see decreases in accrual quality for those periods; the question remains whether the accruals actually represent future cash flows. The comparison of the Dechow–Dichev earnings and net income in Figure 5.8 shows a comparative relationship in that significant reductions in the Dechow–Dichev earnings follow the same trend with significant deductions in net income.

When comparing the testing results of the governmental funds to the primary government, the governmental fund testing does not exactly follow the same patterns of the primary government's testing, but does indicate unusual variations from the model. Although there is some accrual recording in the governmental funds, because of the modified accrual basis of presentation for the financial statements, it is minor in comparison to the full-accrual GAAP presentation of the financial statements for the primary government. Therefore, for Company 3, the Dechow–Dichev Accrual Quality testing is more appropriate for the primary government because of the requirements of the financial statement presentation, but the analysis of the accruals in the governmental funds does point to unusual variations, implying further study. For the governmental funds, the due-from funds and due-to funds accounts classified as current assets and current liabilities respectively represent significant changes to working capital and cash flow and the financial forensic examiner should not ignore these account balances.

The testing of the primary government points to an unusual relationship in YR 3, in view of the fact that the Dechow–Dichev Accrual Quality measurement is comparatively stable despite a significant increase in income, and in YR 3 net income increases while the Dechow–Dichev earnings decrease. In the governmental funds testing, the Dechow–Dichev accrual quality is not stable, suggesting the accruals are not representative of future cash flows. Even though the tests for both the primary government and the governmental funds point to different variations from the model, the financial forensic examiner knows the accruals need further investigative work.

Finally, Figure 5.9 depicts the Dechow–Dichev Accrual Quality comparison to net income for Company 4, and Figure 5.10 illustrates the Dechow–Dichev earnings comparison to net income.

In examining Figure 5.9, the Dechow–Dichev Accrual Quality is reasonably stable for all of the years under study, although in YR 3, net income increases while the accrual quantity remains rather stable, with only 4 basis

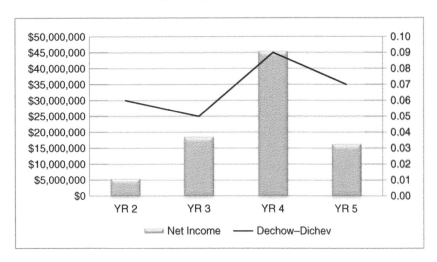

FIGURE 5.9 Dechow–Dichev Accrual Quality and Net Income for Company 4

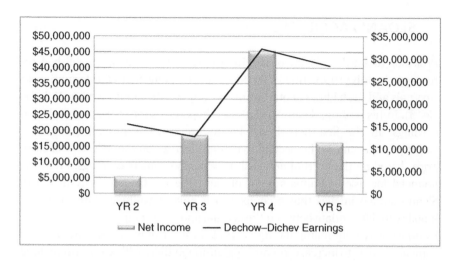

FIGURE 5.10 Dechow–Dichev Earnings and Net Income for Company 4

points separating the lowest and highest calculations. When compared to Figure 5.10, the Dechow–Dichev earnings follow the same trend as net income, with the exception of YR 3. In YR 3, net income increases while the Dechow–Dichev earnings show a slight decrease, more or less representing the same trends of the Dechow–Dichev Accrual Quality where the accruals are stable while net income increases.

Once again, techniques used in analyzing the financial statements of Company 4 indicate the possibility of manipulation considering that stability in the accrual quality while showing significant increases in income. Yet, in understanding the background of the company discussed in Chapter 1 and reviewing the working capital index calculations in Chapter 2, the financial forensic examiner finds a significant event that explains the rationale for the testing. In YR 3, a subsidiary of the company filed for liquidation, subjecting the company to presenting continued accruals of the subsidiary that may or may not represent future cash flows until YR 4, when the company could deconsolidate the subsidiary from the financial statements.

The Dechow–Dichev Accrual Quality and the use of the Dechow–Dichev earnings' calculations are only one method of analyzing accruals in the financial statements. As noted earlier, the financial forensic examiner actually has three new tools to use in analyzing the accruals in the financial statements for possible manipulation. The second method, known as Sloan's Accruals, follows.

SLOAN'S ACCRUALS

Professor Richard G. Sloan of the University of Pennsylvania published his research in July 1996, titled "Do Stock Prices Fully Reflect Information in Accruals and Cash Flows about Future Earnings?" (*Accounting Review*, Vol. 71, No. 3). In his writing, Sloan develops two hypotheses for testing accruals and earnings. In the first hypothesis, his testing concentrates on companies' earnings performance; his second hypothesis focuses on the reflection of stock prices based on the accrual and cash flow components of earnings. From the financial forensic examiner's point of view, the most noteworthy aspect of Sloan's studies implies that a company can take advantage of an investor's inability to differentiate between the accrual and cash components of earnings. In other words, by manipulating accruals in a set of financial statements, a company is able to increase its earnings, although there will be no cash realized from those earnings and the investors would not realize this. This analytical technique works well for focusing on specific periods within a company or for specific groups of companies.

Sloan bases his approach by calculating the implied cash component of earnings from changes in current net operating assets and their relationships to net income. The calculation of Sloan's model is somewhat complex compared to the other accrual models discussed in this chapter, and requires multiple steps to complete the calculations:

- Implied cash component = net income +/– changes in current net operating assets.
- Current net operating assets = current operating assets – current operating liabilities.
- Current operating assets = total current assets – cash and cash equivalents.
- Current operating liabilities = total current liabilities – short-term debt – current portion of long-term debt – income taxes payable.

The accrual component of the model is the change in the current net operating assets.[3] A positive accrual component indicates accruals have increased net income; to calculate the implied cash component, subtract the calculated accrual component amount from net income. If the accrual component is negative, the negative accrual component indicates that accruals have decreased net income; to calculate the implied cash component, add the calculated accrual component amount to net income.

Sloan's theory indicates that if net income has a higher implied cash component, the company projects a stronger financial outlook. The best approach to analyze accruals under Sloan's model is a comparison of net income (loss), the implied cash component, and the accrual component, looking for high levels of accruals compared to net income and the implied cash component. In fact, this should be the preferred method for the financial forensic examiner to use, since it provides both a simple and efficient means of analyzing Sloan's accruals.

Once again, check calculations when negative numbers exist when using a spreadsheet application to calculate the steps of the formula so that the calculations will be correct. High levels of the accrual component when compared to net income and the implied cash component is a red flag and requires additional investigation. The studies of the four companies use the simple but effective approach in analyzing accruals under Sloan's methodology.

The Four Companies: Sloan's Model

Table 5.3 depicts the Sloan Accruals model for Company 1; Figure 5.11 illustrates the components of the model for analysis. Since the accrual component calculation represents changes in net operating assets, the analysis begins with YR 2 for all of the companies.

In Company 1's situation, the financial forensic examiner can readily tell the implication of the accrual component to net income in the table for YR 2, YR 3, and YR 4, but the visual representation in Figure 5.11 allows the financial forensic examiner to see the relationships from a better point of view. In YR 2, it is obvious that the accrual components influence net income, even though the company's financial statements show a loss for the year. Based on the chart's representations for YR 2, the company had a loss prior to adding the accrual components to the financial statements, thus showing the implied cash component at a greater loss. This situation is a signal to the financial forensic examiner to broaden the investigation and use additional analytical techniques, since the implied cash component shows an additional loss.

TABLE 5.3 Sloan's Accruals for Company 1

	YR 2	YR 3	YR 4	YR 5
Net Income	−22,618	1,019	−4,315	−15,441
Accrual Component	8,267	10,814	1,618	−8,468
Implied Cash Component	−30,885	−9,795	−5,993	−6,973

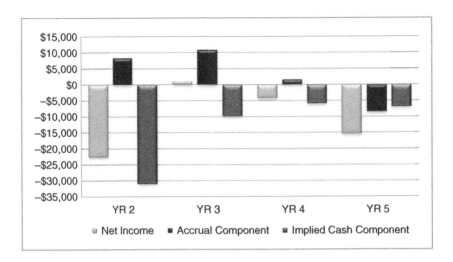

FIGURE 5.11 Sloan's Accrual Comparison for Company 1

YR 3 and YR 4 pose the same issues as YR 2 for the financial forensic examiner. However, YR 5 indicates the accrual component negatively affecting net income. In YR 4, the positive accrual component actually decreases net income, but in YR 5, the accrual component increases net income. In both YR 4 and YR 5, the company reported losses, but the loss is greater in YR 4 due to the impact of the accruals, and in YR 5, the loss is less due to the impact of the accruals. In all of the years under study, the implied cash component is negative and the opposite of Sloan's study that a higher implied cash component projects a stronger financial outlook. Again, this model also questions the reasoning why a company wants to project a weak financial outlook, while the Dechow–Dichev model questions the reasons why a company would continually decrease earnings.

Table 5.4 shows the calculations of the Sloan model components, and Figure 5.12 illustrates the comparison of the components to net income for Company 2.

TABLE 5.4 Sloan's Accruals for Company 2

	YR 2	YR 3	YR 4	YR 5
Net Income	799,532	1,585,639	2,320,650	1,593,947
Accrual Component	1,647,461	−188,003	239,573	1,638,927
Implied Cash Component	−847,929	1,773,642	2,081,077	−44,980

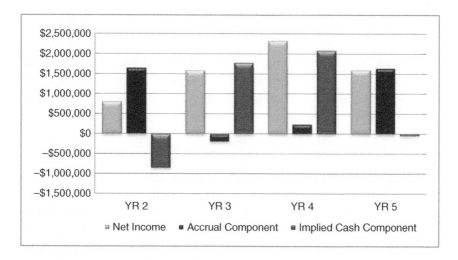

FIGURE 5.12 Sloan's Accrual Comparison for Company 2

With the exceptions of YR 2 and YR 5, YR 3 and YR 4 both show a higher implied cash component compared to net income, with accruals having little effect on net income. However, YR 2 creates a problem for the financial forensic examiner that requires additional study and investigation, because the accrual component positively affects net income while the implied cash component is negative. In addition, Figure 5.12 easily illustrates the issue with YR 5 by showing that net income is mostly the accrual component and the implied cash component shows a loss for the year. Remember that Sloan's research indicates that a positive accrual component suggests that accruals have increased net income. The financial forensic examiner knows that the analysis implies that the financial information for both YR 2 and YR 5 may include manipulation and these years require additional investigation.

Once again, the analyses for the primary government's financial statements and the governmental funds' financial statements are separate because of the effect of the due-to-other funds as other current liabilities and the due-from-other funds as current receivables; in the primary government's financial statements, these amounts are combined with other accruals required by GAAP presentation. Table 5.5 depicts the calculations of the Sloan model components and Figure 5.13 portrays the comparison of the components to net income.

In reviewing Table 5.5, YR 2 is the primary year of concern for the financial forensic examiner in that the positive accrual component suggests

TABLE 5.5 Sloan's Accruals for the Primary Government of Company 3

	YR 2	YR 3	YR 4	YR 5
Net Income	−349,697	1,972,227	1,662,515	3,915,802
Accrual Component	3,130,322	−2,086,924	−3,780,230	−112,825
Implied Cash Component	−3,480,019	4,059,051	5,442,745	4,028,627

that the accruals are increasing net income and the implied cash component is negative. However, considering the opposite end of the spectrum, the negative accruals in both YR 3 and YR 4 reduce net income significantly when compared to the implied cash component for those years. Figure 5.13 illustrates these changes for the financial forensic examiner graphically, allowing a better representation of the relationships compared to the table. Still, the financial forensic examiner needs to review the relationships in the governmental funds' financial statements separately for comparison.

Table 5.6 illustrates the Sloan model components for the governmental funds of Company 3 and Figure 5.14 shows the comparison of Sloan's accruals to net income.

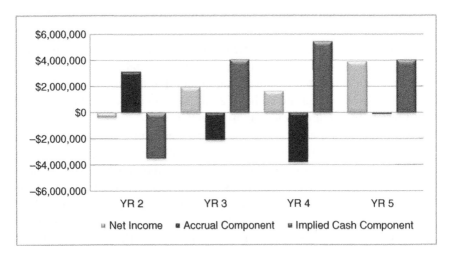

FIGURE 5.13 Sloan's Accrual Comparison for the Primary Government of Company 3

TABLE 5.6 Sloan's Accruals for the Governmental Funds of Company 3

	YR 2	YR 3	YR 4	YR 5
Net income	4,268,304	−3,099,986	−5,649,551	38,653
Accrual Component	4,905,554	−1,253,048	−1,063,082	1,886,136
Implied Cash Component	−637,250	−1,846,938	−4,586,469	−1,847,483

In the case of analyzing the accruals for both the primary government and the governmental funds using Sloan's model, YR 2 is significant for both sets of financial statements and alerts the financial forensic examiner to possible manipulation. For the governmental funds, the accrual component exceeds net income and reduces the implied cash component to a negative number for the year. Sloan's analyses in the governmental funds for YR 3 and YR 4 follow the same trends as those in the primary government. In YR 5, the accrual component does not significantly affect net income for the primary government, but for the governmental funds the accrual component positively affects net income, reducing the implied cash component to a negative number. The financial forensic examiner should not overlook this fact pattern for the governmental funds and should do further studies.

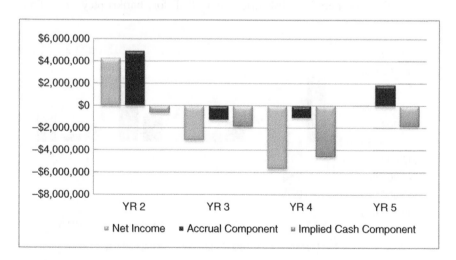

FIGURE 5.14 Sloan's Accrual Comparison for the Governmental Funds of Company 3

TABLE 5.7 Sloan's Accruals for Company 4 (*in thousands*)

	YR 2	YR 3	YR 4	YR 5
Net Income	5,475	18,856	45,343	16,331
Accrual Component	37,171	12,217	14,099	43
Implied Cash Component	−31,696	6,369	31,244	16,288

Table 5.7 illustrates the Sloan accrual calculations for Company 4 and Figure 5.15 displays the relationships of the Sloan accrual components to net income.

For Company 4, the Sloan Accrual Comparison points to YR 2 as a possible issue with earnings manipulation, because the accruals are significantly increasing net income. Although the remaining years under study show positive accrual components, YR 5 suggests the accrual components are not significant to the financial statements and have a paltry influence on net income for the year. Both YR 3 and YR 4 show the accrual components affecting net income, but not to the extent of YR 2. As noted previously, there are several events occurring within the company during these periods that provide reasonable explanations for the changes in the relationships. Although one of the company's subsidiaries had filed for bankruptcy, the final

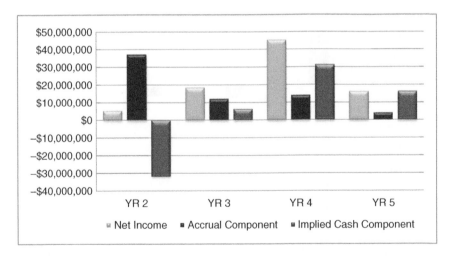

FIGURE 5.15 Sloan's Accrual Comparison for Company 4

deconsolidation process did not occur until YR 4, requiring the company to maintain accruals in the financial statements for the subsidiary until the trustee's approval of the liquidation. Also, in YR 2 the company did receive purchase orders for specialized products that resulted in a backlog of production that carried over into YR 3, thus increasing accruals, which increases net income such as receivables and increases in inventory.

Whereas the Dechow–Dichev model measures the quality of the accruals in terms of cash flows received in future periods, Sloan's model measures the implied cash component of earnings based on the calculation of the accrual component as changes in current net operating assets. Both models, although different in their approach, still link future cash flow from existing accruals. The third model, Jones Nondiscretionary Accruals, provides yet another method of measuring accruals and potential earnings management.

 ## JONES NONDISCRETIONARY ACCRUALS

In 1991, Dr. Jennifer Jones published her study, *Earnings Management During Import Relief Investigations*, which determined that discretionary accruals are used to manipulate earnings, basing her research on the fact that by measuring nondiscretionary accruals one is indirectly measuring discretionary accruals, since the nondiscretionary accruals over time equal zero. To understand the Jones model, the financial forensic examiner must understand the concept of a *discretionary accrual*. A discretionary accrual is an expense recorded on the books that is not required or mandatory, such as accruing expenses for managements' bonuses, compared to a compulsory accrual such as payroll expenses or payroll taxes incurred but not paid at the end of a financial reporting period. Other examples of discretionary accruals are warranty reserves and allowances for uncollectible accounts.

Jones suggests that as nondiscretionary accruals decrease, discretionary accruals increase. Although her research studied the impact of management decreasing earnings for import relief, the implication of her research applies to management positively increasing earnings as well as decreasing earnings. In fact, later research and numerous written studies indicate that management may use discretionary accruals to manipulate earnings to facilitate "income-smoothing" or level out income fluctuations from year to year, quarter to quarter, or month to month so as to attract investors. For these reasons, the financial forensic examiner needs to understand the Jones model and add this analytical technique to his or her toolbox.

The formula for calculating total nondiscretionary accruals in the Jones model is not as complicated as the Sloan model but does require several steps:

$$(1/\text{TA}\,py) + ((\text{Rev}\,cy - \text{Rev}\,py)/\text{TA}\,cy) + (\text{PPE}\,cy/\text{TA}\,py)^4$$

Component Abbreviations

(TA = total assets)
(Rev = revenue)
(PPE = property, plant, and equipment, gross)
(cy = current year)
(py = prior year)

By computing the nondiscretionary accruals as a percentage of total assets, the analysis provides information concerning the discretionary accruals, an important factor for the financial forensic examiner in determining whether the possibility of earnings manipulation exists in the financial information. Thus, if nondiscretionary accruals compared to total assets are lower in one period than in other periods, the analysis indicates that discretionary accruals are higher, suggesting possible manipulation.

The Four Companies: Jones Model

To calculate the Jones Nondiscretionary Accruals for each company, the property, plant, and equipment (PPE) component must be the gross amount and not "net" of accumulated depreciation as in the financial statements. Table 5.8 provides the amount recorded for gross property, plant, and equipment for the four companies so that the financial forensic examiner is able to recalculate the percentages of the Jones Nondiscretionary Accruals for the companies under study. Since property, plant, and equipment appears only in the financial

TABLE 5.8 Gross PPE for the Four Companies

	YR 2	YR 3	YR 4	YR 5
Company 1	136,726	143,328	145,828	153,623
Company 2	3,419,891	3,988,585	4,344,625	4,742,405
Company 3	103,803,762	117,037,722	128,565,154	139,971,563
Company 4	44,429,000	45,070,000	57,528,000	67,011,000

statements of the primary government of Company 3, this model does not include the governmental funds' financial statements. Company 4's financial statements are in thousands and adjusted for presentation in the table.

Figure 5.16 illustrates the calculation of Jones Nondiscretionary Accruals as a percentage of total assets for Company 1.

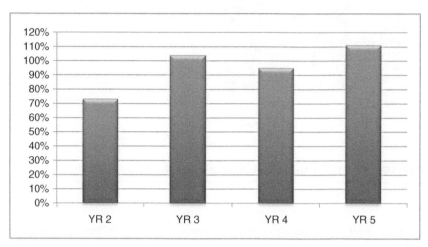

FIGURE 5.16   Jones Nondiscretionary Accruals for Company 1

The important point for the financial forensic examiner to remember in analyzing Jones Nondiscretionary Accruals is that as nondiscretionary accruals decrease, discretionary accruals increase, suggesting the possibility of manipulation of the financial information. The Jones model calculations for YR 3, YR 4, and YR 5 are rather stable in comparison to YR 2. In YR 2, the nondiscretionary accruals are lower, suggesting increases in the discretionary accruals. This model also confirms the low accrual quality in YR 2 calculated by the Dechow–Dichev model and supports the theory that in YR 2, accruals decreased net income in the calculations of the accrual component and the implied cash component in the Sloan model.

Figure 5.17 shows the calculations of Jones Nondiscretionary Accruals as a percentage of total assets for Company 2.

Unlike Company 1, where some of the nondiscretionary accruals are somewhat stable, Company 2's calculations show a continual decrease in nondiscretionary accruals, suggesting increases in discretionary accruals. Nondiscretionary accruals decrease to a negative number in YR 5, and the negative number establishes a new concept of earnings manipulation for the

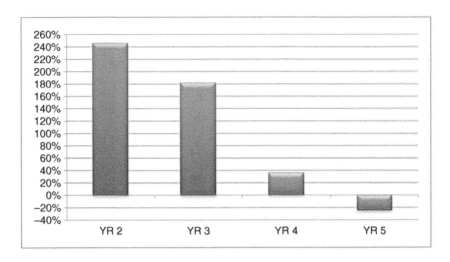

FIGURE 5.17   Jones Nondiscretionary Accruals for Company 2

financial forensic examiner—"income smoothing" or a deliberate attempt to reduce earnings, as indicated in the Jones study.

The Dechow–Dichev analysis suggests an anomaly in YR 4 for Company 2, while the calculations of the Sloan's Accruals signify that in both YR 2 and YR 5 the accrual components directly affect net income. Although the different techniques point to different years that have possible manipulation, the Jones Nondiscretionary Accruals indicate that all years may include possible manipulation through discretionary accruals.

Figure 5.18 shows the calculations of the Jones Nondiscretionary Accruals as a percentage of total assets for the primary government of Company 3.

The calculations of the Jones Nondiscretionary Accruals for the primary government are rather stable for each of the years under study, although YR 2 shows a slight decrease in the nondiscretionary accruals compared to the other years. Both the Dechow–Dichev analysis and the Sloan's accrual analysis indicate possible issues with YR 2 as well. The difficulty with the Jones Nondiscretionary analysis for Company 3 is the combined accruals with the due-from-other-funds and due-to-other-funds accounts included in the nondiscretionary accruals of the primary government, which may distort the calculations. Remember, these accounts should eliminate each other in the governmental funds' financial statements, thus removing them from the Jones Nondiscretionary Accruals; in reality, these funds did not cancel each other out

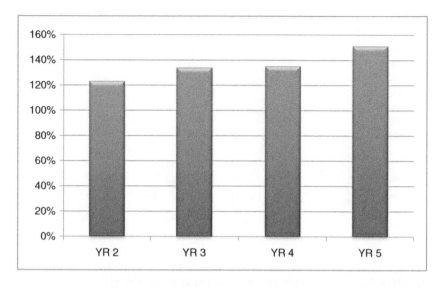

FIGURE 5.18   Jones Nondiscretionary Accruals for the Primary Government of Company 3

to show a zero balance and are thus included in the nondiscretionary accruals calculations.

Figure 5.19 depicts the calculations of Jones Nondiscretionary Accruals for Company 4.

The Jones Nondiscretionary Accruals remain rather stable for both YR 2 and YR 4. YR 3 shows a significant increase in the nondiscretionary accruals, revealing lower discretionary accruals. The analysis for YR 5 signifies the possibility of increased discretionary accruals, since nondiscretionary accruals decreased significantly from YR 4. Once again, the history of the company reasonably explains the anomaly for YR 5, considering that all financial information related to the bankrupt subsidiary no longer sways amounts in the financial statements. The analysis from Sloan's Accruals points out that the accruals did not significantly influence net income for the same year, and the Dechow–Dichev Accrual Quantity analysis shows a rather stable relationship. With this knowledge, the financial forensic examiner is able to determine that the financial statements are free from manipulation.

In the case of the other three companies, the different techniques suggest possible manipulation in one or more years, although the techniques may point to different periods of manipulation. More significant for the financial forensic

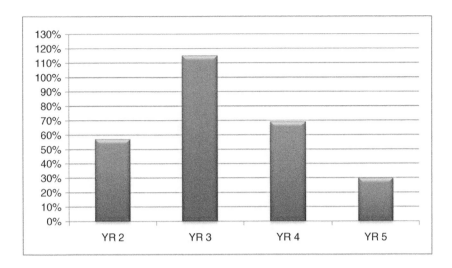

FIGURE 5.19 Jones Nondiscretionary Accruals for Company 4

examiner is the fact that the company history does not provide reasonable explanations for the variances noted in the analyses, indicating additional investigative work is necessary to determine the causes of the variances.

 SUMMARY

The three analytical techniques used in this chapter provide the financial forensic examiner with a means of measuring the impact of accruals in financial statements. Accruals should represent future cash flows for a company, but errors and intentional misrepresentations affect net income in the current period while investors and readers of the financial statements are not mindful of these facts. By using these analytical tools, the financial forensic examiner is capable of studying the impact of accruals on the financial statements and determining where additional investigative work is required.

The Dechow–Dichev Accrual Quality measures the quality of the accruals based on realized cash flow for future periods. While the technique does not determine whether low accrual quality is by error or possible fraudulent activity, it does acknowledge that lower accrual quality means that accruals recorded within the financial statements are unrelated to future cash flows; this is a signal to the financial forensic examiner to investigate further. The model identifies particular actions related to low accrual quality, such as a longer operating cycle, instability in sales, a smaller-sized firm, unpredictable cash flows, and continued losses of earnings. For the financial forensic examiner, this means that the Dechow–Dichev Accrual Quantity provides a process of relating accruals to future cash flows and detecting the possibility of a company boosting earnings for a period without actually receiving the needed cash for continued operations.

The Sloan's Accruals technique calculates the implied cash component of earnings by either subtracting or adding the accrual component to net income. A positive accrual component suggests that accruals have increased net income, while a negative accrual component suggests that accruals have decreased net income. Therefore, positive accrual components require subtraction from net income, while negative accrual components require addition to net income. An important point for the financial forensic examiner to remember is that the preferred method of analysis is to compare the accrual component and the implied cash component to net income. Also, higher levels of accrual components and implied cash components are red flags and require additional investigation, knowing that higher implied cash components project a stronger financial outlook for a company. Negative accrual components may suggest the possibility of income smoothing or intentionally reducing net income.

When using Jones Nondiscretionary Accruals, the financial forensic examiner calculates nondiscretionary accruals, thereby indirectly calculating discretionary accruals. The model suggests that as nondiscretionary accruals decrease, discretionary accruals increase. For financial forensic analysis, discretionary accruals such as warranty reserves, allowances for uncollectible accounts, and management bonuses provide opportunities for a company to manipulate earnings and facilitate income smoothing from period to period. Therefore, the important point for the financial forensic examiner to remember is that lower nondiscretionary accruals suggest increases in discretionary accruals, allowing a company to practice earnings manipulation or income smoothing.

These three techniques assist the financial forensic examiner in locating areas within the financial statements that have unusual relationships, suggesting possibilities of manipulation. In the cases of Company 1, Company 2, and Company 3, the techniques located various unusual relationships requiring further investigative procedures. The financial statements of these three companies include manipulative transactions, but from covering up embezzlement activities instead of earnings manipulation by management, implying that these analytical techniques work well, whether for possible intentional earnings manipulation by management in the case of financial statement fraud or for fraudulent transactions covering up embezzlement schemes.

 ## NOTES

1. Patricia M. Dechow and Illia D. Dichev, "The Quality of Accruals and Earnings: The Role of Accrual Estimation Errors" *Accounting Review*, 77, Supplement: Quality of Earnings Conference (2002): 15.
2. Ibid., p. 15.
3. Richard D. Sloan, "Do Stock Prices Fully Reflect Information in Accruals and Cash Flows about Future Earnings?" *Accounting Review*, 71, no. 3 (July 1996): 293.
4. Jennifer J. Jones, "Earnings Management During Import Relief Investigations," *Journal of Accounting Research*, 29, no. 2 (Autumn 1991): 211.

CHAPTER SIX

Analysis Techniques Using Historical Financial Statements and Other Company Information

HAPTER 2 discusses both the horizontal and vertical analysis techniques used to analyze financial statement information. As mentioned earlier, horizontal analysis measures the changes from period to period for each specific line item in the financial statements, permitting the financial forensic examiner to analyze the trends of the line items. Also discussed in Chapter 2 is the vertical analysis technique that allows a financial forensic examiner to investigate the relationship between accounts in the financial statements based on a common variable. Also termed *common-sizing*, this technique expresses the relationships of line items in the financial statements to a specific base item, such as total assets or total revenues. Sometimes it is much easier to begin a simple analysis of historical financial information that lets the financial forensic examiner determine possible links in financial statement manipulation and earnings before performing additional complex analytical techniques. The two methods discussed in this chapter provide the financial forensic examiner with two additional analytical techniques to add to the toolbox that are fairly simple, and also quite reliable in pointing to questionable irregularities in a company's set of financial statements before completing more complex analytical techniques and additional investigative work.

These two techniques are the *Piotroski F-Score model* and *Lev–Thiagarajan's 12 Signals*. Originally, both models had different applications concerning the analysis of a company's financial statements. The Piotroski F-Score model was used to evaluate a stock's financial strength and determine whether to add or remove a specific stock from an investor's portfolio in order to maximize returns. Yet, in financial forensic analysis, the F-Score provides the financial forensic examiner with information concerning profitability, liquidity, and operating efficiency, all of which are subject to possible manipulation if company performance is inadequate. Lev–Thiagarajan's 12 Signals originally measured the values of corporate securities, but in financial forensics the model measures earnings, risk, and growth, which are often key drivers in financial statement manipulation.

Although these models are simplistic compared to the Beneish M-score model and the models related to testing accruals discussed in Chapter 5, they do provide sufficient information to allow the financial forensic examiner to determine whether extra investigative work is necessary. Each model is applicable to both public and private companies, and various types of entities as illustrated with the four companies. Each model relies on a scoring system for each individual step in the model, and the combined scores of each step fall within general ratings defined by each model. The ratings, used as benchmarks, tell the financial forensic examiner whether the financial statements may include inconsistencies related to possible manipulation. This chapter focuses on the techniques of each model and the application of each model to the four companies.

 ## THE PIOTROSKI F-SCORE MODEL

While Joseph D. Piotroski was an accounting professor at the University of Chicago Graduate School of Business, he wrote "Value Investing: The Use of Historical Financial Statement Information to Separate Winners from Losers" in January 2002 (Selected Paper 84). His research primarily related to valuing a stock's financial strength in order to maximize an investor's portfolio. The goal of his research was to develop simple screens based on financial information that would create a stronger value portfolio and separate strong performers from eventual underperformers.

For the financial forensic examiner, the basis of Piotroski's research allows the financial forensic examiner to apply a simple analysis consisting of nine steps pointing to scores that may indicate possible manipulation of financial statements by defining the company's overall financial position as "weak" versus "strong." The model does not require any market values at all, so its application to private companies' financial statements as well as public companies' financial statements allows the financial forensic examiner to use this technique on all types of financial statements and still find it reliable.

The nine variables[1] or signals in the model measure the profitability, financial liquidity, and the operating efficiency of a company in terms of its overall financial condition. Four of the signals measure profitability in terms of earnings and cash flows:

1. Current-year income
2. Current-year operating cash flow
3. Comparison of current-year income to current-year operating cash flow
4. Comparison of prior-year net income to prior-year operating cash flow

Chapter 3 stresses the importance of measuring cash flows to net income to detect potential manipulation in the financial statements since cash flows normally exceed net income. The fourth signal lets the financial forensic examiner check for unusual changes in the relationships that may indicate potential manipulation of financial information in the Chapter 3 discussions concerning the comparison of net income and cash realized from operations. From the studies of accruals in Chapter 5, continued losses lower accrual quality, suggesting possible manipulation in financial information to improve net income.

Three of the signals measure changes in a company's capital structure and the company's ability to meet future debt obligations:

1. Current-year ratio of long-term debts to total assets compared to prior-year ratio
2. Comparison of current-year current ratio to prior-year current ratio
3. Current-year outstanding shares compared to prior-year outstanding shares

The leverage index of the Beneish M-Score model discussed in Chapter 4 also emphasizes the importance of debt structures and the possibility of manipulating financial information so that a company may show compliance with debt covenants. Changes in outstanding shares measures potential dilution of the stock's worth.

The remaining two signals measure the operating efficiency of the company:

1. Comparison of current-year gross margin to prior-year gross margin
2. Comparison of the percentage increase in sales to the percentage increase in total assets

Chapter 2 discusses the importance of the gross margin, since it measures the financial health of a company. The gross margin index in the Beneish M-Score model allows the financial forensic examiner to measure gross margin deterioration, which may precede earnings manipulation or possible exploitation of inventory or other production costs. Therefore, all of the signals in the F-Score model permit the financial forensic examiner to make preliminary assessments for areas of the financial statement information that require additional analytical techniques.

For the financial forensic examiner to understand the model, one must look at the nine variables and the scoring system of the model before implementing the technique for analysis. The result of analyzing each signal is quite simple: one point if the signal's realization is good and no point if the signal's realization is bad. The sum of the nine signals makes up the F-Score and the final determination of a company's overall quality and the strength of its financial position and its stock. From his research, Piotroski determined that an overall score between eight and nine sends the strongest signals and represents a "high-score" firm with a stronger financial position and stronger stock. A combined overall score of zero or two sends the weakest signals and thus implies poor financial position and the weakest stocks. Scores between three and seven represent the middle ground, where signals mix, providing somewhat conflicting information in the model and suggesting an average financial position for the company with average stock values.

By combining the signals and the scoring system, the F-Score model calculations represent the following items:

- If current-year net income is positive—1 point (0 if negative)
- If current-year operating cash flow is positive—1 point (0 if negative)
- If current-year operating cash flow exceeds net income—1 point (0 if negative)

- If prior-year operating cash flow exceeds prior-year net income—1 point (0 if negative)
- If the ratio of long-term debts to total assets decreases over prior year—1 point (0 if no change or increases over prior year)
- If current ratio increases from prior year—1 point (0 if no change or increases over prior year)
- If outstanding shares are no greater than prior year—1 point (0 if increases over prior year)
- If gross margin increases over prior year—1 point (0 if decreased)
- If the percentage increase in sales exceeds the percentage increase in total assets—1 point (0 if lower or the same)

The financial forensic examiner will follow the use of these signals for additional analysis of the four companies to learn the technique and its application in financial forensic examinations.

Company 1

One way to review the F-Score model for detailed analysis is by putting the information into a tabular format. Table 6.1 depicts the F-Score analysis for Company 1. (CY = current year and PY = prior year, for all tables in this chapter.)

In both YR 2 and YR 4, Company 1's totals illustrate weak financial positions, while both YR 3 and YR 5 barely make the scores for average

TABLE 6.1 Piotroski's F-Score for Company 1

	YR 2	YR 3	YR 4	YR 5
CY Net Income Positive	0	1	0	0
CY Operating Cash Flow Positive	0	1	0	0
CY Operating Cash Flow > Net Income	0	0	1	1
PY Operating Cash Flow > PY Net Income	n/a	0	0	1
Ratio of Long-Term Debts to Total Assets < PY	0	0	0	0
Current Ratio > PY Current Ratio	0	1	0	0
Outstanding Shares No Greater than PY	n/a	n/a	n/a	n/a
Gross Margin > PY Gross Margin	0	0	1	1
% Increase in Sales > % Increase in Total Assets	0	1	0	0
Total Points	**0**	**4**	**2**	**3**

financial performance. Looking at the basic analysis of the financial statements using Piotroski's F-Score, the financial forensic examiner should immediately notice that in YR 2 and YR 3 the current operating cash flow compared to net income signals total zero, illustrating that operating cash flows are less than net income, and consequently depicting an unusual relationship between the two. In addition, the signal for prior-year operating cash flow greater than prior-year net income is zero for both YR 3 and YR 4, once again illustrating an unusual relationship in the financial statements. Remember also from Chapter 3 that the company did not prepare cash flow statements and the calculated cash flow statements did not always equal the cash balance on the financial statements. Knowing that earnings and cash flow are important measures for profitability, the low scores and the unusual relationships require additional analysis.

In conjunction with the weak scores for profitability, Company 1 also exhibits weak signals relating to its ability to meet future debt obligations. Remember from Chapter 1 that one of the shareholders loaned the company funds in YR 2 when the income statement showed a significant loss. However, in YR 3, when the company actually had positive earnings, the shareholder loaned additional money to the company, even when operating cash flows were positive. So far, just analyzing seven of the nine signals reveals that Company 1 is not profitable, and shows unusual relationships concerning operating cash flows compared to net income and its inability to meet future debt obligations.

The final two signals provide contrasting information compared to the other seven signals, in that in YR 4 and YR 5, gross margins increase from the prior year, while in the same period, the percentage increase in sales did not exceed the percentage increase in total assets. Based on the horizontal analyses noted in Figure 2.7 and Figure 2.8 in Chapter 2, total assets and sales decreased in YR 4 and total assets decreased, while sales increased in YR 5. YR 3 also points to an unusual relationship, since gross margins were less than the prior year, but the percentage of change in sales was greater than the percentage of total assets.

The Piotroski F-Score model is simplistic, but see how much information the model shows to the financial forensic examiner for Company 1. Profitability, liquidity, and operating efficiency all suggest weak financial conditions. The overall score barely indicates average performance in both YR 3 and YR 5. By analyzing each signal, the financial forensic examiner learns about several unusual relationships that require additional study. Figure 6.1 illustrates each set of signals, along with the total scores for Company 1.

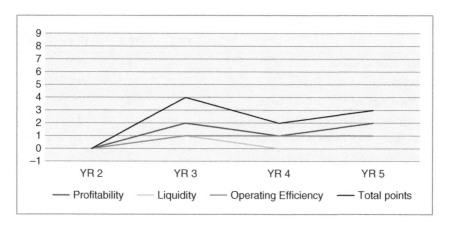

FIGURE 6.1 Piotroski's F-Scores for Company 1

The overall scores for each year under study also are important to the financial forensic examiner. The scores point to an underlying question from other analytical techniques already discussed: why a company would want to continue showing weak financial performance from year to year.

Company 2

Table 6.2 illustrates Piotroski's F-Scores for Company 2.

The table indicates that in YR 3, YR 4, and YR 5, Company 2 has an average financial position. When compared to YR 2 and YR 5, it seems the total points show inconsistent financial positions from year to year, given that YR 1 suggests a weak financial position and the decrease in YR 5 from the prior two years suggests a decline in financial position. As in Company 1, the fact that operating cash flow does not exceed net income is an issue requiring further study. From the analysis of cash flows for Company 2 in Chapter 3, in all years other than YR 5, the calculated ending cash in the cash flow statements did not equal the cash reported in the financial statements, supporting the Piotroski F-Score model in noting the unusual relationships between cash flows and net income. Thus, four of the signals for Company 2 imply weak profitability, with YR 3 and YR 4 scoring 3 points and YR 2 scoring only one point and YR 5 scoring two points.

The next three signals imply that Company 2 is able to meet future debt obligations. In this particular instance, though, the company paid off its debt in YR 3, so these signals are not as significant when compared to the profitability

TABLE 6.2 Piotroski's F-Score for Company 2

	YR 2	YR 3	YR 4	YR 5
CY Net Income Positive	1	1	1	1
CY Operating Cash Flow Positive	0	1	1	1
CY Operating Cash Flow > Net Income	0	1	0	0
PY Operating Cash Flow > PY Net Income	n/a	0	1	0
Ratio of Long-Term Debts to Total Assets < PY	0	1	1	1
Current Ratio > PY Current Ratio	0	1	1	1
Outstanding Shares No Greater than PY	n/a	n/a	n/a	n/a
Gross Margin > PY Gross Margin	0	1	1	0
% Increase in Sales > % Increase in Total Assets	0	0	0	0
Total Points	**1**	**6**	**6**	**4**

signals for the company. Studies relating to the liquidity of Company 2 in Chapter 2 also suggest increases in both working capital and current ratio calculations associated with the company paying off its debt. The LVGI index calculations of the Beneish M-Score model also designate that Company 2 is able to meet future debt obligations, thus illustrating the company's strong financial position related to debt. Thus far, Piotroski's F-Score shows that Company 2's profitability is weak while the company's ability to pay debt is strong.

The last two signals representing the operating efficiency of Company 2 are mixed, considering that in none of the years under study was the percentage increase in sales greater than the percentage increase in total assets. In addition, gross margin increases over the prior year only occurred in YR 3 and YR 4, while gross margins decreased in YR 2 and YR 4, implying Company 2's operating efficiency is weak. By breaking down the signals into their relative parts, the financial forensic examiner is able to determine that, overall, the company's financial performance is rather weak; significant increases in the scoring from YR 2 to YR 3 suggest possible manipulation.

An important point in the last two signals is the change related to gross margins. In Chapter 2, the gross margin calculations were not comparatively stable, especially when compared to the gross margins of Company 4. Remember that gross margins generally remain somewhat stable because when sales increase, so does the cost of sales, and when sales decrease, so should the cost of sales. Once more in Chapter 4, the GMI index of the Beneish M-Score model also suggests changes from year to year and points to continued decreases in GMI from YR 2 through YR 4.

Yet again, the Piotroski F-Score model points to areas in the financial statement information that have unusual relationships and supports the other analytical testing for Company 2 discussed in other chapters. Figure 6.2 shows each set of signals, along with total scores for Company 2.

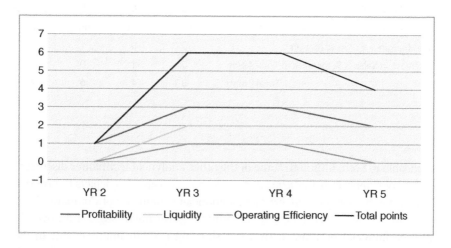

FIGURE 6.2 Piotroski's F-Scores for Company 2

In the case of Company 2, the Piotroski F-Score model implies weak profitability and weak operating efficiency, possible motives for manipulating financial information. One note for the financial forensic examiner to remember is that even though Piotroski's signals are generic and apply to various companies, the analysis of the signals and their importance may change depending on specific circumstances of the company, such as the signals related to measuring a company's ability to meet future debt obligations. These signals were not especially significant to the financial statements for Company 2 because debt was paid and no new debt issued.

Company 3

Since Company 3 has two different sets of financial statements, the primary government and the governmental funds, the Piotroski F-Score model is

TABLE 6.3 Piotroski's F-Score for the Primary Government of Company 3

	YR 2	YR 3	YR 4	YR 5
CY Net Income Positive	1	0	1	1
CY Operating Cash Flow Positive	1	1	1	1
CY Operating Cash Flow > Net Income	1	1	1	1
PY Operating Cash Flow > PY Net Income	n/a	1	1	1
Ratio of Long-Term Debts to Total Assets < PY	0	0	1	1
Current Ratio > PY Current Ratio	0	0	0	0
Outstanding Shares No Greater than PY	n/a	n/a	n/a	n/a
Gross Margin > PY Gross Margin	0	0	1	0
% Increase in Sales > % Increase in Total Assets	0	1	0	1
Total Points	**3**	**4**	**6**	**6**

applicable to both, although some of the other analytical techniques discussed in this book apply only to the primary government. Table 6.3 depicts Piotroski's F-Score for the primary government's financial statements of Company 3.

The overall points scored by the primary government suggest an overall average financial position, with YR 4 showing a slight improvement in its financial position from YR 2 and YR 3 and showing stability in its financial position in YR 5. Both YR 4 and YR 5 also show average earnings and profitability for the primary government while only one year, YR 3, shows negative earnings. Also, in all of the years under study, operating cash flows exceed net income. Both Company 1 and Company 2 did not exhibit this trait, suggesting to the financial forensic examiner that those two companies require additional work. Yet, for the primary government, there are no indicators in the earnings and profitability signals suggesting additional analysis.

Since governments report the majority of long-term debt in the primary government's financial statements, the signals concerning a company's liquidity are important to the analysis of the primary government, unlike Company 2. Piotroski's F-Score signals associated with the company's ability to meet future debt obligations are weak, suggesting the company's inability to meet those future obligations. Both YR 4 and YR 5 suggest a decrease in the ratio of long-term debts to total assets, but all years indicate the current ratios do not increase. In fact, in Table 2.4 in Chapter 2, the current ratios of the primary government tend to decrease every year. Although the LVGI index of the

Beneish M-Score in Chapter 4 seems somewhat stable and within the guidelines of the benchmark, the TCLTA drill-down index shows significant increases in YR 5 and well above the general benchmark of 1, insinuating that the decreases in the current ratio each year are a concern.

In reviewing the signals significant to operating efficiency, the primary government falls within the guidelines of a weak financial position. Although the percentage increase in sales exceeded the percentage in total assets in YR 3 and YR 5, grant revenues play an important role in these calculations. Remember that grant revenues are one variable specific to governmental entities and possibly nonprofit organizations. The gross margin calculations for the primary government found in Chapter 2 actually remove the grant revenues from the calculations to prevent distortion of the gross margins. The horizontal analysis of the primary government found in Chapter 2 also illustrates the importance of grant revenues to operational efficiency. Figure 2.15 shows the significant increases in grant revenues in YR 3 and YR 5 compared to the other years. Considering the effect of grant revenues in YR 3 and YR 5, the primary government shows weakness in operating efficiency.

In reviewing each set of signals for the primary government, the liquidity signals represent a weak financial condition in all four years while profitability remains average. Figure 6.3 illustrates each set of signals, along with total scores for the primary government of Company 3.

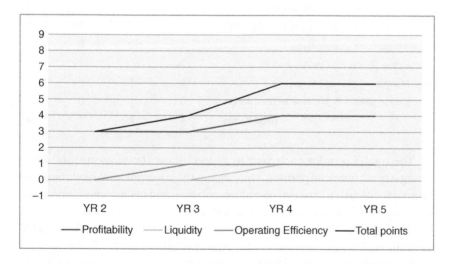

FIGURE 6.3 Piotroski's F-Scores for the Primary Government of Company 3

While the total scores define the primary government's financial statements as having an average financial position, only the signals associated with profitability maintain the same position. Once again, grant revenues also influence the profitability of the primary government, but not to the extent that the scores would be significantly different for those signals. The F-Score does point to issues relating to liquidity, especially the continued declines in current ratios, and implies using other analytical techniques to determine whether anomalies exist in the financial statements. Once more, the financial forensic examiner learns how the due-from-other-funds and the due-to-other-funds balances affect the overall financial statements of the primary government, consequently requiring additional study and analysis.

Table 6.4 depicts Piotroski's F-Scores for the governmental funds of Company 3. Although long-term debt is generally associated with the primary government, the governmental funds' financial statements have long-term debt associated with deferred revenues compared to bonds and other long-term debt recorded in the primary government's financial statements.

TABLE 6.4 Piotroski's F-Scores for the Governmental Funds of Company 3

	YR 2	YR 3	YR 4	YR 5
CY Net Income Positive	1	0	0	1
CY Operating Cash Flow Positive	1	0	0	0
CY Operating Cash Flow > Net Income	0	1	0	0
PY Operating Cash Flow > PY Net Income	n/a	0	1	0
Ratio of Long-Term Debts to Total Assets < PY	1	0	0	1
Current Ratio > PY Current Ratio	1	0	0	0
Outstanding Shares No Greater than PY	n/a	n/a	n/a	n/a
Gross Margin > PY Gross Margin	0	1	0	1
% Increase in Sales > % Increase in Total Assets	0	1	0	0
Total Points	**4**	**3**	**1**	**3**

The total scores for each year in general show the governmental funds having a weak financial position. Once again, the governmental funds imply an unusual relationship between operating cash flow and net income. By now, the financial forensic examiner knows that net income greater than operating cash flow is a red flag that definitely needs additional investigative work to understand the underlying reasons for this type of relationship. YR 5 also presents another sign for the financial forensic examiner, since net income is positive but operating cash flow is negative, according to Figure 3.7 in Chapter 3.

Even though the debt of the governmental funds corresponds to deferred revenues associated with property taxes, Piotroski's F-Scores suggest that the liquidity of the governmental funds is in a weak financial position. Only the scores for YR 2 and YR 5 suggest a stronger liquidity based on the scoring of the ratio of long-term debts to total assets. Although the current ratio calculations for the governmental funds are absent from the calculations in Chapter 2, the current ratios calculations for the government funds follow:

- YR 1 = 4.44
- YR 2 = 4.62
- YR 3 = 3.12
- YR 4 = 1.73
- YR 5 = 1.65

These clearly indicate declining current ratios, implying that liquidity is weak. In understanding governmental funds' financial statements, the financial forensic examiner would find this relationship unusual and suggesting additional scrutiny.

In calculating the gross margins for the governmental funds, the same approach as described in Chapter 2 for the primary government determined the calculations. The calculations for the governmental funds follow:

- YR 1 = .25
- YR 2 = .15
- YR 3 = .33
- YR 4 = .13
- YR 5 = .20

In this instance, total revenues less general and administrative expenses combined with the pension and social security payments represent gross profit. Grant revenues, included in the intergovernmental revenues in the governmental funds (already discussed in Piotroski's F-Score analysis of the primary government's financial statements), include the same patterns for the gross margin increases in the governmental funds. Both YR 3 and YR 5 in the governmental funds show stronger operational efficiency compared to YR 2 and YR 4. With the exception of YR 3, all other years under study point to weak operating efficiency.

For the governmental funds, YR 4 has the lowest score, indicating an overall weak financial condition, while YR 2 seems to have the strongest

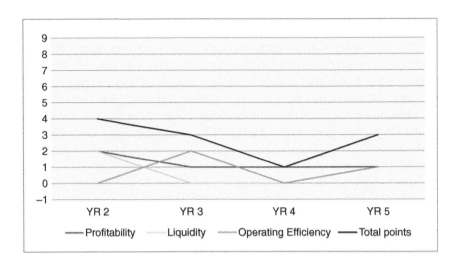

FIGURE 6.4　Piotroski's F-Scores for the Governmental Funds of Company 3

financial condition for the years under study. Figure 6.4 illustrates each set of signals along with total scores for the governmental funds.

Although YR 2 shows stronger profitability scores, the score declines in YR 3 and then remains steady for both YR 4 and YR 5. Piotroski's F-Scores indicate that profitability is in a weak financial position and the profitability scores show an inconsistent relationship between net income and operating cash flow. Liquidity is also weak, having its strongest point in YR 2. Yet operating efficiency increases in both YR 3 and YR 5, while there are no points earned for YR 2 and YR 4. The overall changes from year to year are particularly puzzling, because the changes in the other scores from YR 3 to YR 4 drop significantly and then increase significantly from YR 4 to YR 5, while the only scores remaining constant for this period are the profitability signals. This type of trend should concern the financial forensic examiner and needs additional study.

Company 4

Company 4's Piotroski's F-Scores are illustrated in Table 6.5.

With the exception of YR 2, the total scores indicate an overall average financial position for the company, with YR 4 and YR 5 showing stability in the firm's financial position. YR 3 shows the highest total score and a significant improvement in the firm's financial position compared to YR 2. Remember that

TABLE 6.5 Piotroski's F-Scores for Company 4

	YR 2	YR 3	YR 4	YR 5
CY Net Income Positive	0	1	1	1
CY Operating Cash Flow Positive	0	1	1	1
CY Operating Cash Flow > Net Income	1	1	0	1
PY Operating Cash Flow > PY Net Income	n/a	1	1	0
Ratio of Long-Term Debts to Total Assets < PY	1	1	1	1
Current Ratio > PY Current Ratio	1	1	1	1
Outstanding Shares No Greater than PY	0	0	0	0
Gross Margin > PY Gross Margin	0	1	1	0
% Increase in Sales > % Increase in Total Assets	1	1	0	1
Total Points	**4**	**8**	**6**	**6**

in YR 1 the external auditors issued a going-concern opinion for that year. The F-Scores in YR 2 mirror the consequences of the subsidiary filing for bankruptcy, and the financial results of the subsidiary shown as discontinued operations in the financial statements until YR 4, when the financial statements no longer contain the effects of the bankrupt subsidiary. Knowing this fact pattern, the lower total scores in YR 2 are reasonable, and the facts provide a basis for the increase in YR 3.

In reviewing the signals measuring profitability, YR 2 is the lowest score, implying weak earnings and cash flows, especially since both net income and operating cash flow for the year are negative. The financial forensic examiner already knows the underlying causes of these measurements, but there is an unusual relationship in YR 4 concerning net income and operating cash flow. Once more, there is a reasonable explanation for this difference, as shown in Figure 3.9 in Chapter 3, as well as in the company's general information in Chapter 1. In YR 4, the financial statements include a non-cash gain and tax benefit related to the deconsolidation of the subsidiary that is included in net income but deducted in cash from operations. Figure 3.10 in Chapter 3 offers an excellent visual presentation of the effect of these transactions in YR 4 and the unusual relationship caused by this event.

While the company did not receive perfect totals for the signals representing liquidity, the scores do imply that Company 4 is able to meet its future obligations, giving the impression of a strong financial position in this area. The only weakness in these signals correlates to the changes in outstanding shares from year to year. Outstanding shares increase from year to year, suggesting possible dilution to the stock and therefore a weak financial position. While the outstanding shares are missing from the financial information in Chapter 1, the Statements of Consolidated Shareholder's Equity convey the necessary information for the increases, along with information provided in Chapter 2 discussing the conversion of debt to stock that took place in YR 2. Other additions to stock include shares sold to outside investors, shares to outside directors, and stock options offered under the company's employee stock option plan. Knowing these facts, the financial forensic examiner can easily understand the F-Scores for this signal and consider that overall liquidity is strong.

The scores for the two remaining signals measuring the operating efficiency of the company insinuate an average financial position, just like the overall F-score totals. Although the scores do not show increased profit margins in every year, Table 2.6 in Chapter 2 illustrates a comparatively stable profit margin for Company 4. Figure 4.36 in Chapter 4 concerning the GMI index for the company also shows little difference from year to year. From a financial forensic analysis perspective, declining gross margins from year to year may induce pressure on management to manipulate earnings. However, the stability of the gross margins from Company 4 indicates reasonable performance.

Figure 6.5 shows each set of signals for Company 4, along with total F-Scores, and enhances the analysis of Piotroski's F-Scores for the company.

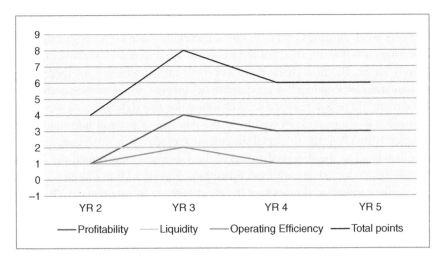

FIGURE 6.5 Piotroski's F-Scores for Company 4

The graphical presentation makes it rather easy for the financial forensic examiner to see the increase in overall financial condition in YR 3 and stability in the financial condition of the company in YR 4 and YR 5. Both profitability and operating efficiency increase while liquidity remains stable, not only for YR 3, but for the other years as well. In the review of the SGI calculations for Company 4 in Chapter 4, YR 3 signified significant growth from the company receiving special orders for the year, once again supplying a reasonable explanation for the change. These special orders also explain the significant increase in profitability from YR 2 to YR 3 and the increase in the total points.

Piotroski's F-Score analysis of financial statements allows the financial forensic examiner to review unusual relationships concerning profitability, liquidity, and operating efficiency of a company, as well as providing an indication of overall financial condition. But this simple analysis does more than just provide information concerning the financial condition of a company, because it also gives valuable information to a financial forensic examiner concerning areas of questionable changes and unusual relationships requiring additional investigative work. Part of this extra investigative work includes finding reasonable explanations for unusual changes and then finding support documentation to validate the explanations, as in the case with Company 4. While this will not expose fraudulent activity, it does allow the financial forensic examiner to move on to another area that may not have accurate support for unusual changes or that might have unusual relationships that may contain fraudulent activity.

LEV–THIAGARAJAN'S 12 SIGNALS

As with Piotroski's F-Score, Lev–Thiagarajan's 12 Signals began as a study associated with securities valuation. In 1993, Baruch Lev and S. Ramu Thiagarajan co-authored a paper published in the *Journal of Accounting Research* (Vol. 31, No. 2), titled "Fundamental Information Analysis." In their study, the authors identified a set of signals, referred to as *fundamental signals*, used by analysts in valuing securities. These signals aim to measure earnings quality and future growth. The significance of their research to the application of financial forensic analysis involves the fact that these signals capture important characteristics of earnings determination, and are especially effective when considering the current macroeconomics at the time of evaluation.

Where Piotroski's F-Score contains nine signals, Lev–Thiagarajan's model contains twelve fundamental signals. Some of these signals, such as the order backlog, labor force, the use of LIFO, and the audit qualification, are not part of the financial information included in financial statements and require additional information about the company, as opposed to the F-Score analysis, which uses information strictly from the financial statements. The 12 Signals do contain a set of conditions and a scoring system similar to the F-Score system, but this model is not quite as simplistic. Similar to the F-Score analysis, larger positive total fundamental scores suggest a high quality of earnings, while larger negative total fundamental scores imply a low quality of earnings. Therefore, it is important that the financial forensic examiner understand the scoring system of the components to perform the analysis correctly. Not every signal will be applicable to every analysis, but this does not change the effectiveness of the analysis. The discussions concerning the 12 Signals include the forensic application for each component. Each of the twelve factors in the analysis is equally weighted. The following list defines the Lev–Thiagarajan's 12 Signals[2] and the scoring system for each signal.

- Inventory
  - % Δ Inventory – % Δ Sales
  - Positive value = negative signal
- Accounts Receivable (A/R)
  - % Δ A/R – % Δ Sales
  - Positive value = negative signal
- Capital Expenditures
  - % Δ Industry Benchmarks – % Δ Capital Expenditures
  - Disproportionate decrease to benchmarks = negative signal
- R&D Costs
  - % Δ Industry Benchmarks – % Δ R&D Expenditures
  - Disproportionate decrease to benchmarks = negative signal
- Selling and Administrative Expenses (S&A)
  - % Δ S&A – % Δ Sales
  - Positive value = negative signal
- Gross Margin (GM = defined as Sales – Cost of Sales)
  - % Δ Sales – % Δ GM
  - Negative value = negative signal
- Allowance for Doubtful Accounts (ALL)
  - % Δ Gross A/R – % Δ ALL
  - Positive value = negative signal
- Effective Tax Rate (ETR)
  - Δ ETR

- Effective Tax Rate = Tax Expense/Pretax Income
  - Negative value = negative signal
- Order Backlog
  - % Δ Sales – % Δ Order Backlog
  - Positive value = negative signal
- Labor Costs
  - % Δ Sales per Employee
  - Positive value = negative signal
- LIFO Earnings
  - Use of LIFO = positive signal
- Audit Opinion
  - Unqualified opinion = positive signal
  - Qualified opinion = negative signal
  - Disclaimed opinion = negative signal
  - Adverse opinion = negative signal

The first signal associates changes in inventory compared to changes in sales. If the increases in inventory from the prior year exceed the increases in sales from the prior year, the signal is negative. Positive signals associated with inventory increases include the possibility of management hedging against future price increases or management's attempt to reduce the extra costs incurred when inventory runs out. While it is possible that a positive result would not be a negative signal, the authors defined the main reason for finding inventory increases a negative signal related to production smoothing, which essentially is another method of earnings management similar to income smoothing. In essence, the buildup of inventory increases current-year income at the expense of future earnings, definitely a potential issue for the financial forensic examiner.

Other issues related to increases in the changes of inventory when compared to changes in sales include management's expectations of future earnings and sales. Inventory increases may suggest difficulty in generating sales, and/or management expects earnings to decline by attempting to lower inventory levels by reducing sales. Finally, there is also a question of whether inventory includes either slow-moving or obsolete inventory not written off in the current period. Again, these are concerns for the financial forensic examiner, because management may decide to manipulate earnings to show a high level of quality earnings.

Increases in the changes of accounts receivable compared to sales present several issues for the financial forensic examiner. First, there is the question of manipulating earnings by recording fictitious sales and receivables. Second, a company may be increasing credit terms because of the difficulty in selling products. Then there is the concern that increased credit terms also decrease future earnings. The authors consider this second signal almost as important as the first signal in determining a company's quality of earnings. Yet again, this signal enables the financial forensic examiner to determine whether unusual relationships or unusual variations exist in the company's financial statements, including recording fictitious sales to increase earnings that will not provide future cash flows for a company.

Unlike the first two signals, the signal regarding capital expenditures and research and development costs compared to sales is rather weak, so the authors determined that industry benchmarks might be more useful. The theory for these two signals is that liquidity and cash flows spur a company's decision to increase capital expenditures or pursue additional research and development. From a financial forensic examiner's perspective, a disproportionate increase in capital expenditures may suggest the possibility of earnings manipulation by capitalizing costs rather than expensing them, thus improving the bottom line of the company.

Negatives for the next two fundamental signals, gross margins and sales and administrative expenses, question a company's ability to continue long term or whether management lost control of managing costs, since the negatives indicate increased costs over increased sales compared to the prior year. When gross margins decrease compared to sales, the overall concept of this pattern is one of questioning the long-term performance of the company, lowering the quality of earnings, and tempting management to manipulate earnings. Yet, in the case of Company 2, the fluctuating gross margins were associated with fictitious invoices covering up embezzlement activities. As a rule, sales and administrative costs are somewhat fixed. When sales and administrative expenses increase compared to sales, the condition suggests that management is not controlling the company's costs, or that there has been an unusual struggle with sales. Increased sales and administrative expenses may also result from hiding embezzlement activities. As a lesson to the financial forensic examiner, unusual variations or changes may suggest fraudulent activity other than earnings manipulation.

The signal regarding the allowance for doubtful accounts is especially important to the financial forensic examiner because this account is discretionary in nature, meaning the amounts are subject to management's estimates and assumptions and subject to manipulation. Remember in Chapter 5 that Jones Nondiscretionary Accruals indirectly calculate discretionary accruals where Jones's research indicated that management used discretionary accruals to manipulate earnings or to facilitate income smoothing. The authors also consider a positive value a sign of future earnings decreases associated with inadequate provisions that increase current-year earnings at the expense of future earnings.

One would not normally consider a significant change in a company's effective tax rate as a signal of earnings quality and possible earnings manipulation, but the key is in the formula used to calculate the effective tax rate. The use of pre-tax income in the formula is the key, noting that a negative signal suggests the inability to maintain earnings over time as pre-tax income decreases, thus decreasing the effective tax rate. Remember, though, some changes in the effective tax rate may be mandatory, caused by statutory rate changes, so the financial forensic examiner needs to determine the underlying causes for the changes.

The remaining four fundamental signals relate to information other than the information noted in the financial statements, but are still useful in the overall analysis if the information is available. For example, a change in order backlogs compared to operations is a good indicator of a company's future earnings. A decrease in the order backlog compared to sales suggests lower future earnings due to decreased demand for the company's products, or that recorded sales include fictitious sales with no future cash flows. By comparing labor costs as sales per employee, the changes in this ratio actually summarize the efficiency of the labor and the change in the number of employees, defining the quality of earnings and potential benefits from a corporate restructuring, including labor force reductions. The authors consider LIFO a closer estimate of current costs compared to the use of FIFO, but in instances where inventory turnover is quick, the differences between the two methods may be minimal. Still, the use of LIFO is a positive signal. The audit opinion signal is self-explanatory since anything other than an unqualified opinion would send a negative message to investors and potential investors.

When using the Lev–Thiagarajan's 12 Signals model for analyzing the four companies, the periods under study begin with YR 2, since the model requires calculations linked to changes from the prior year. Instead of using ones and zeros, as in the Piotroski F-Score model, the Lev–Thiagarajan's 12 Signals model for the four companies requires the use of "positive" and "negative." The calculations will be in both a tabular format and a visual one that better presents the negative signals. Total scores represent the overall quality of earnings in each year for each company. It is important for the financial forensic examiner to remember that each signal may not be applicable but that will not change the result of the analysis.

Company 1

Unlike the other companies that follow, Company 1 is relatively easy to analyze using the 12 Signals, because many of the more pertinent signals are not applicable to this company, such as inventory, allowance for doubtful accounts, and the effective tax rate. Table 6.6 depicts the summary of the company's scores for Lev–Thiagarajan's 12 Signals.

TABLE 6.6   Summary of Lev–Thiagarajan's 12 Signals for Company 1

Signals	YR 2	YR 3	YR 4	YR 5
Inventory	n/a	n/a	n/a	n/a
Accounts Receivable	Negative	Negative	Negative	Positive
Capital Expenditures	n/a	n/a	n/a	n/a
R&D Costs	n/a	n/a	n/a	n/a
S&A Expenses	Negative	Positive	Negative	Negative
Gross Margin	Positive	Positive	Negative	Negative
Allowance	n/a	n/a	n/a	n/a
Effective Tax Rate	n/a	n/a	n/a	n/a
Order Backlog	n/a	n/a	n/a	n/a
Labor Costs	n/a	n/a	n/a	n/a
LIFO Earnings	n/a	n/a	n/a	n/a
Audit Opinion	n/a	n/a	n/a	n/a
Positives	1	2	0	1
Negatives	2	1	3	2
N/A	9	9	9	9

Even though there are multiple items that are not applicable to Company 1, there is sufficient information relating to the remaining signals that shows areas of unusual changes for the financial forensic examiner. For example, the negative signals in the accounts receivable changes compared to sales imply decreases in future earnings and/or increasing credit terms. The negative signals also point to the possibility of earnings manipulation. After completing the accrual analysis for Company 1 in Chapter 5, those studies indicated unstable accrual quality; accrual components in YR 2, YR 3, and YR 4 positively affected net income while negatively affecting net income in YR 5, and there was an increase of discretionary accruals in YR 2 suggesting the possibility of earnings manipulation. The accrual studies for Company 1 lean toward the same conclusions for accounts receivable in the 12 Signals.

The results of the selling and administrative expenses also provide clues for the financial forensic examiner. Management controls these types of costs, so if a company sees a decline in sales, these expenses should also decline. Increases in these costs compared to sales suggest that management is not controlling costs or that the company is having an unusual event that is decreasing sales, but then that indicates an unusual relationship between the accounts receivable signal and the selling and administrative expenses signal for YR 3. The SGAI index for Company 1, discussed in Chapter 4, also indicates totals in excess of the benchmark for YR 2, YR 4, and YR 5, confirming the negative signals. Considering the years with negative signals combined with the SGAI index results, the negative signal for selling and administrative expenses should concern the financial forensic examiner simply because two separate analytical techniques hint of unusual changes, suggesting the possibility of fraudulent transactions hiding embezzlement activities.

Figure 6.6 illustrates Lev–Thiagarajan's 12 Signals for Company 1 by totaling the results of the calculations for the signals. By showing the negative signals as negative on the chart, the chart provides a more accurate picture of earnings quality for each of the years under study.

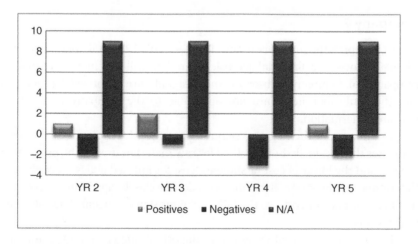

FIGURE 6.6 Lev–Thiagarajan's 12 Signals for Company 1

The illustration easily shows all of the signals not applicable to Company 1, and most of these exceptions are in Chapter 1's general information about the company. Inventory is not applicable since the company does not have an inventory, and the effective tax rate is not applicable since the company is an S-corporation, transferring taxes to the individual stockholders. The company did not provide for an allowance for doubtful accounts but directly wrote off any bad debts instead. The discussions related to gross margins in both Chapter 2 and Chapter 4 indicate that any type of analysis concerning gross margins is ineffective because the cost of sales for Company 1 strictly relates to payroll costs and no manufacturing costs. Chapter 4 does consider the effect of these costs to the GMI index, and the results of the index analysis determined that payroll operations required additional study.

Ignoring the items that are not applicable to Company 1, the negatives outweigh the positives in all of the years under study, with the exception of YR 3. It becomes intuitively obvious to the financial forensic examiner that in the years under study, the company is experiencing poor earnings quality, with very little change occurring from YR 2 through YR 5. The big question for the financial forensic examiner is, "Why the improvement in YR 3?". Even though gross margin is positive in YR 3, it is also positive in YR 2, so the change in YR 3 actually relates to the only year that selling and administrative expenses is positive. Other discussions and analyses already label this account with red flags that require additional work.

Company 2

Table 6.7 depicts the summary of Lev–Thiagarajan's 12 Signals for Company 2. At first glance, the financial forensic examiner will see more information compared to Company 1 because more signals are identified for analysis and that only four items are not applicable to the company or have no available information.

To understand the negative signals concerning LIFO earnings, the company uses the first-in, first-out method for raw materials used in the production process and the lower of cost or standard cost for finished goods. According to the authors of the study, these methods do not closely approximate replacement cost or current costs, so the LIFO earnings signal is negative for all years under study.

The first signal, inventory, is a very important one based on the authors' research, and inventory increases in excess of sales increases imply multiple issues for the financial forensic examiner, including difficulties in generating

TABLE 6.7 Summary of Lev–Thiagarajan's 12 Signals for Company 2

Signals	YR 2	YR 3	YR 4	YR 5
Inventory	Positive	Positive	Negative	Negative
Accounts Receivable	Positive	Positive	Positive	Positive
Capital Expenditures	Positive	Positive	Negative	Negative
R&D Costs	n/a	n/a	n/a	n/a
S&A Expenses	Positive	Positive	Negative	Positive
Gross Margin	Positive	Negative	Negative	Positive
Allowance	Positive	Negative	Positive	Negative
Effective Tax Rate	Negative	Negative	Negative	Positive
Order Backlog	n/a	n/a	n/a	n/a
Labor Costs	n/a	n/a	n/a	n/a
LIFO Earnings	Negative	Negative	Negative	Negative
Audit Opinion	n/a	n/a	n/a	n/a
Positives	6	4	2	4
Negatives	2	4	6	4
N/A	4	4	4	4

sales or expectations that earnings may decline if management attempts to lower inventory levels by reducing sales prices. Yet the main reason these increases receive negative signals is the connection to the concept of production smoothing. In the discussions in Chapter 2 regarding the calculations of Company 2's stock sales, the stock sales ratios are rather consistent, suggesting the possibility of production smoothing, especially when compared to the changes in sales. Another factor for the financial forensic examiner to consider is the possibility of the inventory including either obsolete or slow-moving inventory not written off, thus increasing current-year earnings at the expense of future earnings.

While the accounts receivable signal is positive for all years under study, the allowance for doubtful accounts signal is negative in YR 3 and again in YR 5. Both the accounts receivable and the allowance for doubtful accounts are accruals discussed in Chapter 5. Remember that the allowance for doubtful accounts is a discretionary accrual subject to management's estimates and assumptions, often a target for earnings manipulation. In reviewing the changes, it is rather odd that the allowance is negative every other year under study, while in the other years, it is positive, suggesting that the financial forensic examiner do additional studies to determine the pattern of changes. Even though the accounts receivable signal is positive for all years, the Sloan's Accruals analysis in Chapter 5 implies that in both YR 2 and YR 5, the accrual components positively affect net income, definitely signs that the financial forensic examiner needs to perform more studies.

The gross margin signals remain negative for both YR 3 and YR 4, suggesting a negative impact long term, yet the signal improves and remains positive in YR 5. The GMI study in Chapter 4 also supports changes from year to year, alerting the financial forensic examiner that such changes as noted in the 12 Signals are unusual and require more study. The trend of the decline is of importance to the financial forensic examiner considering the increases in gross profits from YR 2 noted in Chapter 2. Additionally, in YR 4, the decrease in cost of sales is greater than the decrease in sales. Moreover, the embezzlement activities ceased during YR 5, thus stopping the manipulation of the financial statements.

The effective tax rate signal is negative for all years except YR 5. Yet, a decrease in the effective tax rate creates the negative signal under the 12 Signals model. In reviewing the financial statements for Company 2, the company overpaid taxes in YR 3 and YR 4, explaining the negative signals for those years. In YR 5, the effective tax rate increases, but not quite to the rates in YR 1 and YR 2 because of the overpayment of taxes in YR 3 and YR 4 creating the positive signal for YR 5. When considering these facts, the financial forensic examiner finds the decreases in the effective tax rate understandable.

Figure 6.7, showing the totals for Lev–Thiagarajan's 12 Signals for Company 2, illustrates an interesting change in the earning quality for the years under study.

When the financial forensic examiner first looks at the chart, it becomes apparent that overall earnings quality decreases during the years under study. In successive years from YR 2, as positive signals decrease, negative signals increase. While the decreases in earnings quality in the years under study may signal inefficient company operations and raise doubts about the company's ability to continue long term, this company's financial information contained multiple false transactions hiding embezzlement activities, diverting cash flows needed for operations. Often in the situation of embezzlement, especially by trusted personnel, the company is completely unaware of the activity until cash flows shrink to the point that a company is unable to pay its bills as they become

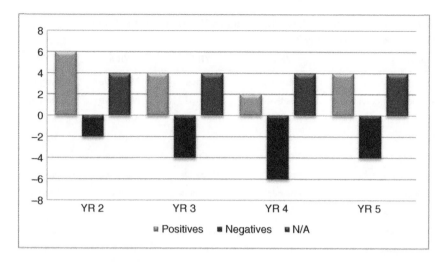

FIGURE 6.7 Lev–Thiagarajan's 12 Signals for Company 2

due. Thus, a lesson for the financial forensic examiner is that continued declines in earnings quality require additional examination.

Company 3

Company 3 is a governmental entity, but the Lev–Thiagarajan's 12 Signals model is an appropriate analysis, even though some of the signals may not apply. As with Piotroski's F-Score, the Lev–Thiagarajan's 12 Signals study applies to both the primary government and the governmental funds. Table 6.8 shows the summary of the primary government's scores for Lev–Thiagarajan's 12 Signals.

For the most part, the inventory signal remains negative throughout the years under study. The calculations for the inventory signal are somewhat different from the original formula, since governmental operations are different from manufacturing entities. Inventories in governmental entities relate to items used in providing services, so the actual calculation consists of the changes in the charges for services revenue account subtracted from the changes in inventory. There is also a modification to the formula for the sales part of the equation for gross margins. Sales totals do not include grant revenues and transfers from the private trust fund to correlate with the change for the gross margin calculations discussed in Chapter 2.

TABLE 6.8   Summary of Lev–Thiagarajan's 12 Signals for the Primary Government of Company 3

Signal	YR 2	YR 3	YR 4	YR 5
Inventory	Negative	Positive	Negative	Negative
Accounts Receivable	Positive	Positive	Negative	Negative
Capital Expenditures	n/a	n/a	n/a	n/a
R&D Costs	n/a	n/a	n/a	n/a
S&A Expenses	Negative	Positive	Positive	Positive
Gross Margin	Positive	Negative	Negative	Negative
Allowance	Positive	Negative	Positive	Positive
Effective Tax Rate	n/a	n/a	n/a	n/a
Order Backlog	n/a	n/a	n/a	n/a
Labor Costs	n/a	n/a	n/a	n/a
LIFO Earnings	Negative	Negative	Negative	Negative
Audit Opinion	Positive	Positive	Positive	Positive
Positives	4	4	3	3
Negatives	3	3	4	4
N/A	5	5	5	5

Since inventory is rather minor in the operations of the primary government, the negative signals are not surprising because the inventory is not part of a production process, therefore suggesting a longer turnover time. Most governments consider a buildup of inventory practical and maintain a sufficient quantity on hand for the business-type entity projects. Thus, the negative signal in this instance does not suggest difficulties in generating sales or an issue of production smoothing. However, the financial forensic examiner does need to be aware of the possibility of the inventory containing obsolete items not written off. The government also values inventory using the first-in, first-out method, creating the negative signal for LIFO earnings.

The formula for the accounts receivable signal also contains the same change for sales as for the gross margin signals in that the sales do not include grant revenues because the grant revenues are actually reimbursable costs. All grant costs incurred, but the reimbursements not yet received, are deferred revenues, not accounts receivable. The accounts receivable signal is positive for YR 2 and YR 3, but earnings quality appears to decrease in YR 4 and YR 5 as the signal is negative for those years. For the financial forensic examiner, the negative signals suggest the possibility of recording unrealized revenues such as fictitious sales or extensions of credit that might influence future earnings.

As a side note of interest, the notes to the financial statements for any of the years under study did not include any specific information relating to the makeup of the accounts receivable balances, something that a financial forensic examiner should question. In association with the accounts receivable signal, the allowance signal is positive with the exception of YR 3, suggesting that the primary government's allowance for doubtful accounts appears adequate in relation to accounts receivable. In fact, the horizontal analysis of the primary government in Chapter 2 shows significant increases in the allowance for doubtful accounts for both YR 4 and YR 5.

Because the primary government gross margins do not relate to production activities, this signal is not quite as relevant compared to an entity that produces products for sale. Yet the signal does provide some useful information in view of the fact that the calculations do not include grant revenues that may vary from year to year, distorting the signals. In the case of the primary government, the gross margin signal is predominantly negative with the exception of YR 2, decreasing to negative in YR 5. The actual calculation in YR 5 for the gross margin signal is zero and considered a negative signal because of the significance of the decline. Negative signals for gross margins question the long-term performance of a company, or for a government, the inability to control and monitor costs effectively. The significant increase in the gross margin for YR 2 implies a possible unusual change from the prior year, and requires additional study by the financial forensic examiner.

High, uncontrollable costs may suggest possible embezzlement activities within the governmental entity, whether the implication comes from the negative signals for gross margins or negative signals for selling and administrative costs. Signals for selling and administrative expenses are positive with the exception of YR 2. While the GMI index found in the Beneish M-Score model for both the primary government and the governmental funds is not an effective analytical tool, the SGAI index in the Model shows similar results to the 12 Signals because both types of analysis indicate that YR 2 is unusual. Another aspect of governmental entities is that selling and administrative expenses are generally more stable and very seldom adjusted for changes in revenues.

Figure 6.8 shows the overall earnings quality for the primary government, suggesting an overall low earnings quality.

In both YR 4 and YR 5, negative signals outweigh the positive signals, whereas in YR 2 and YR 3, positive signals outweigh the negative signals. In

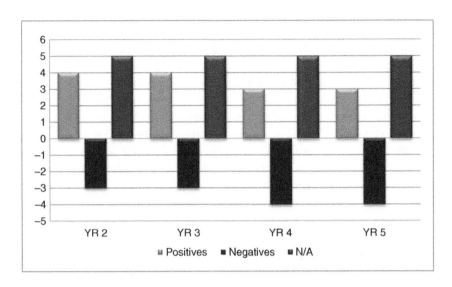

FIGURE 6.8 Lev–Thiagarajan's 12 Signals for the Primary Government of Company 3

YR 3, the inventory signal is positive while in all of the other years it is negative. Previous discussions already note that the inventory signal is not especially relevant to the primary government. Although the audit opinion is positive for all of the years, meaning that the financial statements had an unqualified opinion, in hindsight this signal was not effective because the financial statements contain numerous fictitious entries hiding embezzlement activities not discovered during the audit process.

Table 6.9 illustrates the summary of Lev–Thiagarajan's 12 Signals for the governmental funds of Company 3 for comparison with the summary of the primary government.

Aside from the change related to the allowance for doubtful accounts by adding one more item as nonapplicable, the summary provides some interesting information for the financial forensic examiner. According to the financial statements of the governmental entity, the governmental funds did not record any provision for bad debts, hence the reason for the change in the allowance for doubtful accounts.

The most persuasive evidence suggesting anomalies in the financial statements is in Table 6.9 regarding accounts receivable, selling and administrative expenses, and gross margins. Looking closely at the table, each one of

TABLE 6.9 Summary of Lev–Thiagarajan's 12 Signals for the Governmental Funds of Company 3

Signal	YR 2	YR 3	YR 4	YR 5
Inventory	Negative	Positive	Negative	Negative
Accounts Receivable	Negative	Positive	Negative	Positive
Capital Expenditures	n/a	n/a	n/a	n/a
R&D Costs	n/a	n/a	n/a	n/a
S&A Expenses	Negative	Positive	Negative	Positive
Gross Margin	Positive	Negative	Positive	Negative
Allowance	n/a	n/a	n/a	n/a
Effective Tax Rate	n/a	n/a	n/a	n/a
Order Backlog	n/a	n/a	n/a	n/a
Labor Costs	n/a	n/a	n/a	n/a
LIFO Earnings	Negative	Negative	Negative	Negative
Audit Opinion	Positive	Positive	Positive	Positive
Positives	2	4	2	3
Negatives	4	2	4	3
N/A	6	6	6	6

the signals flips every year. If these signals are negative one year, then they are positive the following year. The inventory signals in the governmental funds follow the same trends as the primary government. In YR 5, the negative inventory signal makes the only difference in the governmental funds by adding one additional negative signal for the year. Inventory is valued using the first-in, first-out method, and the audit opinion mirrors the primary government.

Figure 6.9 better illustrates the changes between the positive signals and the negative signals.

As the 12 Signals study points out, the signals show the financial forensic examiner that information within the financial statements from year to year contains anomalies that require additional investigative work. Areas requiring additional investigative work include accounts receivable and selling and administrative expenses. As mentioned earlier, the gross margin signal is not as effective for governments, but even this signal flips like the other ones. The fact that different signals flip each year is an additional sign that something is amiss in the financial information.

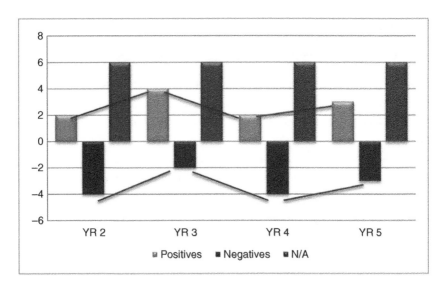

FIGURE 6.9 Lev–Thiagarajan's 12 Signals for the Governmental Funds of Company 3

Company 4

Finally, Table 6.10 illustrates the summary of Lev–Thiagarajan's 12 Signals for Company 4.

The company uses the first-in, first-out method in calculating inventory, so the LIFO earnings signal is negative for each of the years under study. The company also discloses in all of its financial statements in the years under study that the order backlog is not an appropriate indicator of future operating performance because the backlog contains "firm orders," representing less than three months of production. Therefore, the order backlog signal is not an appropriate analysis for this company.

Even though the company had poor performance in YR 1 with the external auditors issuing a *going-concern paragraph* in the audit opinion, the audit opinion was an unqualified one, indicating positive signals for the remaining years under study. More important is the earnings quality improvement shown in some of the more important signals. Inventory, one of the more important signals, suggests that the changes in inventory do not exceed the changes in sales, representing positive future earnings growth. The positive signals also imply that management is not practicing production smoothing or holding

TABLE 6.10 Summary of Lev–Thiagarajan's 12 Signals for Company 4

Signal	YR 2	YR 3	YR 4	YR 5
Inventory	Negative	Positive	Positive	Positive
Accounts Receivable	Negative	Positive	Negative	Positive
Capital Expenditures	Negative	Negative	Positive	Positive
R&D Costs	n/a	n/a	n/a	n/a
S&A Expenses	Positive	Positive	Positive	Negative
Gross Margin	Negative	Negative	Negative	Positive
Allowance	Negative	Positive	Positive	Negative
Effective Tax Rate	Negative	Positive	Negative	Positive
Order Backlog	n/a	n/a	n/a	n/a
Labor Costs	n/a	n/a	n/a	n/a
LIFO Earnings	Negative	Negative	Negative	Negative
Audit Opinion	Positive	Positive	Positive	Positive
Positives	2	6	5	6
Negatives	7	3	4	3
N/A	3	3	3	3

slow-moving or obsolete inventory for future write-downs, signifying important facts for the financial forensic examiner.

Although the accounts receivable signals are mixed, the signal is positive in YR 5. The allowance for doubtful accounts also has mixed signals, showing negative signals in YR 2 and YR 5 and positive signals in YR 3 and YR 4. The company's product mix is partly responsible for these signals, because some of the products do have extended credit terms. The important issue here for the financial forensic examiner is that the company discloses this information in the financial statements. Remember that a lack of appropriate disclosures in financial statements may hide possible earnings management, whether by complete omission or including false information. The allowance for doubtful accounts is a discretionary accrual, and negative signals suggest the possibility of an inadequate provision that affects future earnings. However, discussions in Chapter 5 concerning the accrual testing for Company 4 show that accrual quality remains relatively stable in YR 5, and the accruals did not significantly influence net income for the same year. Knowing these details, the financial forensic examiner is able to conclude the negative signal does not represent earnings manipulation.

The negative signals regarding capital expenditures in both YR 2 and YR 3 are understandable as they pertain to the company's guarded finances associated with the bankrupt subsidiary. In YR 4, the company is able to divest itself of the bankrupt subsidiary and focus its attention on capital improvements, as shown by the positive signals in both YR 4 and YR 5. The same situation also applies to the negative signal for the effective tax rate in YR 4. As discussed in Chapter 3, in YR 4, the company had a rather large non-cash gain and a tax benefit associated with the deconsolidation of the bankrupt subsidiary. Once again, the financial forensic examiner finds reasonable explanations for the negative signal normally suggesting decreased future earnings and decreased earnings quality.

Clearly, the negative gross margin signals show the effect of the bankrupt subsidiary, since all of the years except YR 5 are negative. Naturally, the negative signals also imply questions about long-term performance for the company, but the change in YR 5 implies the company is improving earnings quality by reversing the signal to positive. The GMI index for this company, discussed in Chapter 4, also shows the effect of the bankrupt subsidiary and the improvement starting in YR 4 upon the dissolution of the subsidiary.

Figure 6.10 illustrates the changes between the positives and negatives for Company 4, easily showing the improvement in the earnings quality for the years under study.

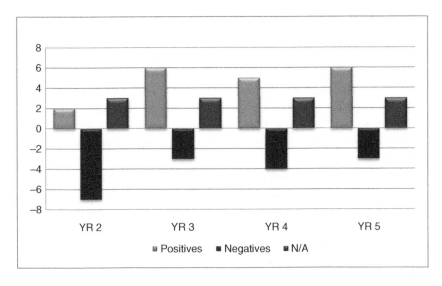

FIGURE 6.10 Lev–Thiagarajan's 12 Signals for Company 4

Although the positive signals slightly decrease in YR 4, they do remain comparatively stable from YR 3 through YR 5, suggesting higher earnings quality. The financial forensic examiner should expect to see low earnings quality in YR 2, considering the going-concern issue in YR 1 and the bankruptcy filing of one of the company's subsidiaries, so the high negative scores in YR 2 are not surprising. The slight decrease from YR 3 to YR 4 is not surprising, either, since the company received special orders in YR 3 that increased sales. The chief issue in Company 4 for the financial forensic examiner is that all unusual changes had reasonable explanations confirmed with disclosures in the financial statements, implying no manipulation of earnings or false transactions were in the financial statements under study.

 ## SUMMARY

The two simple methods of analyzing financial statements discussed in this chapter provide sufficient information to allow the financial forensic examiner to determine where additional investigative work is necessary. Piotroski's F-Score allows the financial forensic examiner to apply a nine-step analysis of financial statements to measure a company's profitability, financial liquidity, and operating efficiency. These factors determine whether a company's overall financial performance is weak or strong, with weak scores suggesting stress to improve performance, thus developing the environment for possible earnings manipulation.

The individual variables in the Piotroski F-Score model assist the financial forensic examiner in finding unusual relationships or changes that may suggest possible manipulation of financial information. The four signals measuring profitability stress the importance of measuring cash flows to net income, a crucial analysis determined in Chapter 3 for finding unusual relationships within a set of financial statements, because net income normally should be lower than cash from operating activities. Chapter 5 discusses how continued losses lower accrual quality by allowing accruals to affect net income positively without providing future cash flows.

The three signals measuring changes in a company's capital structure allow the financial forensic examiner to determine whether the company is able to meet its future debt obligations and establish whether compliance with debt covenants may influence management's decisions to manipulate earnings. The signals measuring the operating efficiency let the financial forensic examiner measure the overall financial health of a company. Gross margin deterioration may precede earnings manipulation or possible exploitation of inventory or other production costs. In circumstances related to Company 2, gross margin deterioration meant covering up embezzlement activities by recording fictitious invoices in cost of sales.

Lev–Thiagarajan's 12 Signals measure the earnings quality and future growth of a company, capturing important characteristics of earnings determination for the financial forensic examiner. Even though not every signal will apply to each company, the information from the applicable signals is sufficient for determining the need of additional investigative study, because each signal is equally weighted. Some of the more relevant components of the 12 Signals include inventory, accounts receivable, gross margins, allowance provisions, capital expenditures, and selling and administrative expenses, with the inventory and accounts receivable signals as the leading indicators for future earnings and growth. All of these areas are important to financial forensic analysis for determining possible earnings manipulation or finding false information within the financial statements.

A negative inventory signal suggests possible earnings management associated with production smoothing, or whether inventory includes slow-moving or obsolete inventory not written off in the current year. Negative signals associated with accounts receivable hint of possible earnings manipulation by recording fictitious sales and receivables, or by extending credit terms beyond normal company operations. When capital expenditures are negative, management may have concerns with the adequacy of current and future cash flows and may boost earnings by incorrectly capitalizing costs still below industry standards for the year. Negative signals for gross margins and selling and administrative expenses question a company's ability to continue long-term or whether management is not supervising and monitoring its costs.

Both Piotroski's F-Score and Lev–Thiagarajan's 12 Signals total performance scores give the financial forensic examiner sufficient information to determine unusual changes from year to year. For example, the governmental funds of Company 3 provide an excellent example of conflicting scores from year to year, as shown in Lev–Thiagarajan's 12 Signals, suggesting the possibility of some form of manipulation in the financial statements. Both methods are easy for the financial forensic examiner to complete in a comparatively insignificant amount of time. From the financial forensic examiner's perspective, both the individual components of each model and the total scores of each model suggest areas of unusual variations or relationships that point out the need for additional investigative work in a very efficient and effective way.

NOTES

1. Joseph D. Piotroski, "Value Investing: The Use of Historical Financial Statement Information to Separate Winners from Losers," *Journal of Accounting Research*, 38, Supplement (January 2002): 7–9.
2. Baruch Lev and S. Ramu Thiagarajan, "Fundamental Information Analysis," *Journal of Accounting Research*, 31, No 2 (Autumn 1993): 193.

CHAPTER SEVEN

Benford's Law, and Yes—Even Statistics

T HIS BOOK would not be complete without a chapter devoted to the use of Benford's Law and the use of statistics in analyzing financial statement information, and interpreting the results of these techniques without having an advanced educational degree in mathematics or statistics. There are many articles and books written on Benford's Law and its use, not only in auditing, but in financial forensics as well. In addition, there are many articles and books written on the use of statistics in business applications, from evaluating portfolios and investments to managing operations and even auditing and forensic accounting applications. Some of the more common statistical applications used in this chapter include correlation and regression analysis, Z-score tests, and descriptive statistics. Even basic data analyses, such as checking for duplicate numbers or gaps in numbers, are simple tools available to financial forensic examiners. Covering all types of statistical tests, along with detailed study of Benford's Law, is not within the scope of this chapter, but the financial forensic examiner needs to be aware that there are multiple other statistical tools available to assist in financial forensic examinations, along with additional information relating to the opportunities of using Benford's Law in financial forensic examinations. While these techniques generally dissect the detailed financial information that makes up a financial account balance, some of these tools are also useful in finding unusual variations in financial statements.

Even though the financial statements may not contain all of the financial transactions or other financial information, something the financial forensic examiner must consider, these tools are capable of pointing to unusual relationships and variations in the financial statements, even when the financial information is missing or altered. The key to these techniques is that their applications draw a roadmap to areas requiring more investigative work. Using only these techniques generally does not provide sufficient evidence for trial, but using them in combination with other techniques provides the financial forensic examiner with the detailed evidence required for prosecution. Nonetheless, used alone, they assist the financial forensic examiner in planning effective and efficient investigations and deserve a place in his or her toolbox.

There is somewhat of a learning curve before using these tools correctly, but the time spent learning these techniques is well worth the investment. In-depth discussions related to these techniques follow, but there are some simple points to keep in mind concerning these techniques and their applications in financial forensic analysis. *Benford's Law* analyzes naturally occurring numbers and does not require expensive data analysis tools to use. Many digital analysis software packages, such as IDEA, ACL, and ActiveData, include Benford's Law in their software programs. Even though it is effective in detecting data manipulations, it does have its limitations. Most important, it is a test of reasonableness and points to variations in the actual frequencies of the digits of numbers compared to the expected frequencies of digits in Benford's Law.

Some of the simpler statistical testing applications that allow the financial forensic examiner to find unusual variations within the data do not require sophisticated software, since the statistical techniques discussed in this chapter use the formulas found in Microsoft Excel. Once the financial forensic examiner understands the fundamental process of the formulas, the analysis is quite easy to perform. Correlation analysis allows the financial forensic examiner to measure relationships such as cost of sales to sales, and often reveals unusual relationships. Regression analysis identifies the relationship between variables, such as sales to cost of sales, and actually allows the financial forensic examiner to look at a relationship between two variables and make predictions about the numerical values of the second variable based on the relationships between the two. Both correlation and regression analysis require the financial forensic examiner to use professional judgment in reaching conclusions, thus requiring the use of other empirical techniques, such as the *z-test*, *t-tests*, and *chi-square tests*. These represent only three of the many statistical tests available to the financial forensic examiner for use. These types of tests are generally useful for large sets of data and samples from a population.

 ## BENFORD'S LAW

Benford's Law, described as a digital analysis technique, was made famous in 1938 by a physicist, Frank Benford, even though Simon Newcomb, an astronomer and mathematician of the 1880s, originally identified the trend of the digits of numbers. Simon Newcomb observed a developing pattern in library books of logarithms where pages that dealt with low digits showed more wear and tear from use when compared to pages with higher digits. Benford's research expanded Newcomb's observations and determined the existence of a distribution law applicable to numerical data, defining the frequencies of digits in each position of the number for naturally occurring numbers. Table 7.1 illustrates the expected digital frequencies discovered by Benford.

For example, the probability of the digit 1 used as a first digit is 30% and the probability of the numbers 1, 2, or 3 used as a first digit is 60%. In addition, notice that the digit 0 and the digit 9 are the least-used numbers according to their frequencies. Not all data follows Benford's Law, as discussed below. Benford tested more than 20,000 different observations and a wide variety

TABLE 7.1   Benford's Law: Expected Digital Frequencies

Digit	First	Second	Third	Fourth
0	N/A	.11968	.10178	.10018
1	.30103	.11389	.10138	.10014
2	.17609	.10882	.10097	.10010
3	.12494	.10433	.10057	.10006
4	.09691	.10031	.10018	.10002
5	.07918	.09668	.09940	.09998
6	.06695	.09337	.09940	.09994
7	.05799	.09035	.09902	.09990
8	.05115	.08757	.09864	.09986
9	.04576	.08500	09827	.09982

of data to determine the expected frequencies documented in Table 7.1. He then documented his research in a paper titled "The Law of Anomalous Numbers," published in the *Proceedings of the American Philosophical Society* (Vol. 78, No. 4) in March 1938.

When testing large sets of data, his research also discovered that the distribution law did not work on numbers that did not occur naturally, so the financial forensic examiner must define the numbers to test as naturally occurring numbers. *Naturally occurring* numbers come from real-life sources such as population numbers, death rates, or financial transactions without human intervention. Numbers such as product serial numbers, ZIP codes, assigned address numbers, customer account numbers, or any other assigned numbers that are not naturally occurring numbers, will not follow Benford's Law, including numbers with human intervention, making Benford's Law useful in financial forensic examinations. Numbers that contain a minimum or maximum value, such as hourly wage rates, will not follow Benford's Law. Larger data sets are preferable to avoid the possibility of negative results from the testing.

Although Benford's Law was discovered in 1938, its use as a forensic accounting technique was not recognized until the studies and research performed by Mark Nigrini, Ph.D., in the 1990s. By using the information in Table 7.1, the financial forensic examiner is able determine anomalies in data based on numerical sequence. Because human choices are not random, invented numbers, often the result from hiding fraudulent activity such as earnings management or embezzlement, do not follow Benford's Law, with the actual frequencies of the digits generally straying significantly from the expected frequencies. Therefore, Benford's Law effectively analyzes 100% of a population in a comparatively short time, making the technique applicable to various accounting records such as disbursement journals, checks, deposits, and transfers.

Although there are many applications to the use of Benford's Law in underlying financial information generally representing large sets of data, sufficient research also suggests the use of Benford's Law in analyzing financial statements for number bias, even in smaller sets of data. To determine whether a small set of data, such as the data found in financial statements, is applicable to Benford's Law analysis, the financial forensic examiner may find it useful to implement a simplified statistical approach in determining the appropriateness of the data. If the mean of the population is greater than the median of the population and the skew of the population is positive, the use of Benford's law is appropriate. It is important for the financial forensic examiner to remember that the use of Benford's Law for these purposes is actually a test of reasonableness and not necessarily a test for fraudulent activity, yet it may be useful as an early indicator of anomalies in financial statement information, suggesting the possibility of fraudulent activity.

Since Benford's Law defines logical patterns of the digit sequence in naturally occurring numbers, there are multiple ways Benford's Law may be applied. The financial forensic examiner may choose to use the *first-digit* analysis, the *second-digit* analysis, the *first-two-digits* analysis, the *first-three-digits* analysis, or the *last-two-digits* analysis. Each one has specific attributes that the financial forensic examiner must consider before choosing the appropriate method for analyzing the data. The financial forensic examiner generally will find variations in the data analysis, but the use of the *z-statistic* allows the financial forensic examiner to determine the significance of the difference.

For example, the first-digit test is an initial test of reasonableness in the expected frequencies for numbers 1 through 9. This may provide a large amount of data to review, but the results should point in the right direction. The second-digit test, also a basic preliminary test of reasonableness, was used in the research by Charles Carslaw in his "Anomalies in Income Numbers: Evidence of Goal Oriented Behavior," published in *The Accounting Review* (Vol. 63, No. 2, April 1998), to detect improvements to net income or ordinary income by rounding numbers to enhance the bottom line. The first-two-digits test, measuring the actual frequencies of the first two digits of numbers from 10 through 99, is a more refined test that finds anomalies in data that may not turn up in the first- or second-digit test, thus reducing the amount of false-positives that may occur when using Benford's Law. The first-three-digits test measures the actual frequencies of the first three digits of numbers 100 through 99 and is most effective on larger sets of data. Finally, the last-two-digits test is also effective in finding rounded numbers possibly invented by fraudulent activity or in identifying recurring patterns in the last two digits that may not be immediately apparent.

The calculation of the z-statistic is very complex and beyond the scope of this book, but several digital analysis software programs that include Benford's Law analysis perform these calculations for the financial forensic examiner. The important detail for the financial forensic examiner to remember is that if the z-statistic for a point not following Benford's Law is greater than 1.96 when using a 5% significance level, the detailed information requires further study. The 5% level means that there is a 5% probability that the difference between the expected frequency and the actual frequency is due to chance. When using a 1% significant level, if the z-statistic for a point not following Benford's Law is greater than 2.58, there is a 1% chance the difference is due to chance. Various statistical tables found in books associated with statistics provide the z-statistics referenced here and at other various levels of significance. While the information seems rather complex, by using the z-statistic, the financial forensic examiner is able to determine if the variations require additional examination. The studies of the four companies that follow illustrate the use of the z-statistic in determining whether the anomaly requires further study.

The underlying theme for the financial forensic examiner to remember is that invented numbers such as amounts on fraudulent invoices do not follow the sequences of Benford's Law. Additionally, Benford's Law is actually a test of varying degrees of reasonableness depending on the selection of the digit test, and has many practical applications in a financial forensic investigation. Over a stretch of time, the financial forensic examiner expands his or her ability to determine what data sets are applicable for the Benford's Law analysis, thus developing the roadmap to areas requiring specific additional work while performing an effective and efficient investigation.

In studying the financial statements of the four companies using Benford's Law, the use of descriptive statistics determines the appropriateness of the data by determining that the mean is greater than the median and the skew of the data is positive. The analysis uses a 5% significant level, and points outside the frequencies of Benford's Law use a comparison of the calculated z-statistic to 1.96 when using a 5% significant level and 2.576 when using a 1% significant level. The analysis of each company's financial statements also includes an individual analysis of each company and a combined analysis of all the years under study. For purposes of testing financial statements, the definition of financial statements includes both the balance sheet and income statement combined. Because the data set is small, the author has found that the best method to use for financial statement analysis is the first-two-digits analysis, refining the reasonableness test to pick up variations in the actual frequencies in account number balances that either a first-digit or second-digit test may miss and reduce the incidence of false-positives. In addition, pictorial graphs of each analysis include not only the actual frequencies and Benford's Law frequencies, but the upper- and lower-limit boundaries as well, so that the financial forensic examiner is easily able to see the results of the tests. To comply with the parameters of Benford's Law, the data set does not include numbers representing totals, and negative numbers become positive numbers for analysis.

Benford's Law data, including the z-statistic calculations, is generated by ActiveData (www.informationactive .com).

Company 1

Even though the analysis of each financial statement uses the first-two-digits test, Figure 7.1 illustrates an example of the first-digit test for YR 1 of Company 1 to show that normal variations are possible and do not represent variations in the frequencies that require additional examination. To determine that the financial information for YR 1 meets the criteria for testing with Benford's Law, the relationship between the mean and median of the population, along with the skew of the population, determines whether the data meets the requirements for Benford's Law analysis.

- Mean = 1,908.8621
- Median = 4,590
- Skewness = 2.5917

The chart provides a nice illustration of variations that may normally occur in the analysis of Benford's Law. The actual frequencies of digits 1, 4, 5, and 9 exceed the expected frequencies of Benford's Law, suggesting the possibility that information in the data may include manipulated numbers. Yet the actual frequencies of the digits 3, 6, and 8 are below the expected frequencies. This is a

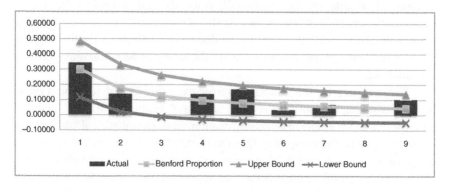

FIGURE 7.1   First-Digit Test of YR 1 for Company 1

normal occurrence; when the actual frequency of one digit exceeds the expected frequency of Benford's Law, another digit will respond with actual frequencies less than the expected frequencies. By adding the upper-limit boundaries and the lower-limit boundaries to the chart, the financial forensic examiner has a better perspective concerning the significances of the differences.

Remember, the first-digit test is really just a preliminary test for reasonableness; to refine the Benford's Law analysis to financial statements with smaller sets of data, it is more appropriate to use the first-two-digits test as a test of reasonableness. Figure 7.2 illustrates the first-two-digits test YR 1 for Company 1.

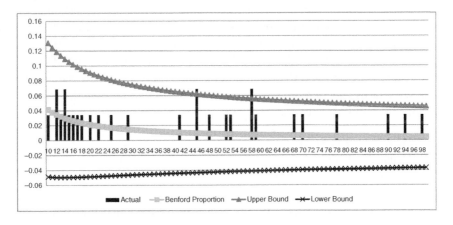

FIGURE 7.2 First-Two-Digits Test of YR 1 for Company 1

Even though the first-digit test did not find any unusual variations in the Benford's Law analysis, the first-two-digits test did find two points that are in excess of the upper-limit boundaries. As stated earlier, the first-two-digits test is more refined and will find variations not discovered with either the first-digit or the second-digit test and aids in reducing the false positives that may occur in the analysis.

The next step for the financial forensic examiner is to determine if these variances are significant and require additional examination. The financial forensic examiner is able to do this by examining the z-statistic calculations for these two points and comparing them to the threshold of 1.96. The z-statistic for point 45 is 2.336, and 2.779 for point 58. Both of these are clearly over the 1.96 threshold and require additional examination. Some digital analysis software allows the financial forensic examiner to drill down to the actual sets of data frequencies that create the variances and points to the specific details of the variance. For reference here, the variations noted in the Benford's Law analysis correlate to the actual frequencies associated with the first two digits of the account balances related to labor costs recorded as cost of sales, general, and administrative expenses. Point 58 has the largest variance from the threshold and relates strictly to the actual frequency variance in the first two digits of the account balance associated with general and administrative expenses. General and administrative expenses include the total of all expenses as noted in the SGAI index testing with the Beneish M-Score model.

The first-two-digits test for YR 2 did not disclose any unusual actual frequency variances either in excess of the upper-bound limits or below the lower-bound limits, thus allowing the omission of the illustrations for YR 2. However, the first-two-digits test for YR 3, YR 4, and YR 5 show variations. The descriptive statistics for YR 3 confirm that the data is appropriate for using Benford's Law.

- ■ Mean = 22,314.24
- ■ Median = 5,791
- ■ Skewness = 2.2094

Figure 7.3 shows the Benford's Law analysis of YR 3 for the company.

Once more, there are two points exceeding the upper-limit boundaries, point 50 and point 54. The z-statistic for point 50 is 2.17, and the z-statistic for point 54 is 2.85. Both are obviously above the 1.96 threshold, indicating that further additional investigation is necessary. Aside from variances in the actual

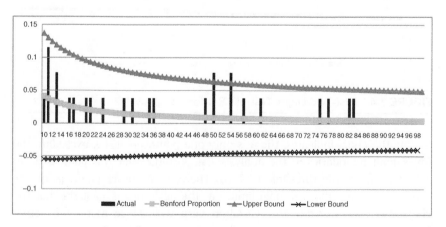

FIGURE 7.3   First-Two-Digits Test of YR 3 for Company 1

frequencies of the first two digits of the account balances for general and administrative expenses, there is also a variance associated with the first two digits of the account balance for accounts payable. Even though Benford's Law is just a test for reasonableness and the findings in YR 3 do not correspond to findings in some of the other tests, there is still the indication that something is amiss. The Sloan's Accruals test of YR 3 does indicate that the accrual component for that year positively affected net income, and the implied cash component is negative while net income is positive. Remember also the discussions in Chapter 1 noting that management did not always record the same type of expense in the same account classification from year to year.

Figure 7.4 displays the first-two-digits test of YR 4 for Company 1 and the descriptive statistics follow.

- ▦ Mean = 20,628.56
- ▦ Median = 5,882
- ▦ Skewness = 2.2915

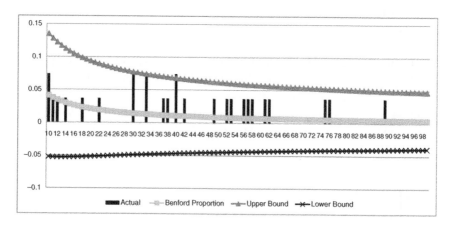

FIGURE 7.4 First-Two-Digits Test of YR 4 for Company 1

As the chart indicates, there is only one point, point 40, exceeding the upper-limit boundaries in the analysis. The z-statistic for this point is 2.26, definitely above the threshold of 1.96. There is one other point, point 30, actually equaling the threshold limit, but the difference is so slight that the chart does not illustrate this variation very well. Once more, the actual frequency variation occurs in the first two digits of the account balances representing general and administrative expenses. Point 30's variation is associated with the first two digits in the amounts for cash and accounts receivable, but since these do not actually exceed the threshold, the financial forensic examiner does not need to perform additional studies for point 30 even though point 40 requires additional study.

Figure 7.5 illustrates the first-two-digits test of YR 5 for Company 1 and the descriptive statistics follow.

- Mean = 22,210.6539
- Median = 5,559.50
- Skewness = 2.2876

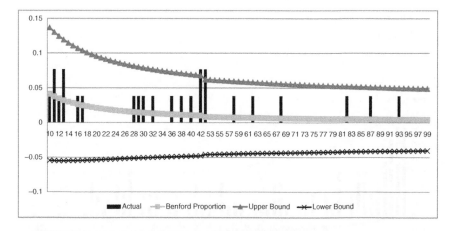

FIGURE 7.5 First-Two-Digits Test of YR 5 for Company 1

YR 5 also has two points that exceed the upper-limit boundaries, point 42 and point 52. By now, the financial forensic examiner should recognize the developing pattern that in four of the five years under study, the Benford's Law analysis shows at least two points that exceed the upper-limit boundaries each year. The z-statistic for point 42 is 2.407, definitely above the threshold of 1.96, while the z-statistic for point 52 is 2.782, also above the threshold. Aside from the actual frequencies for the first two digits of the cash balance as one of the areas of variation, the other variations also relate to the actual frequency variations for the first two digits of the account balance for general and administrative expenses. Even though the financial forensic examiner is only performing tests for reasonableness, the fact that the majority of the years under study show variations above the upper limits of the expected frequencies of Benford's Law should alert the financial forensic examiner that additional inspections are necessary.

There is one more test for the financial forensic examiner to review concerning the Benford's Law analysis of the financial statement numbers—combining all five years into one set of data. Combining all of the financial statements' numbers into one set of data, thereby increasing the size of the set of data, also allows analysis of an overall picture of the financial statements over a five-year period. Figure 7.6 shows the Benford's Law analysis for all five years under study. The descriptive statistics for the data under analysis follow.

- ▩ Mean = 21,613.2977
- ▩ Median = 5,820
- ▩ Skewness = 2.2333

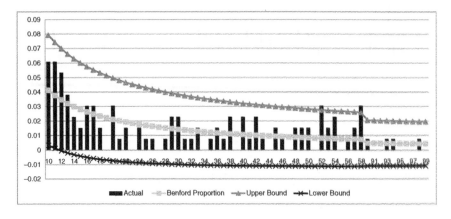

FIGURE 7.6   First-Two-Digits Test for All 5 Years of Company 1

Even though the chart shows numerous points exceeding the expected frequencies of Benford's Law, there are only two points exceeding the upper-limit boundaries, points 52 and 58. Of the two points, the greater difference between the z-statistic and the threshold of 1.96 is point 58, with a z-statistic of 2.5724. The z-statistic for point 52 is 2.3308. It is not surprising that one point creating the variance connects to the actual frequency variance for the first two digits in the account balances of general and administrative expenses, since this area is already questionable from the analyses of each year. However, in this particular test, the general and administrative expense actual frequency deviations occur in YR 1, YR 4, and YR 5. One other point not targeted in each yearly analysis is the area of the actual variance in the first two digit numbers of the account balance representing depreciation, especially in YR 4. Looking back at Chapter 4, the DEPTA index for Company 1 showed a significant decrease in YR 4 when compared to YR 3.

Because there is little difference between the mean and median in the descriptive statistics of the cash flow statements for YR 2, YR 3, and YR 4, along with very little skew to the population, the use of Benford's Law for analyzing the cash flow statements of Company 1 is not an acceptable procedure. However, knowing the expected frequencies of the digit 0, the financial forensic examiner is able to scan cash flow statements looking for numbers whose last digit is zero, suggesting the possibility of rounding or manipulated numbers in the financial statement. Remember from Chapter 3 that it is extremely difficult to manipulate a cash flow statement, so unusual variations or manipulations in the financial statement are not easy to hide in the cash flow statements. In addition, Company 1 did not prepare cash flow statements. However, the last-two-digits test in Benford's Law is an excellent test of reasonableness concerning rounding issues in financial statements, including cash flow statements, if the data meets the criteria for the use of Benford's Law.

Company 2

The Benford's Law analysis for YR 1 did not show any unusual variances in the actual frequencies of numbers outside the upper- and lower-limit boundaries of the test, so the illustration of the test is not necessary. However, the analysis for YR 2 shows two points that exceed the threshold of 1.96. The descriptive statistics for YR 2 follow.

- Mean = 4,687,159.863
- Median = 1,964,925.5
- Skewness = 2.4293

Since the descriptive statistics show the data is appropriate for Benford's Law analysis, Figure 7.7 illustrates the first-two-digits test of YR 2 for Benford's Law.

Point 22 and point 29 both extend beyond the upper-limit boundaries, but point 29 has the greater difference when compared to point 22. When reviewing the z-statistics, the z-statistic for point 22 is 2.164 and the z-statistic

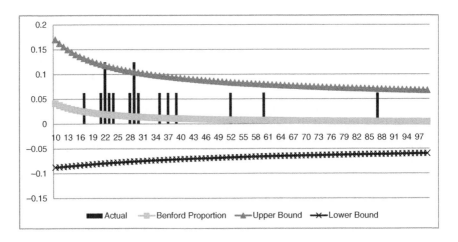

FIGURE 7.7   First-Two-Digits Test of YR 2 for Company 2

for point 29 is 2.625. The two actual frequency variations creating the variance for point 29 include the actual frequencies in the first two digits of account balances associated with accounts receivables and accounts payables. Oddly enough, the TARTA index and the TAPTA index for Company 2, found in Chapter 4, show the calculations for YR 2 in excess of the general benchmark of 1, even though the first-two-digits test is just a test for reasonableness. The unusual variance for point 22 is associated with the actual frequency deviations of the first two digits in the account balances for fixed assets and miscellaneous income. Although these variations are closer to the threshold of 1.96 compared to point 29, the financial forensic examiner still needs to do additional analysis.

YR 3 has only one area that exceeds the upper-limit boundaries in the Benford's Law analysis, yet the variance is more significant compared to the variances in YR 2. The descriptive statistics for YR 3 follow.

- ▪ Mean = 6,037,495.851
- ▪ Median = 1,586,612
- ▪ Skewness = 2.480

Figure 7.8 displays the Benford's Law analysis for YR 3. For information purposes, point 95 is actually below the line of the upper bounds with a z-statistic of 1.587, since the chart does not make this distinction as clearly as it should be.

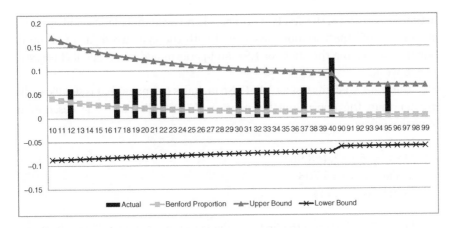

FIGURE 7.8 First-Two-Digits Test of YR 3 for Company 2

The chart makes it plain that point 40 significantly exceeds the upper-limit boundaries. The z-statistic for point 40 is 3.224, 1.264 points above the threshold of 1.96. So far, in the study of both Company 1 and Company 2, point 40 stands out with the greatest actual frequency variance from the threshold, naturally suggesting that the financial forensic examiner should do an additional detailed study of the underlying data. The actual frequency deviations for point 40 include the first two digit numbers of the account balances for cash and sales. Remember, the cash flow statements were not prepared with the financial statements, and the constructed cash flow statement did not agree with the cash totals in YR 3, nor in YR 2. However, the Benford's Law analysis for YR 2 did not find actual frequency variances in the numbers of the cash balance as a variance. According to the SGI index in Chapter 4, the calculations for both YR 2 and YR 3 exceed the general benchmark of 1, YR 2 more significantly than YR 3.

The differences in the testing between the two years for these account balances concern Benford's Law itself, because the first two digits of the numbers of these account balances in YR 2 fall within the expected frequencies of Benford's Law, whereas in YR 3 the first two digits of these account balances did not. Benford's Law is not actually measuring an account balance itself, but rather measuring the first two digits of each account balance, and that is why the first-two-digits test for YR 2 did not find the same issues as the first-two-digits test for YR 3. The important issue for the financial forensic examiner to remember is that the first-two-digits test is a test of reasonableness of the actual frequencies of the first two numbers in an account balance, and as such, should identify the variations associated with the first two digits of account balances above the threshold of 1.96 and perform additional detailed investigative work.

The first-two-digits test for YR 4 also includes one point that is significantly greater than the upper-limit boundaries of Benford's Law. The descriptive statistics follow.

- ⬚ Mean = 5,652,448.961
- ⬚ Median = 1,615,708
- ⬚ Skewness = 2.534

Figure 7.9 illustrates the first-two-digits test of YR 4, identifying the point of significant variation in the Benford's Law analysis.

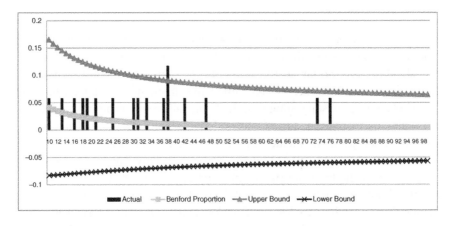

FIGURE 7.9   First-Two-Digits Test of YR 4 for Company 2

From the chart, the financial forensic examiner easily determines that point 38 definitely exceeds the upper-limit boundaries. In fact, the z-statistic for point 38 is 3.004, once again identifying a variation at least one point over the threshold. The actual frequency deviations in point 38 include the first two digits of the account balances for inventory and sales. Once more, this difference is above the threshold of 1.96 and definitely requires further research.

The first-two-digits test, shown in Figure 7.10 for YR 5, shows only one point above the upper-limit boundaries. The descriptive statistics for YR 5 follow.

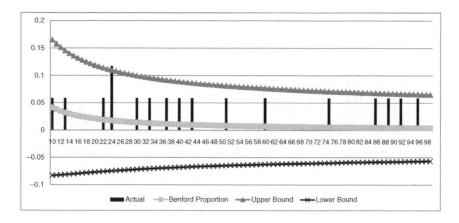

FIGURE 7.10   First-Two-Digits Test of YR 5 for Company 2

- Mean = 4,894,840.288
- Median = 963,459
- Skewness = 2.371

Point 24 is the only point in YR 5 where the actual frequencies of the first two digits of the data set are above the z-statistic threshold of 1.96.

From the chart, the financial forensic examiner easily sees that point 24 is marginally above the upper-limit boundaries. The z-statistic for point 24 is 2.2029 and represents deviations in the actual frequencies from the expected frequencies in the first two digits of the account balances for fixed assets and costs of sales. In YR 5, the company actually had a non-cash entry reducing both fixed assets and payables from a non-cash transaction sale, making one of the manufacturing facilities a separate entity. There have been several other analyses relating to cost of sales, including the GMI index of the Beneish M-Score model and multiple discussions concerning the use of fraudulent invoices found in the cost of sales area.

For Company 2, the Benford's Law analysis for all of the financial statement balances under study somewhat contrasts the study in Company 1 because the deviations noted in this analysis include deviations not noted in each individual analysis and little consistency between the two. The descriptive statistics for the data set, including all of the financial statement data under study, follow. Figure 7.11 shows the Benford's Law analysis for all years under study.

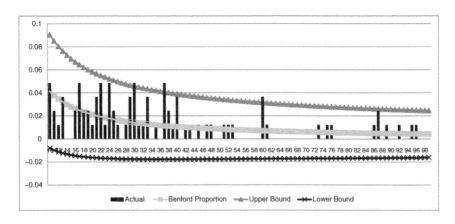

FIGURE 7.11   First-Two-Digits Test of All Years for Company 2

- Mean = 4,675,840.41
- Median = 1,332,990
- Skewness = 2.7062

There are three actual frequencies exceeding the upper-limit boundaries of the expected frequencies for the set of data with all of the financial information for the years under study: points 30, 37, and 60. The z-statistic for point 30 is 2.1738, point 37 is 2.6322, and point 60 is 2.5002, with point 37 having the greatest difference from the threshold of 1.96. While the Benford's Law analysis for all years under study for Company 1 is consistent with some of the findings in the individual studies, this analysis, for the most part, has separate findings associated with deviations of the actual frequencies from the expected frequencies. These deviations are associated with the first two digits of account balances of the allowances for doubtful accounts for YR 2 and YR 3, deferred taxes for YR 4 and YR 5, depreciation for YR 5, cash for YR 1, and stockholder's equity for YR 2.

There is one deviation in this analysis that is consistent with the individual analyses, and that is the deviation in the actual frequencies connected to the first two digits of the account balances for sales. This analysis pointed to the sales in YR 5, while the individual analyses pointed to sales in both YR 3 and YR 4. One advantage of using Benford's Law on all of the years under study is the ability to see if there are consistencies in this analysis compared to the individual yearly analysis of the financial statements. While all actual frequencies greater than the benchmark of 1.96 require additional investigative work, so should any consistencies.

Company 3

Because Company 3 is a governmental entity and prepares multiple financial statements with each set of financial statements presenting information differently, the primary government's financial statements and the governmental funds' financial statements will require separate analysis using Benford's Law. Beginning with the primary government, the first-two-digits test of YR 1 finds one difference in the actual frequencies of the first two digits compared to the expected frequencies of Benford's Law, exceeding the threshold of 1.96. As usual, before using Benford's Law, the financial forensic examiner must calculate the descriptive statistics to ensure the use of Benford's Law is appropriate. The descriptive statistics follow:

■ Mean = 8,593,560.64
■ Median = 1,579,370
■ Skewness = 2.8164

Figure 7.12 displays the first-two-digits test of YR 1 for the primary government.

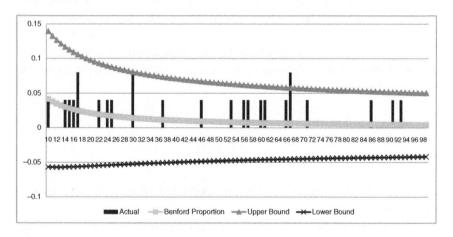

FIGURE 7.12 First-Two-Digits Test of YR 1 for the Primary Government of Company 3

Point 67 has a z-statistic of 3.350, definitely above the threshold of 1.96, indicating that the actual frequencies of the first two digits of the numbers involved exceeded the expected frequencies, requiring additional examination. The first two digits of the account balances that represent point 67 are the first two digits of account balances for notes receivable and fixed assets. Since the actual frequencies of the first two digits associated with notes receivable and fixed assets exceed the threshold limit, the financial forensic examiner must pursue further inspection techniques by reviewing the detailed information making up these account balances. Remember in the financial statements that fixed assets is a net number that comprises both gross fixed assets and accumulated depreciation, so both account balances require further study.

For comparison between the first-two-digits test and the first-digit test, the first-digit test of YR 1 for the primary government identified one point that exceeded the threshold of 1.96. The z-statistic for point 6 is 2.2617. Since only one digit is under investigation, the first-digit test identified five first-digit account balances where the first-digit actual frequency exceeded the expected frequency at the 5% significant level. While the first-digit test tells the financial forensic examiner to study five different account balances, the first-two-digits test tells of the need to study only two account balances. The accounts included in the first-digit test included not only fixed assets and notes receivable, but also accounts receivable, accrued liabilities, and charges for services.

While the first-two-digits test for YR 1 pointed out only one area with variations between the actual and expected frequencies, the same test for YR 2 highlights three areas where actual frequencies exceed expected frequencies over and above the upper-limit boundaries. The descriptive statistics for YR 2 follow, showing that the data meets the requirements of a data set that may use Benford's Law for analysis.

- Mean = 9,204,487.16
- Median = 2,861,106
- Skewness = 2.6946

Figure 7.13 illustrates the first-two-digits test of YR 2 for the primary government.

The three first two digits whose actual frequencies exceed the expected frequencies are points 40, 41, and 69, with z-statistics of 2.392, 2.434, and 3.411, respectively. Point 69 has the greatest variance from the threshold of 1.96 and the first two digits of the account balances associated with this

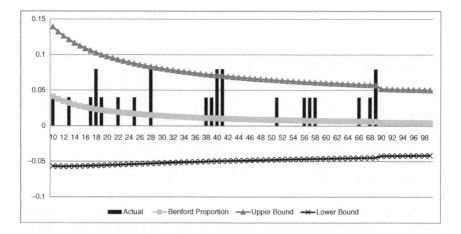

FIGURE 7.13 First-Two-Digits Test of YR 2 for the Primary Government of Company 3

variance include fixed assets, same as in YR 1, and grant revenues. The first two digits of account balances associated with point 41 prove to be more interesting in terms of testing for reasonableness, since they represent interest income and interest expense. What is so interesting about these two accounts is that interest income is $410,530 while interest expense is $410,930, exactly a $400 difference. In exercising professional skepticism, the financial forensic examiner should definitely question the amounts and the difference for these accounts in order to determine whether the amounts include manipulations. The first two digits of the account balances in the last variation include deferred revenues and other revenues. Since all three of these points exceed the threshold of 1.96, they do require additional study.

The first-two-digits tests for YR 3, YR 4, and YR 5 include only one point each that exceeds the threshold of 1.96. The descriptive statistics for each of these years follow:

YR 3:

- Mean = 9,800,901.24
- Median = 2,463,413
- Skewness = 2.8204

YR 4:

- Mean = 9,685,203.32
- Median = 1,282,307
- Skewness = 2.9830

YR 5:

- Mean = 9,699,194.704
- Median = 1,299,373
- Skewness = 3.1816

Figure 7.14 shows the first-two-digits test of YR 3 for the primary government; both YR 4 and YR 5 discussions and illustrations follow YR 3.

The Benford's Law test of the first two digits for YR 3 shows only one point, point 53, that not only exceeds the upper-limit boundaries but also has a z-statistic of 2.891, which is above the threshold limit of 1.96. The first two digits of the account balances whose actual frequencies exceed the expected frequencies of Benford's Law include investments and net assets. Neither of these account balances contained actual frequencies in excess of the threshold in the previous tests, but the financial forensic examiner still needs to review the underlying detailed information that makes up these account balances to

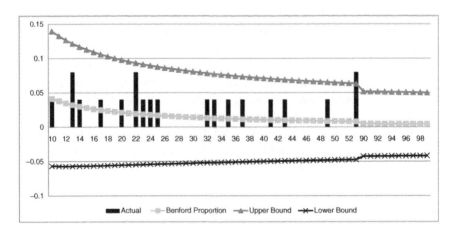

FIGURE 7.14 First-Two-Digits Test of YR 3 for the Primary Government of Company 3

determine whether the underlying information contains unusual deviations that may suggest the possibility of fraudulent activity. There is always the possibility that the account net assets contains accounting transactions directly posted to the account rather than flowing through income or expense, in an attempt to manipulate earnings.

Figure 7.15 displays the results of the Benford's Law analysis of YR 4 for the primary government.

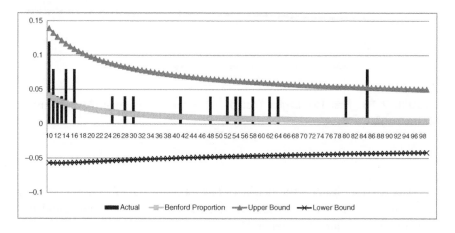

FIGURE 7.15   First-Two-Digits Test of YR 4 for the Primary Government of Company 3

The only first two digits whose actual frequencies exceed the expected frequencies in Benford's Law apply to point 85. The z-statistic for point 85 is 3.863, definitely above the threshold of 1.96, so the financial forensic examiner knows that any account balance whose first two digits are 85 requires additional examination. For YR 4, these account balances are fixed assets and accrued liabilities. The Benford's Law tests for both YR 1 and YR 2 already identified the fixed assets balance as having actual frequencies greater than the expected frequencies in those periods. Although the account balance accrued liabilities has actual frequencies in excess of the threshold for YR 4, the financial forensic examiner must investigate further. Remember also that the accrued liabilities include the due-to-other-funds account balances, and these accounts will affect the outcome of the test. The Benford's Law analysis for the governmental funds will test both the due-from-other-funds and the due-to-other-funds accounts.

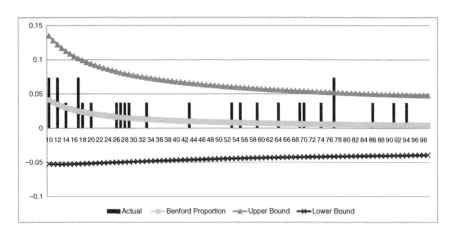

FIGURE 7.16 First-Two-Digits Test of YR 5 for the Primary Government of Company 3

Figure 7.16 displays the Benford's Law analysis for YR 5 of the primary government. One set of two-digit numbers exceeds the upper-limit boundaries of Benford's Law for YR 5, point 77.

The z-statistic for point 77 is 3.477, 1.517 over the threshold of 1.96. The actual frequencies for the first two digits of the account balances in this variation are the first two digits of the amounts for the allowance for doubtful accounts and notes receivable. While both of these account balances require detailed inspections of underlying data, the allowance for doubtful accounts is also a discretionary accrual based on management's estimations and judgment and is sometimes prejudicial to management's notions and concepts, allowing management to manipulate earnings.

When using Benford's Law for analyzing the financial statement data for all of the years under study, the analysis finds one point where the first two digits of numbers associated with account balances not only exceed the upper-limit boundaries, but also exceed the threshold of 1.96. Point 53 has a z-statistic of 2.442 and includes the first two digits of the account balances for net assets in YR 1 and YR 3, investments in YR 3, and depreciation expense in YR 5. YR 3's analysis of the financial statement data using Benford's Law already identified both investments and net assets, suggesting consistency with the analysis for all of the years under study. Yet depreciation expense and net assets for YR 1 are new discoveries related to this analysis, suggesting the financial forensic examiner needs to review the underlying transactions for these account balances.

Having completed the Benford's Law analysis for the primary government's financial statements and based on testing the reasonableness of account balances using the differences in the actual frequencies of the first two numbers in the account balances versus the expected frequencies, the primary government's analyses did not find as many consistencies as in Company 1 and Company 2. Now the financial forensic examiner needs to compare the governmental funds' financial statements and see whether there are similarities between the two sets of financial statements. Remember, the primary government financial statements also include the elements of the governmental funds' financial statements.

The first-two-digits test for YR 1 of the primary government found only one point showing the actual frequency in excess of the expected frequency and in excess of the z-statistic. The Benford's Law analysis of YR 1 for the governmental funds, in Figure 7.17, shows three points where the actual frequencies of the first two digits are in excess of the upper-limit boundaries and in excess of the z-statistic threshold of 1.96. The descriptive statistics for YR 1 follow.

- ▓ Mean = 2,239,295.913
- ▓ Median = 970,971
- ▓ Skewness = 0.91426

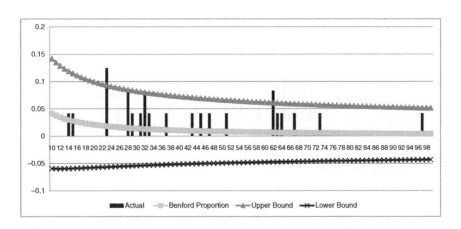

FIGURE 7.17 First-Two-Digits Test of YR 1 for the Governmental Funds of Company 3

Points 23, 32, and 62 are the three first two digits that exceed the upper-limit boundaries of Benford's Law and also have z-statistic scores higher than the threshold of 1.96. Point 23 has a z-statistic of 3.116, but does not have the greatest difference from the threshold. Point 32 has a z-statistic of 2.096 while point 62 has a z-statistic of 3.276, the greatest difference from 1.96. Starting with point 62, the first two digits of numbers of account balances that are greater than the threshold of 1.96 include other revenues and debt service payments. The second set of first two digit numbers included in point 23 include the account balances associated with cash, inventory, and due-to-other funds. Finally, the last first two digit numbers of account balances included in point 32 include due-from-other funds and accrued liabilities.

Once more, the Benford's Law analysis for YR 2 of the governmental funds shows three points, point 34, 38, and 39, that exceed the upper-limit boundaries and have z-statistics greater than 1.96. The descriptive statistics for YR 2 follow.

- ▪ Mean = 2,997,941.96
- ▪ Median = 3,073,334
- ▪ Skewness = .5728

The skewness calculations of the governmental funds are not as great as the other companies reviewed, but as long as the skewness is positive, the data meets the requirements for use with Benford's Law. Figure 7.18 illustrates the first-two-digits test of YR 2 for the governmental funds.

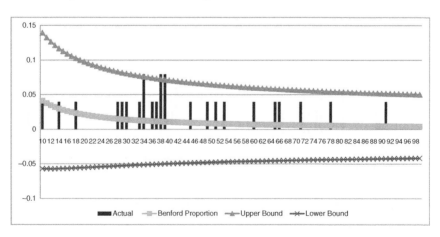

FIGURE 7.18 First-Two-Digits Test of YR 2 for the Governmental Funds of Company 3

The actual frequencies of the first two digits in point 34 having a z-statistic of 2.126 actually have the lowest z-statistic when compared to the 5% significant level of 1.96. Point 38 has a z-statistic of 2.307, while point 39 has a z-statistic of 2.350. The first two digits of numbers of account balances associated with point 34 include due-to-other funds and interest expense. Point 38 includes the first two digits of account balances for inventory and notes receivable. The final point, point 39, includes the first two digits of account balances for due-from-other funds and debt service. The due-from-other funds, due-to-other funds, and debt service also have actual frequencies greater than 1.96 in the first-two-digits test of YR 1. Remember also that in YR 2, Benford's Law pointed out variations in both interest income and interest expense.

The first-two-digits test for YR 3 displays only one point, point 86, that is greater than the upper-limit boundaries and exceeds 1.96. The descriptive statistics for YR 3 follow.

■ Mean = 3,056,219.875
■ Median = 1,588,586.5
■ Skewness = .77703

Figure 7.19 shows the first-two-digits test of YR 3 for the governmental funds.

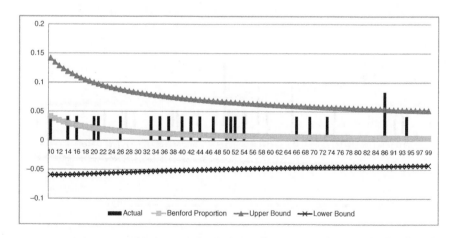

FIGURE 7.19 First-Two-Digits Test of YR 3 for the Governmental Funds of Company 3

A financial forensic examiner can easily tell that the actual frequencies of the first two digits in the financial statement data that comprise point 86 are significantly over the upper-limit boundaries. Actually, the z-statistic for point 86 is 3.984. There are only two account balances where the first two digits represent the variations of point 86, capital outlay and general and administrative expenses. As with any actual frequency that exceeds the 5% significant level threshold of 1.96, the financial forensic examiner must review the underlying data of the financial statement account balance to determine whether the account balance contains fraudulent activity.

The first-two-digits test for YR 4 includes three points where the actual frequencies of the first two digits exceed the expected frequencies of Benford's Law. Figure 7.20 illustrates the first-two-digits test, and the descriptive statistics follow.

- Mean = 2,879,473.542
- Median = 963,151.5
- Skewness = .8100

Although the illustrations noted so far in the study of the companies more than display the types of deviations found so far, this illustration includes one point, point 54, whose z-statistic is 5.2438, the highest difference so far when compared to the threshold of 1.96. The first two digits of point 54 include the first two digits of the account balances for investments, accounts receivable,

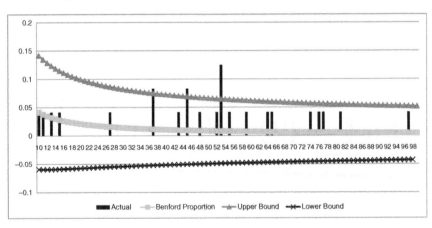

FIGURE 7.20 First-Two-Digits Test of YR 4 for the Governmental Funds of Company 3

and prepaid expenses. The second set of first two digit numbers whose actual frequencies exceed the expected frequencies of Benford's Law is point 45. The first two digits of account balances associated with point 45 include accounts payable and charges for services. The last point, point 37, includes the first two digits of account balances for deferred revenues and tax revenues.

If the financial forensic examiner has a good understanding of governmental accounting, the account relationships in those accounts where the actual frequencies exceed the expected frequencies in the governmental funds become apparent. Taxes billed, but not yet received, comprise a large portion of accounts receivable. Property taxes also comprise a portion of deferred revenues. Even though the first-two-digits test is a test of reasonableness, all of the accounts associated with the exceptions noted in the first-two-digits test for YR 2 require a study of the underlying data that represents the account balances in the financial statements.

The descriptive statistics that follow signify the financial statement data for YR 5 applicable for using Benford's Law for analysis. The first-two-digits test for YR 5 shows only one point, point 59, where the actual frequencies of the two digits are in excess of the expected frequencies. Figure 7.21 displays the first-two-digits test for YR 5.

- Mean = 2,930,032.64
- Median = 1,123,927
- Skewness = .9535

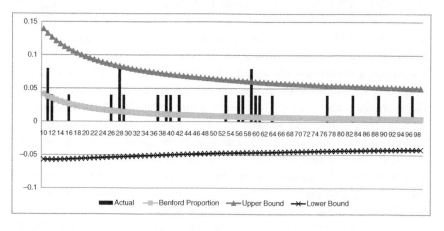

FIGURE 7.21 First-Two-Digits Test of YR 5 for the Governmental Funds of Company 3

The z-statistic for point 59 is 3.096, definitely exceeding the threshold of 1.96. The actual frequencies of the first two digits that exceed the estimated frequencies noted in Benford's Law apply to the first two digits of account balances associated with cash and accrued liabilities. Once more, since the actual z-statistic for point 59 exceeds 1.96, the financial forensic examiner needs to review the underlying data to ensure the account balances do not contain fraudulent transactions.

The first-two-digits test for all of the years under study shows four points where the actual frequencies of the first two digits exceed the upper-limit boundaries in the Benford's Law analysis and exceed the 5% significant level, requiring additional investigations of the underlying data for these areas. The descriptive statistics for all of the years under study follow.

- Mean = 2,831,428.207
- Median = 1,109,795
- Skewness = .8163

Point 37 has a z-statistic of 3.482 and the first two digits of the account balances connected to this point include interest expense for YR 1, accrued liabilities for YR 2, deferred revenues for both YR 3 and YR 4, and tax revenues for both YR 4 and YR 5. Both the deferred revenues and tax revenues for YR 4 are consistent with Benford's Law analysis for YR 4. The z-statistic for point 45 is 2.193 and includes the first two digits of the account balances for accounts receivable for YR 1, charges for services for both YR 2 and YR 4, and accounts payable for YR 4. Both accounts payable and charges for services in YR 4 are consistent with the Benford's Law analysis for YR 4. Point 53's z-statistic is 3.564, the largest variation from 1.96 compared to the other three points. The first two digit numbers of the account balances associated with point 53 start with other revenues for YR 2, investments for YR 4, accounts receivable for YR 4, prepaid expenses for YR 4, and capital outlay for YR 5. Investments, accounts receivable, and prepaid expenses for YR 4 are consistent with Benford's Law findings for YR 4. The final point, point 97, has a z-statistic of 2.678. The first two digit numbers of the account balances connected to point 97 include the pension and social security payments for YR 1 and general and administrative expenses for both YR 4 and YR 5. None of these items existed in any of the previous first-two-digits tests.

When using Benford's Law as a test of reasonableness, the testing for the primary government, and especially the governmental funds, show areas where the financial forensic examiner needs to examine the underlying data that comprise the account balances to determine if the data includes fraudulent transactions. Constantly finding variations in the first-two-digit tests, testing not only for each year but for all of the years under study, raises questions as to whether the financial statements are free from manipulated data, definitely requiring additional analytical and investigative techniques.

Company 4

By using Benford's Law as a test of reasonableness on Company 4, the financial forensic examiner begins to understand that not all variations in the number frequencies relate to fraudulent activity, but may connect with actual events occurring during the same time that affects the analysis. Yet until the financial forensic examiner investigates the underlying causes of these variations, it is possible that the variations suggest possible fraudulent activity. The descriptive statistics for YR 1 follow, and Figure 7.22 illustrates the results of the first-two-digits test for the same year. Remember the financial statements for Company 4 are in thousands and so are the Benford's Law analyses.

- Mean = 36,416.05263
- Median = 20,977
- Skewness = 2.522

In YR 1, there are two points illustrated where the actual frequencies of the first two digits of numbers in the set of data exceed the expected frequencies of

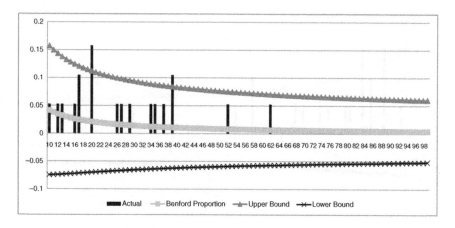

FIGURE 7.22 First-Two-Digits Test of YR 1 for Company 4

Benford's Law. The z-statistic for point 20 is 3.341, while the z-statistic for point 39 is 2.8403. Both exceed the 5% significance level and require additional study. The first two digits of the account balances connected to point 20 include fixed assets, the current portion of long-term debt and sales. The first two digits of account balances associated with point 39 include accounts receivable and other assets. Usually, the Benford Law test comes first, prior to other analytical techniques, so these accounts require additional study in order to determine whether the anomalies suggest possible fraudulent activities. By investigating the underlying data, the financial forensic examiner could determine whether the anomalies represent actual occurrences or possible fraudulent activity.

Figure 7.23 displays the first-two-digits test for YR 2 after completing the descriptive statistics to determine the data appropriate for using Benford's Law. The descriptive statistics follow:

- Mean = 38,158.78947
- Median = 18,416
- Skewness = 2.5438

There are three points where the actual frequencies of the first two digits of the data exceed the expected frequencies of Benford's Law in YR 2. Point 15 has a z-statistic of 2.7346, point 20 has a z-statistic of 3.3412, and point 46 has a z-statistic of 3.1542. All three points exceed the 5% significance z-statistic of 1.96, so they do require additional investigative procedures. When reviewing the information concerning point 20, the first two digits of the account

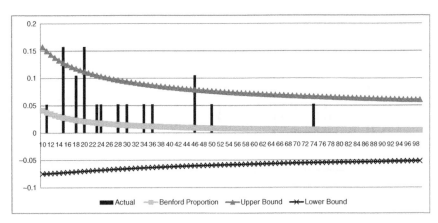

FIGURE 7.23   First-Two-Digits Test of YR 2 for Company 4

balances connected to this point include other assets, current portion of long-term debt, and cost of sales. Point 46 includes the first two digits of the account balances connected to stockholders' equity and other expenses. Finally, point 15 includes the first two digits of the account balances associated with prepaid expenses, miscellaneous income, and general and administrative expenses.

The descriptive statistics for YR 3 that follow designate the data appropriate for analysis with Benford's Law:

- Mean = 51,473.15789
- Median = 16,131
- Skewness = 2.6193

Since the first-two-digits test found only one point where the actual frequencies of the data exceed the expected frequencies of Benford's Law, the illustration of the test is not necessary. The z-statistic for point 16 is 2.8653, definitely exceeding the threshold of 1.96. The first two digits of the account balances connected to point 16 include other assets, other liabilities, and notes payable. The first-two-digits tests for both YR 1 and YR 2 identified variations in other assets as well as YR 3. From the notes to the financial statements, other assets include such items as goodwill; intangible assets, such as patents and production rights; and deferred tax assets, to mention a few. The asset quality index (AQI) of the Beneish M-Score model includes these items for testing, as well as other assets. The leverage index (LVGI) of the Beneish M-Score model tests current portion of long-term debt as well as long-term debt payable over time.

As with YR 3, the first-two-digits test for YR 4 found only one point where the actual frequencies of the two digits in the financial statement data exceed the expected frequencies in Benford's Law, so the illustration of the test is not necessary. However, the descriptive statistics follow, since they measure the appropriateness of the data before applying Benford's Law.

- Mean = 63,688.36842
- Median = 18,370
- Skewness = 2.5067

The z-statistic for point 24 is 3.7606, and since it is greater than the threshold of 1.96, the financial forensic examiner must perform additional studies on the data. The first two digits of the account balances connected to point 24 include the allowance for doubtful accounts, income tax expense, and general and administrative expenses. The allowance for doubtful accounts is a discretionary accrual measured by using Jones Nondiscretionary Accruals. The testing of the discretionary accruals in Chapter 5 shows the accruals remaining comparatively stable in YR 4. By using the SGAI index of the Beneish M-Score model, the financial forensic examiner is able to use a second analytical technique to review the general and administrative expenses.

The following descriptive statistics ensure that the financial statement data of YR 5 is appropriate prior to using Benford's Law for analysis:

- Mean = 64,727.61
- Median = 23,556
- Skewness = 2.406421

The first-two-digits test for YR 5 shows three points where the actual frequencies in the first two digits of the financial statements exceed the upper-limit boundaries in Benford's Law as well as the expected frequencies. Figure 7.24 displays the first-two-digits test for YR 5.

The three points displayed as anomalies in the expected frequencies of the first two digits include points 23, 33, and 39. The z-statistic for point 23 is 3.7926 and represents the greatest variation in the actual frequencies from the expected frequencies of Benford's Law. The z-statistic for point 39 is 2.9431 while the z-statistic for point 33 is 2.6391. The first two digits of the account balances associated with point 23 include cash, other assets, and general and administrative expenses. The first two digits of the account balances connected

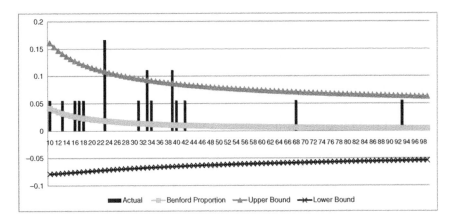

FIGURE 7.24   First-Two-Digits Test of YR 5 for Company 4

to point 39 include inventory and accounts payable, and the first two digits of the account balances connected to point 33 include fixed assets and other expenses. The financial forensic examiner can use the TAPTA (total accounts payable to total accruals), a drill-down of the Beneish M-Score model, to test accounts payable, and TITA (total inventory to total assets), another drill-down of the Beneish M-Score model, to test inventory, and, of course, detailed examination of the underlying documents that make up the account balances.

When combining all of the financial statements under study into one set of data, the descriptive statistics that follow find the data appropriate for using in Benford's Law:

- Mean = 50,475.61702
- Median = 17,906.5
- Skewness = 2.67964

The first-two-digits test for all of the years under study shows three points, points 20, 34, and 39, where the actual frequencies of the first two digits in the account balances exceed the upper-limit boundaries as well as the threshold of 1.96. The z-statistic for point 20 is 3.229, representing the greatest difference from the threshold. Interestingly, all of the first two digits of the account balances connected to point 20 include findings in one of the previous years' studies with the exception of one account balance, prepaid expenses for YR 4. The z-statistic for point 39 is 2.4395. The first two digits of the account balances connected to point 39 are all associated with findings in one of the prior years' studies. The z-statistic of point 34 is 2.143, representing the least distance from the threshold of 1.96. The first two digits of the account balances associated with point 34 include accounts payable in YR 1, inventory in YR 2, and cost of sales in both YR 4 and YR 5. This is the first finding for all of the accounts connected to point 34.

Even though the financial statements for Company 4 are free from fraudulent transactions and earnings manipulation, Benford's Law still finds variations in the actual frequencies of the first two digit numbers of amounts in the financial statements compared to the expected frequencies. These variations do not necessarily suggest possible fraudulent activities because the first-two-digits test of Benford's Law is a test of reasonableness. However, the variations essentially suggest the analysis of the first two digits of those accounts fail the reasonableness test. Yet, the variations do point to areas where the financial forensic examiner needs to perform additional work. The additional work may include other uses of Benford's Law on detailed data, inspection of the underlying documents representing the area under question, other analytical techniques, or a combination of any of these. In the instance of Company 4, a combination of analytical techniques and inspections provided sufficient information to determine the financial statements did not contain earnings manipulation or fraudulent transactions in the underlying data.

Benford's Law offers the financial forensic examiner a method to determine the reasonableness of the financial data and provides a roadmap to variations that require further investigative work and an excellent tool to drill down effectively through large sets of data to particular items. Even though designed for large sets of data, Benford's Law is also an effective tool in analyzing financial statements as long as the data meets the requirements necessary to use the analysis, as in the studies of the four companies. Just remember that the data in the financial statements must not include totals and negative numbers when determining the appropriateness of the data. The same restraints also apply to trial balances; when the data is appropriate, Benford's Law points to possible variations requiring additional investigative techniques in trial balances as well as financial statements.

SIMPLE STATISTICS

Often overlooked, basic statistical techniques have a place in the financial forensic examiner's toolbox. The tests included in this chapter are very basic, do not require advanced mathematical knowledge, and are very effective in pointing to anomalies in financial statements suggesting possible fraudulent activities. However, the financial forensic examiner must understand some of the more common statistical terms in order to relate the tests to financial forensics:

- A *population* is all that one wants to study or analyze.
- A *variable* represents a characteristic of each item in the population.
- A *sample* is a group of items within the population.
- *Variation* describes how the items in the population are different from each other.
- The *mean* is the mathematical average of a population or a sample.
- The *median* is the middle value of a list of numbers sorted from the smallest to the largest number.
- The *standard deviation* measures the spread of either the population or the sample.

These statistical terms are used within this chapter's testing.

Statistical data in this chapter is generated by Microsoft Excel and its Data Analysis feature (http://office .microsoft.com/en-us/excel/).

Since the financial statement data for the four companies represents small sets of data, only some of the statistical tools available in Excel are useful for these sets of data. Many of the other statistical tools in Excel provide the financial forensic examiner with pragmatic evidential matter, especially some of the statistical testing related to comparing sample data to a population or another sample. Many of the statistical tools are extremely useful when analyzing samples of the detailed information underlying the financial statement information.

One tool that is quite useful for the analysis of each company's financial data is the descriptive statistics tool in the Data Analysis pack of Excel, which provides a summary of statistical information rather than using the individual formulas found in Excel. This tool easily calculates the mean, median, and standard deviation, along with other information related to the data that allows the financial forensic examiner to determine the inconsistencies of the data. However, there are individual formulas in Excel that will also calculate these. While the median and the standard deviation individual formulas are easy to identify, the AVERAGE (range) actually calculates the median. The mean, median, and the standard deviation are important statistical measures used in the analysis of the financial statements for each of the four companies. Although the discussions related to statistical testing concern the population, in many instances the term *sample* also applies. For example, the years under study form the population for the statistical tests in this chapter, while each of the individual years under study represents a sample of the population.

Understanding the shape of the population is also important in determining which statistical theories to use in analyzing the data. A very easy method to understand the shape and spread of the data is to use a *scatter plot*. The scatter plot provides the financial forensic examiner the ability to determine the shape of the data visually, rather than using a histogram to determine it. A scatter plot is also useful in finding outliers of the population that may represent unusual variations in the data or the

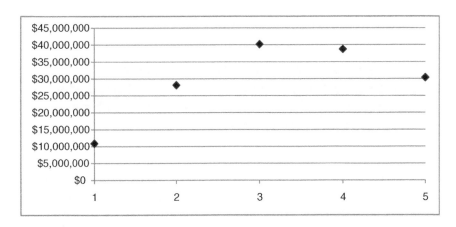

FIGURE 7.25   Scatter Plot of a Normal Distribution

correlation between two sets of data. Figure 7.25 provides an example of how the data falls within the population. The shape is very important in that it illustrates the famous *bell curve* known in statistics as a characteristic of a symmetrical normal distribution. The slight slant to the curve relates to the small size of the population, which can sometimes distort the shape. This is an important factor in performing additional analytics.

One other method that is relatively easy for the financial forensic examiner to use is to calculate the first and third quartile of the population using the formula in Excel and, adding these numbers to the minimum, median, and maximum calculations from the descriptive statistics, sort from lowest to highest number, then graph the results using a pie chart. By segregating the data in the chart, the financial forensic examiner obtains a better overall picture of the spread of the data. Figure 7.26 shows the same data as Figure 7.25, using a pie chart to show the dispersion of the maximum, median, and minimum of the population.

By using the pie chart, the financial forensic examiner is able to determine the spread of the data across the population, noting that both the median and the minimum percentages closely total the maximum percentage. Once again, a smaller set of data will somewhat distort the characteristics of a symmetrical normal distribution, but the chart does indicate some symmetry in the population. In some of the testing, the financial forensic examiner will not see this type of distribution.

When the population is normally distributed and have the characteristics of the data shown in both Figures 7.25 and 7.26, there is a statistical theorem noted in statistical books as the "Empirical Rule" that allows the financial

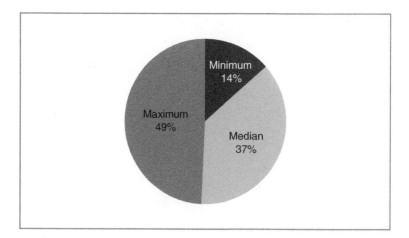

FIGURE 7.26 Pie Chart of a Normal Distribution

forensic examiner to analyze the data easily. The theorem provides a simple analysis of the data that ultimately points to variations in the data, but first the financial forensic examiner must calculate the standard deviation and the mean of the population. Once those calculations are complete, the financial forensic examiner follows these basic rules:

- Approximately 68% of the data values fall within one standard deviation of the mean.

  Mean + or − Standard Deviation

- Approximately 95% of the data values fall within two standard deviations of the mean.

  Mean + or − (2 × Standard Deviation)

- Approximately 99.7% of the data values fall within three standard deviations of the mean.

  Mean + or − (3 × Standard Deviation)

So far, the financial forensic examiner knows how to analyze a population using the Empirical Rule, but that applies only to symmetrical normal distributions. Many times the population will not follow the characteristics of a normal distribution. Figure 7.27 illustrates a scatter plot of data that does not conform to the characteristics of a normal distribution.

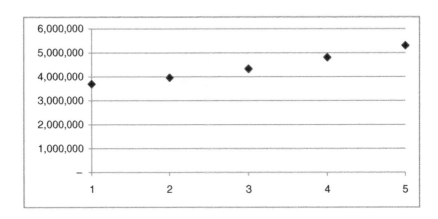

FIGURE 7.27   Scatter Plot for a Different Type of Distribution

The financial forensic examiner can easily see the difference in this type of distribution compared to the normal distribution because there is *no bell-shaped curve* to the data. Figure 7.28 displays the pie chart for the data and, once again, the financial forensic examiner can see the differences in the percentages, indicating the data is not symmetrical.

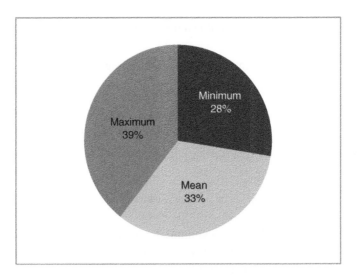

FIGURE 7.28   Pie Chart for a Different Type of Distribution

There are other types of distributions that will exhibit different characteristics compared to Figures 7.27 and 7.28, but will not display the characteristics of a symmetrical normal distribution, so the Empirical Rule will not apply. Another theorem will apply to these types of distributions, but is rarely used. When the scatter plot of a population illustrates anything but a bell-shaped curve, *Chebyshev's Theorem*, found in statistical books, applies to these types of distributions. The theorem also uses both the mean and the standard deviation, so the financial forensic examiner must complete the descriptive statistics first. Although the process is somewhat similar to the Empirical Rule, there are differences:

- At least 75% of all data will lie in the range of the mean + or − (2 × standard deviation).
- At least 89% of all data will lie in the range of the mean + or − (3 × standard deviation).
- At least 94% of all data will lie in the range of the mean + or − (4 × standard deviation).

Now the financial forensic examiner knows two important tests to apply to a population to analyze for possible variations. Other statistical tests used in examining the financial data of each of the four companies will include discussions, because they may not be appropriate for all sets of data.

Company 1

The financial statement balances for accounts receivable begin the financial statement analysis for Company 1, since the DRSI index of the Beneish M-Score model in Chapter 4 shows all of the years, with the exception of YR 5, over the general benchmark of 1. Figure 7.29 displays the scatter plot for the accounts receivable balances.

This chart includes a regression line to assist the forensic examiner in determining the variability of the data. The type of regression line that best represents the data should have an *R-squared* calculation that equals 1. This particular regression line is a *polynomial regression line* that has an R-squared calculation closest to 1. The shape of the data in the chart indicates that the distribution of the data is somewhat skewed to the right, so the Empirical Rule will not be effective, but the financial forensic examiner can use Chebyshev's Theorem to assess the data. To use this technique, the financial forensic examiner needs to calculate both the mean and the standard deviation of

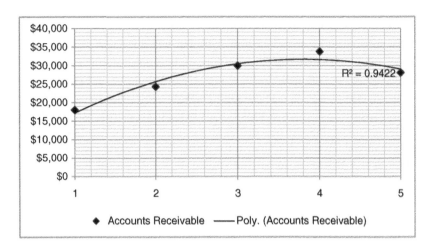

FIGURE 7.29 AR Scatter Plot for Company 1

the population. The mean and the standard deviation of the financial data associated with accounts receivable are $26,859 and $5,373.01, respectively. By using the formula in Excel, "STDEVP," the financial forensic examiner is able to find the standard deviation of the population, which is the total of the years under study. The entire set of data falls within the 75% rule of Chebyshev's Theorem, with boundaries of $16,113 and $37,605.

The scatter plot with the polynomial regression tells the financial forensic examiner a lot of information, showing that both YR 1 and YR 5 are significantly lower than the calculated trend, while YR 4 is significantly higher than the calculated trend. While the DSRI index did not show YR 5 above the general benchmark, YR 4 exceeds the general benchmark of 1. Even though the DRSI index measures the changes from year to year, the financial forensic examiner can still use this measure as a comparison of trends between the two different analyses.

Probably the best analysis for accounts receivable for Company 1 is to compare the accounts receivable balances with the sales balances in a scatter plot. Figure 7.30 illustrates the scatter plots for both accounts receivable and sales in one chart, along with their respective linear regressions.

The financial forensic examiner will find some interesting variations in this plot concerning the relationships with sales and accounts receivable. For example, in YR 2, sales decrease and accounts receivables increase, suggesting the possibility of delayed payments and/or extensions of credit. Yet in YR 3,

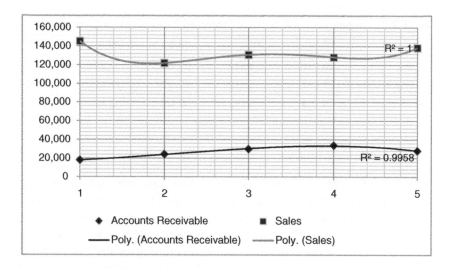

FIGURE 7.30 Scatter Plot for AR and Sales of Company 1

sales increase as well as accounts receivable. The DSRI for YR 3 was also in excess of the general benchmark of 1, as well as the SGI index.

Since there is a relationship between sales and accounts receivable, the financial forensic examiner can use the regression analysis technique to determine the reliability of the accounts receivable balances based on sales. The financial forensic examiner must first adjust sales for actual cash sales, since these amounts do not relate to the accounts receivable balances. In the case of Company 1, about 5% of total sales are cash sales, so the sales figures require adjusting by this amount. When using regression analysis, though, one must be careful in the notations for the x and y values, because the y values in the regression analysis are recalculated for projected amounts. Thus, for Company 1's situation, the sales amounts are the x values and the y values are the accounts receivable balances.

It is also wise to use a confidence level in determining the projected amounts, and the analysis here and all of the other regression analyses in this chapter use a 95% confidence level. The regression analysis in Excel does require the data to be in a columnar format, or the analysis will not be correct. Table 7.2 illustrates the results of the regression analysis for accounts receivable. Remember that regression analysis is just another method of determining the reasonableness of the data, but does point to variations in the financial data for the financial forensic examiner to study further.

TABLE 7.2 Comparison of Actual and Projected Receivables for Company 1

	YR 1	YR 2	YR 3	YR 4	YR 5
Actual A/R	18,011	24,345	29,994	33,807	28,138
Projected A/R	22,674	30,638	27,569	28,425	24,989
Difference	−4,663	−6,293	2,425	5,382	3,149

Another area of concern noted in the study of Company 1 when using the Beneish M-Score model is depreciation expenses. However, performing additional statistical analysis is not necessary, since the change in accumulated depreciation from year to year is the same as the depreciation expense recorded in that year. Although the scatter plot for depreciation is not required for illustration purposes, the chart does indicate an unusual anomaly in YR 3 that also affects the DEPI index calculations for YR 4. Both depreciation expense and accumulated depreciation fall within the 75% rule of Chebyshev's Theorem.

Small populations, such as with the financial data of each of the four companies, do limit the types of statistical testing used on these sets of data and pose a challenge to the financial forensic examiner. Sometimes the best statistical test to use is the scatter plot because it is simple to prepare, and, by adding an appropriate trend line available in Excel to show the trend of the data, variations become quite apparent. Scatter plots work well for either small or large sets of data for a simple, quick method of finding outliers in the sample or population. For the type of data found in Company 2's financial statements, scatter plots and regression analysis are effective tools that do not require advanced mathematical degrees to understand; they are easy to use and it is easy to understand the results from the testing.

Even for small sets of data, such as the data for each of the four companies, there is yet another statistical tool useful to the financial forensic examiner, showing any extreme inconsistencies in the data that require additional study—the *Z-score*. The formula for the Z-score is not that complicated, since it only requires the actual data point, the mean, and the standard deviation, whether they come from a sample or a population.

$$Z = (\text{Data Point} - \text{Mean})/\text{Standard Deviation}$$

There is an easier way to calculate the Z-score just by using the STANDARDIZE formula in Excel. This Excel formula is the same as the formula shown for the Z-score. The Z-scores used in the analysis of the four companies

TABLE 7.3   Z-Scores for Specific Financial Statement Balances of Company 1

Account	YR 1	YR 2	YR 3	YR 4	YR 5
Accounts Receivable	−1.6467	−0.4679	0.5835	1.2931	0.2380
Sales	1.5131	−1.3662	−0.2569	−0.5663	0.6762
Depreciation	−0.7806	−0.8696	1.8759	−0.3250	0.0993
General and Administrative Expenses	−0.8908	0.2482	−0.9035	−0.2598	1.8059

use the population standard deviation as part of the calculations, since the analysis relates to all five years under study; otherwise, the standard deviation calculation to use is the standard deviation of the sample. Table 7.3 illustrates the Z-score calculations for accounts receivables, sales, depreciation, and sales and administrative expenses, representing the areas in question in some of the prior testing.

Now the financial forensic examiner knows that in both YR 1 and YR 4, the accounts receivable balances have excessive inconsistencies that require further investigation. The financial statement balances for sales have excessive variations in the data for both YR 1 and YR 2, suggesting that the financial forensic examiner needs to perform additional investigative work because the Z-score indicates extreme inconsistencies within the underlying data. Depreciation has one year, YR 3, where the Z-score indicates the underlying data has some unusual outliers that require further investigation while the Z-score for general and administrative expenses points to YR 5 for additional investigative work.

Company 2

Upon completing the discussion associated with the importance of the Z-score, the statistical analysis of the financial statements for Company 2 and the remaining three companies begins with the Z-score calculations for account balances identified in the various indices of the Beneish M-Score as having indices greater than the benchmarks. Table 7.4 displays the Z-score calculations for these financial statement account balances.

From Table 7.4, the financial statement data for YR 1 has quite a bit of variability, since all of the Z-score calculations show excessive data measurements from the mean while the other years are not that consistent. The measurement of the data in the Z-score analysis relates to the number of standard deviations from the mean, so a negative one would indicate a

TABLE 7.4   Z-Scores for Specific Financial Statement Balances of Company 2

Account	YR 1	YR 2	YR 3	YR 4	YR 5
Accounts Receivable	−1.6813	1.4540	0.1664	−0.0915	0.1524
Inventory	−1.6409	0.2658	−0.3156	0.2504	1.4403
Sales	−1.7927	−0.1451	1.0044	0.8673	0.0661
Cost of Sales	−1.8005	−0.1037	1.0366	0.8228	0.0477
Depreciation	−1.4183	−0.8347	0.2152	0.7280	1.3097
General and Administrative Expenses	−1.7846	0.1618	1.2853	0.3688	−0.0312

measurement of distance that is one standard deviation less than the mean, while a positive one would indicate a measurement of distance that is one standard deviation more than the mean. While the measurement may appear small, remember both the Empirical Rule and Chebyshev's Theorem, and a measurement in excess of 1 is significant. As with Company 1, the amounts noted in the table all fall within the 75% rule of Chebyshev's Theorem.

Excluding YR 1, the Z-scores for both depreciation and general and administrative expenses show the need for additional study. The Z-score for general and administrative expenses in YR 3 indicates variability, suggesting unusual variations in the data for that year. The Z-score for depreciation suggests unusual variability in YR 5. Remember that in YR 5, Company 2 had a non-cash sale relating to one of its production facilities becoming an independent company, so the effect of these transactions influences the Z-score of depreciation for YR 5.

Sales and cost of sales definitely relate to each other, and previous discussions in the other chapters indicate that cost of sales should normally be consistent with changes in sales. By using a scatter plot with smooth lines for comparison, the financial forensic examiner can better see the relationship between sales and cost of sales. Figure 7.31 illustrates the sales and cost of sales relationship for Company 2.

The financial forensic examiner should expect these lines to be parallel because the company's products are unique and the overall profit margins on the different types of products do not change from year to year, since any increases in production costs pass over to the consumer. While the variation is subtle, the two lines are not parallel and not proportioned equally, especially between YR 2 and YR 3 and once again between YR 4 and YR 5. Compare the lines in Figure 7.31 to the lines in Figure 7.34 for Company 4, and the variations are more noticeable.

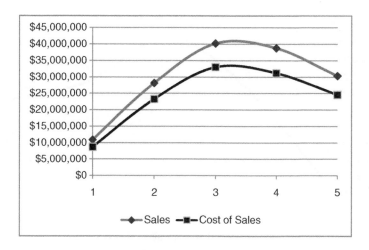

FIGURE 7.31 Sales and Cost of Sales for Company 2

Since the relationship of sales and cost of sales posed several suggestions of unusual variations, the financial forensic examiner can perform a regression analysis in Excel comparing the actual cost of sales to predicted cost of sales based on the trends of sales. Table 7.5 shows the results of the regression analysis of the financial statement balances for cost of sales.

The regression analysis does not show much of a difference in YR 1, but the analysis does question the reasonableness of the data for the years under study. Another interesting factor for YR 5 concerns the difference in the predicted cost of sales and the variability of the inventory Z-score for YR 5. These areas, needless to say, require additional study of the underlying data that makes up the financial statement balances for these accounts.

Although the Z-score calculations for general and administrative expenses in Table 7.4 show unusual variability in the data, there is another way to review the difference visually by preparing a dual-axis chart showing the shape

TABLE 7.5 Regression Analysis of Cost of Sales for Company 2

COS	YR 1	YR 2	YR 3	YR 4	YR 5
Actual	8,737,104	23,312,675	33,082,011	31,270,725	24,613,108
Predicted	8,811,756	22,957,353	32,826,572	31,649,409	24,770,532
Difference	−74,652	355,322	255,439	−378,684	−157,424

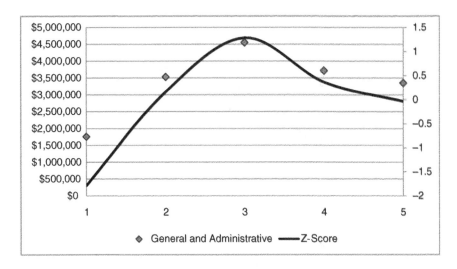

FIGURE 7.32 General and Administrative Expenses and the Z-Scores of Company 2

of the data for general and administrative expenses along with the calculations of the Z-score. Figure 7.32 displays the dual-axis chart for both the Z-score and the actual general and administrative expenses for Company 2.

By doing the dual-axis chart, the financial forensic examiner gets a better picture of the extreme variations in the data shown by the Z-score calculations. For example, from the chart, both YR 1 and YR 3 show variations, suggesting further additional work. In YR 1, the Z-score is over a negative one, but also shows a great distance between the x statistic and the data. However, in YR 3 the data shows an extreme variance in the opposite direction from the other years under study with the Z-score in excess of a positive one and a significant increase in the expense for the year. Both YR 2 and YR 4 show little variation in both the data and the Z-score while YR 5 shows only a slight difference.

Company 3

As with all of the other analyses already completed for Company 3, the basic statistical analyses apply to each of the primary government's financial statements and the governmental funds' financial statements. Like Company 2, the analysis begins with the Z-scores from some of the more significant areas in the financial statements, such as receivables, payables, tax revenues, general

TABLE 7.6 Z-Scores for Specific Financial Statement Balances of the Primary Government of Company 3

	YR 1	YR 2	YR 3	YR 4	YR 5
Accounts Receivable	−0.1165	−0.9193	−0.7724	−0.0731	1.8813
Accounts Payable	−1.0574	−0.5092	1.0773	−0.8375	1.3269
Tax Revenues	−1.8871	0.5669	0.6395	−0.1480	0.8287
General and Administrative Expenses	−1.6531	0.9417	1.0014	−0.5546	0.2646
Depreciation	−1.2505	−0.7928	−0.1558	0.6722	1.5270
Property, Plant, and Equipment	−1.4262	−0.7257	0.0468	0.7196	1.3854
Accumulated Depreciation	−1.1630	−0.5453	0.1007	0.8451	1.6705

expenses, depreciation expenses, and the components of property, plant, and equipment, since these account balances only appear in the primary government's financial statements. Table 7.6 displays the Z-scores for accounts receivable, accounts payable, tax revenues, general and administrative expenses, depreciation expenses, and the components of property, plant, and equipment.

When reviewing the Z-scores for some of the more significant account balances in the financial statements, the financial forensic examiner finds several areas that have excessive variability over both YR 1 and YR 5. While the accounts receivable balances and the account payable balances have excessive variability in YR 5, tax revenues and general and administrative expenses have excessive variability in YR 1, along with accounts payable. The depreciation expense account balances and the account balances of property, plant, and equipment depreciation have excessive inconsistencies in YR 1 and YR 5, as well as accumulated depreciation. Figure 7.33 illustrates the comparison of accumulated depreciation (A/D), adjusted for retirements and sales, and depreciation expenses.

To compare accumulated depreciation changes with the only changes from year to year related to depreciation expense and not the sales or retirements of assets, adjustments are necessary to the accumulated depreciation amounts for retirements and sales of assets. The adjustment amounts follow:

- YR 1 = 30,600,337
- YR 2 = 33,901,472
- YR 3 = 38,212,382

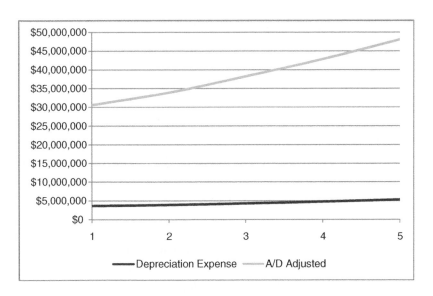

FIGURE 7.33 Comparison of A/D and Depreciation of the Primary Government of Company 3

- YR 4 = 42,803,301
- YR 5 = 48,035,860

The chart practically speaks for itself, as the financial forensic examiner can easily see that depreciation expense is slowly increasing while the adjusted accumulated depreciation is increasing at a faster rate. Table 7.7 shows the change in the adjusted accumulated depreciation from year to year and the depreciation expense recorded in the financial statements. Undoubtedly, the financial forensic examiner needs to do additional investigative work by reviewing the underlying financial data for those years where excessive variations occur.

TABLE 7.7 Comparison of Changes in A/D to Depreciation of the Primary Government for Company 3

	YR 2	YR 3	YR 4	YR 5
Change in A/D (adjusted)	3,301,135	4,310,910	4,590,919	5,232,599
Depreciation	3,966,022	4,333,368	4,810,923	5,303,901
Difference	664,887	22,458	220,004	71,342

TABLE 7.8 Z-Scores for Specific Financial Statement Balances of the Governmental Funds for Company 3

	YR 1	YR 2	YR 3	YR 4	YR 5
Accounts Receivable	−1.5391	−0.3871	−0.1496	0.6477	1.4281
Due-From Funds	−1.0690	−0.8014	−0.4668	0.8041	1.5331
Due-To Funds	−1.1758	−0.7445	−0.4118	0.8707	1.4614
Deferred Revenues	−1.7703	−0.1680	0.2208	0.4625	1.2551
Taxes	−1.5370	−0.6683	0.1271	0.9527	1.1257
General and Administrative Expense	−1.7442	0.1731	−0.3346	0.9466	0.9591
Transfers In	−0.6296	1.4958	0.8081	−1.2318	0.4425
Transfers Out	0.0654	0.7837	1.3434	−0.8017	−1.3908

One comparison in the chart that requires additional scrutiny is the variability in YR 3 for both accounts payable and general and administrative expenses. Although there is a relationship between general and administrative expenses and accounts payable, regression analysis is not appropriate unless the financial forensic examiner removes all cash elements from the general and administrative expenses. Because of the cash element involved in the account balance for general and administrative expenses, the financial forensic examiner must review the underlying data for these account balances. Since tax revenues presented in the primary government's financial statements are full accrual, a more appropriate analysis is in the governmental funds financial statements analyses that follow.

Table 7.8 displays the Z-scores for some of the relevant financial statement accounts for the governmental funds, including accounts receivable, due-from-other funds, due-to-other funds, deferred revenues, taxes, general and administrative expenses, transfers in, and transfers out.

When looking at the table, the financial forensic examiner should quickly realize the pattern between YR 1 and YR 5 for most of the account balances under study. Tax revenues relate to both accounts receivable and deferred revenues, while the due-from funds and the due-to funds are associated with the transfers in and transfers out. To pair the relationships for the due-to and due-from accounts with transfers in and transfers out, the due-from account is associated with the transfers out while the due-to account is associated with the transfers in.

Because of the relationships of the due-to and due-from accounts with the transfers in and out, the financial forensic examiner can use regression analysis

TABLE 7.9 Regression Analysis of the Transfers In Balances of the Governmental Funds for Company 3

	YR 1	YR 2	YR 3	YR 4	YR 5
Actual Transfers In	6,350,000	7,815,000	7,341,000	5,935,000	6,479,000
Predicted Transfers In	7,177,073	7,032,877	6,921,673	6,492,934	6,295,442
Difference	−827,073	782,123	419,327	−557,934	183,558

to determine the reasonableness of the account balances for the transfers in or out. Table 7.9 displays the regression analysis testing the reasonableness of the transfers in based on the due-to-other-funds account balances, while Table 7.10 displays the regression analysis testing the transfers out based on the due-from-other-funds account balances.

Even though the regression analysis is just another test of reasonableness, the statistical analysis does show that the financial forensic examiner must perform additional investigative work related to these account balances by inspecting the underlying documentation associated with these account balances.

By using these simple statistical analyses on the primary government's financial statements and the governmental funds' financial statements, the financial forensic is putting together a roadmap showing areas within the financial statements that have excessive variability and unusual variation suggesting the possibility of fraudulent activity. By pinpointing these areas, the financial forensic examiner is able to focus on only those areas with excessive inconsistencies and not areas that have minor variability and fluctuations, with the governmental funds at the heart of the investigative process.

TABLE 7.10 Regression Analysis of the Transfers Out Balances of the Governmental Funds for Company 3

	YR 1	YR 2	YR 3	YR 4	YR 5
Actual Transfers Out	4,753,000	5,120,000	5,406,000	4,310,000	4,009,000
Predicted Transfers Out	5,167,694	5,055,508	4,915,270	4,382,553	4,076,976
Difference	−414,694	64,492	490,730	−72,553	−67,976

Company 4

Even though the financial statements of Company 4 do not include any fraudulent activity, the basic Z-test still defines areas where there may be excessive variability or unusual variations. Company 4's statistical analyses might show variations. It is the financial forensic examiner's responsibility to determine the *causes* for the excessive variability to assess whether the unusual variations or excessive inconsistency are fraud related. Table 7.11 illustrates the Z-scores for some of the more pertinent financial statement account balances for Company 4.

TABLE 7.11 Z-Scores for Specific Financial Statement Balances of Company 4

	YR 1	YR 2	YR 3	YR 4	YR 5
Accounts Receivable	−1.4301	−0.7347	0.3129	1.4749	0.3769
Inventory	−1.7657	−0.2716	0.3283	1.2012	0.5078
Sales	−1.3632	−1.0031	0.3702	1.0538	0.9423
Cost of Sales	−1.3662	−0.9994	0.3672	1.0397	0.9586
General and Administration Expenses	−1.4118	−0.9508	0.3873	1.0178	0.9575
Depreciation	1.6092	0.1773	−0.8172	−1.2725	0.3032

Knowing the background history of the company from discussions in previous chapters, the financial forensic examiner should expect excessive variability and unusual variations in the first four years under study, with YR 5 showing more stability as the company's operations are no longer influenced by the bankruptcy of the subsidiary. Table 7.11 does not show any excessive variability in YR 5. Since the reasons for the unusual and excessive variations noted in Table 7.11 appear in other discussions, the only item discussed here includes sales and cost of sales because of the importance of the relationship of these two account balances.

Figure 7.34 displays this relationship for Company 4. Remember that this relationship is generally consistent and lines in the graph should be parallel.

When reviewing Figure 7.34, the financial forensic examiner can see that for the most part the lines are parallel even though gross profit, the space between the lines, is increasing. Unlike Company 2, the product mix for Company 4 can affect the overall gross margins when there is a sufficient quantity of sales for a particular product. However, even these sets of circumstances do not swerve the cost of sales lines significantly. When comparing Figure 7.34 with Figure 7.31, the financial forensic examiner will begin to see

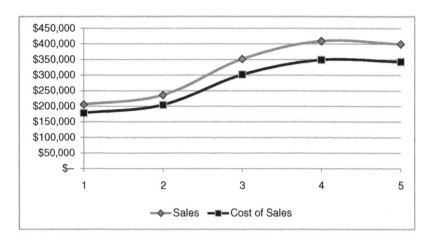

FIGURE 7.34 Scatter Plot of Sales and Cost of Sales for Company 4

the subtle differences in graphical presentations and train the mind to focus on minute details.

 ## SUMMARY

Even though the study of financial statements may involve small sets of data, the financial forensic examiner does have additional analytical tools that will effectively analyze small sets of data and point to areas of excessive and unusual variations. Using the tools appropriately for the smaller sets of data is a priority; incorrect usage of the tools provides the financial forensic examiner with false information. Once the analytical tests define the areas of unusual variations, the investigation can focus on the underlying data that makes up the financial statement account balances. These tools provide the financial forensic examiner with the ability to assess the reasonableness of the data.

Benford's Law analyzes naturally occurring numbers, such as the numbers in the financial statement account balances, and points to variations of the actual frequencies of the digits of numbers compared to the expected frequencies found in Benford's Law. The financial forensic examiner must first determine that the numbers meet the requirements in order to use Benford's Law, make negative numbers positive, and remove all totals and subtotals before beginning the analysis. To use Benford's Law for small sets of data, the financial forensic examiner must determine that the mean is greater than the median and the skewness of the small set of data is positive; otherwise, Benford's Law cannot be used for testing the data.

For analyzing financial statements, the first-two-digits test is a more refined test of reasonableness and can find anomalies in the actual frequencies of account balances that may not show in the first-digit test. The z-statistic of 1.96 is the threshold to use when comparing the actual frequencies of the numbers to the expected frequencies when using a 5% significant factor, and is 2.58 when using a 1% significance factor. Regardless of the significance factor, if the calculated z-statistic exceeds the threshold, the financial forensic examiner must investigate further.

The fundamental theme that makes Benford's Law an excellent tool for the financial forensic examiner is that invented numbers do not follow Benford's Law. While the use of Benford's Law in analyzing financial statements only points to unusual variations in the numbers presented on the financial statement, it is an excellent tool to use when investigating underlying data such as invoices, payroll records, sales records, and other numerical data defined as naturally occurring numbers. By using the pictorial graphs presented in the analysis of each of the four companies, combining the results of the Benford's Law test, along with the upper-limit and lower-limit boundaries, the financial forensic examiner is able to find variations that merit further study because there will always be some natural variation in the test.

Correlation analysis allows the financial forensic examiner to measure relationships within the financial statements, such as sales and cost of sales, while regression analysis allows the financial forensic examiner to make predictions about the numerical values of the second variable, cost of sales, based on the values of the first variable, sales. Regression analysis is a test of reasonableness, like Benford's Law, but it also points to possible irregularities in the financial information. Both correlation and regression analysis require professional judgment, requiring the financial forensic examiner to perform other empirical techniques to support the conclusions of these tests, especially for prosecution.

One of the best methods to understand correlation is to use a scatter plot. The scatter plot is also useful in finding the outliers of the data, especially by adding the linear regression trend line or one of the other types of trend lines available in Excel that meet the testing requirements. The shape of the data determines which analysis is appropriate, the Empirical Rule or Chebyshev's Theorem. Many times, the shape of the data will not allow the use of the Empirical Rule, but the financial forensic examiner can use Chebyshev's

Theorem as a simple analysis of the data that shows unusual variations. Both the Empirical Rule and Chebyshev's Theorem apply to either a population or a sample. When using the Empirical Rule, the financial forensic examiner should focus attention to data that falls outside of the rule, which states that approximately 68% of the data values fall within one standard deviation of the mean. The threshold for Chebyshev's Theorem is data that falls outside the rule that at least 75% of all data will lie within the range of the mean + or – the standard deviation multiplied by 2.

Since the use of analytical techniques for small sets of data is a challenge for the financial forensic examiner studying financial statements, the appropriate techniques are necessary if the financial forensic examiner wants to avoid the false-positive issues when using an inappropriate analytical test. Another useful technique for small sets of data is the Z-score, which shows excessive variability in the data. By calculating the Z-score for significant account balances in the financial statements, the financial forensic examiner can easily find the accounts with excessive inconsistencies and perform additional investigative studies of the underlying information that makes up the account balances.

All of the tests included in this chapter provide the financial forensic examiner with methods of finding unusual inconsistencies in data, requiring further investigative work to determine whether the unusual variations suggest the possibility of fraudulent activity. These tests, along with tests included in the other chapters, provide the financial forensic examiner with sufficient information to focus the investigative process on the specific areas requiring greater attention. While possibilities of fraudulent activity may exist in other areas, the areas shown by these techniques will point the way to unusual variations where there is a strong possibility of fraudulent activity, thus making the investigation more effective and efficient.

NOTE

1. Mark J. Nigrini, "A Taxpayers Compliance Application of Benford's Law," *Journal of the American Taxation Association*, 18 (Spring 1996): 72–91.

CHAPTER EIGHT

Grading the Four Companies

FTER GOING through all of the techniques and tools discussed within the pages of this book, the case studies require summation, with each company given either a passing or a failing grade. It is relatively straightforward to summarize testing outcomes, as the financial forensic examiner need only keep a scorecard as tests are completed. The failing grades should point to areas with unusual variations, unusual relationships, or excessive variability in the financial statements from period to period that suggest the possibility of fraudulent activity. Naturally, the next step in the investigative process includes the gathering of sufficient evidence for prosecution. Here are a few points to remember about analytical tools and techniques:

- Analytical procedures, by themselves, are not sufficient evidence for prosecution.
- Not every test within the scope of this book is necessary for every engagement.
- Use multiple techniques.
- Apply results of these tools and techniques to benchmarks.

- Financial records are not always inclusive of all transactions, so the financial forensic examiner must consider the possibility of transactions occurring outside of the financial records.

There are other types of analytical techniques and tools available to the financial forensic examiner not discussed within the scope of this book. Some of these tests include analyses of trends over a period of time, aging, Monte Carlo simulations, and stratification. A *trend analysis* is most effective when multiple periods are available for analysis—the more periods available for analysis, the more accurate the testing. *Stratification* is merely segmenting a population into groups of items exhibiting similar value amounts and then sampling each stratum separately. *Aging* allows the financial forensic examiner to sort the population by date, showing older transactions that may require additional study. *Monte Carlo simulation* is a mathematical technique used to approximate the probability of certain outcomes by running multiple trial runs that essentially analyze risks. However, other tools may be easier to use and provide similar results. These also point the financial forensic examiner to areas of unusual variations that require additional investigation.

In determining the final grades for the four companies used as case studies, the scorecard will show each step of the analytical process, beginning with the more simple analytical techniques and moving to more sophisticated analytical tools, building the roadmap necessary for the financial forensic examiner to develop an effective and efficient investigation. Even though each analytical technique was part of each company's case study for illustration purposes, as the progress of the grading continues, the financial forensic examiner should be able to determine which tests met the needs of the investigation of each company and apply the process to future investigations.

COMPANY 1

Beginning with the financial statements illustrated in Chapter 1, the first step for the financial forensic examiner is to complete some very basic ratios, including liquidity and profitability ratios. The liquidity ratios discussed in Chapter 2 focus on a company's ability to pay its debts, an area of particular interest to the financial forensic examiner. The liquidity ratio analyses for Company 1 point out inconsistencies in the company's ability to manage operations effectively, with the different liquidity ratios showing significant fluctuations from year to year and suggesting the company is unable to meet its debt obligations for future years. The profitability ratios discussed in Chapter 2 measure a company's ability to make a profit, definitely an area of interest to the financial forensic examiner, since a company wants to represent that it is doing well financially. Unfortunately, the profitability ratios for Company 1 do not indicate stability, showing variations in the ratio analyses from year to year. Thus, the conclusions reached for these tests include the following notations:

■ The company is not managed effectively and is unable to pay its debts.
■ The company is unable to sustain a profit from year to year.

Remember that these analytical techniques are very basic and any conclusions reached at this point are premature.

Horizontal analysis examines the changes in the line items of the financial statements from year to year; in other words, it develops trends in the financial statements for further study. The most effective method for reviewing trends is to calculate the percentages of changes from period to period rather than dollar-amount changes, so the magnitude of the change is very apparent. In using the big-picture concept for Company 1, there are several fluctuations occurring throughout the years under study, beginning with YR 2 because YR 1 is the foundation of the calculations for YR 2. The list follows.

■ Cash changes dramatically year over year.
■ Accounts receivable changes decrease each year.
■ Sales fluctuate from year to year, either increasing or decreasing from the previous year.
■ Accounts payable varies from year to year, decreasing in YR 2 and YR 3, significantly increasing in YR 4, and then decreasing in YR 5.
■ Total expenses decrease in both YR 2 and YR 3 and then increase significantly in both YR 4 and YR 5.

Of special importance is the variations in the analysis for the line item general and administrative expenses, since these should be relatively consistent from year to year.

Not only are the line item changes important, the financial forensic examiner must also look at relationships, even with the simplest of analytical tools and techniques. Since the financial statements of the company only have accruals related to accounts receivable and payable, changes in cash become relative to the relationships. In the situation of Company 1, the horizontal relationships are inconsistent with the horizontal analysis, showing YR 1 as the exception. For the rest of the years under study, the changes in cash are not reasonable, considering the changes in the other account relationships. These inconsistencies in the horizontal analysis should supply the financial forensic examiner with the basic assumption that the financial information is troublesome and requires additional analysis.

The findings in the horizontal analysis support the first two indications of the troublesome findings from the basic liquidity and profitability ratio calculations, but the horizontal analysis starts to point to broad areas in the financial information that appear to have some inconsistencies, such as cash, accounts receivable, accounts payable, notes payable, sales, and especially general and administrative expenses. Yet, these areas are still too broad for the financial forensic examiner to be efficient, so the other analytical techniques will allow the financial forensic examiner to further refine the process, focus on areas most worthy of future study, and remove areas that may have reasonable explanations for unusual changes.

The next step for the financial forensic examiner is to use vertical analysis to put the variances in the horizontal analysis into perspective. Vertical analysis, also called *common-sizing*, relates the line items of the financial statements to a specific base item. The financial forensic examiner may use vertical analysis on the balance sheet, the income statement, and even the cash flow statement. In the instance of Company 1, vertical analysis furnishes the financial forensic examiner with several interesting points:

- After YR 1, accounts receivable remains relatively stable.
- Cash varies significantly from year to year.
- Fixed assets increases in YR 2 and YR 5.
- Accounts payable decreases in YR 3, appearing unusual compared to the other years under study.
- After YR 1, general and administrative expenses remains comparatively stable, decreasing in YR 5.
- Salaries, on the other hand, fluctuate significantly from year to year.
- Total expenses vary significantly from year to year.

Comparing the vertical analysis to the horizontal analysis, the financial forensic examiner finds both conflicting information and corroborating information that confirms that the financial information contains unusual inconsistencies that require explanation.

When analyzing the vertical analysis of the cash flow statements, the financial forensic examiner finds some additional information related to specific line items in the income statement:

- Significant fluctuations are noted in depreciation expense.
- Extreme variations are found in the changes for both accounts receivable and accounts payable.
- Significant change is found in purchases of fixed assets for YR 3.

By far, the most important point in the calculated cash flow statements relates to YR 3 and YR 5. In both of these years, the ending cash balances on the books do not agree with the calculated ending balances in the cash flow statements.

As stated in Chapter 3, cash flow statements provide the financial forensic examiner with valuable information, including the discovery of possible incentives to commit fraud or conceal fraudulent activity. Whereas it is easy to manipulate the balance sheet and the income statement, it is not easy to manipulate a cash flow statement. When the financial statements do not contain cash flow statements, the financial forensic examiner should build a cash flow statement in order to determine the uses and sources of cash.

Since the prior analytical techniques suggest unusual variations, the comparison of net income from operations and cash realized from operations (CRO) is an effective way to measure net income, along with calculating the cash realization ratio. Increases in net income and decreases in cash flows create inconsistencies in how a company operates and are warning signs to the financial forensic examiner. Fraudulent transactions may occur anywhere on the financial statements, but the results of fraudulent activity generally flow to the income statement. Even off-book fraud, such as skimming and theft of inventory, will eventually show in cost of sales as these costs increase and sales do not. Analyzing net income and cash realized from operations reveals unusual variations between net income and cash, requiring further analysis.

Generally, the cash realization ratio will be less than 1, although variances differ greatly by industry. From an operational position, a company's CRO should be higher than net income because of non-cash transactions, such as depreciation and amortization expenses, that affect net income, but not cash. The financial forensic examiner should remember also that there are ways a company can temporarily boost cash flows by extending payables, reversing expenses from prior periods, or billing customers before shipping the product. The CRO calculations for Company 1 show YR 2 outside the normal range of expectations, with a calculation of 1.16. When presenting the CRO and net income visually in a dual-axis chart, the financial forensic examiner finds that the relationships between the two are not parallel as they should be.

In Piotroski's F-Score model, this analysis also illustrates weak financial positions in both YR 2 and YR 4, with YR 3 and YR 5 scores barely hitting the average mark. More importantly, the model confirms that cash flows and earnings are weak. The model also points out that in YR 3, current operating cash flow is positive, along with net income, yet the shareholder loaned additional money to the company in that year. From Piotroski's F-Score model, the financial forensic examiner finds that profitability, liquidity, and operating efficiency receive low scores, indicating weak financial performance and thus reducing the worth of the company's stock to each of the shareholders.

Using Lev–Thiagarajan's 12 Signals, the financial forensic examiner finds several results that also corroborate the findings from other analyses and show specific areas that require additional study. The findings follow:

- Negative signals are noted for accounts receivable when compared to sales for all years, except YR 5.
- Negative signals are noted for general and administrative expenses for all years, except YR 3.

Even though not all of the 12 Signals apply to Company 1, the testing turned up these clues as areas that require further additional study.

Upon completing the analyses already discussed, the financial forensic examiner has multiple tests that indicate areas of unusual relationships or significant variations in accounts receivable, accounts payable, sales, and general and administrative expenses. Other areas not as consistent, but still unusual, include fixed assets and depreciation expenses. From this knowledge, the financial forensic examiner can now use additional sophisticated analytical techniques that measure variability in specific areas of the financial statements. By using Benford's Law, the financial forensic examiner can measure the first two digits of account balances within the financial statements to discover specific account balances whose actual frequencies of the first two digits exceed the expected frequencies of Benford's Law and exceed the z-statistic threshold.

Using Benford's Law requires the financial forensic examiner to test each year under study. The first two digits of the account balances that exceeded the threshold follow:

Findings for YR 1

- Labor costs recorded as cost of sales
- General and administrative expenses

Findings for YR 2

- No variations exceeding the expected frequencies of the first two digits test of account balances

Findings for YR 3

- General and administrative expenses
- Accounts payable

Findings for YR 4

- General and administrative expenses
- Cash
- Accounts receivable

Findings for YR 5

- Cash
- General and administrative expenses

Findings for All Years Combined

- General and administrative expenses
- Cost of sales
- Depreciation

Remember that for the purpose of testing, general and administrative expenses includes all of the itemized expenses in the income statement, excluding depreciation and interest. Even though Benford's Law is a test of reasonableness, this technique also verifies variability in general expenses for most of the years under study. The test also confirms inconsistencies in both accounts receivable and payable, although not as consistently as general and administrative expenses.

The Beneish M-Score and the indices are excellent analytical tools for studying specific relationships in a set of financial statements by giving the financial forensic examiner a general benchmark, usually 1, to use in determining the results of the tests. Not only do the indices offer detailed studies of key balances in the financial statements, the TATA index also offers further detailed analysis by breaking down the components of total accruals to total assets formula. The overall Beneish M-Score formula provides the financial forensic examiner with a broad overview of the financial statements by comparing the calculation to the benchmark of −2.22. Remembering the movement of negative numbers, −2.21 is greater than −2.22 and −2.23 is less than −2.22. If the calculation is greater than −2.22, it suggests possible manipulation in the financial statements. The overall Beneish M- Score calculations for Company 1 are −1.95, −3.49, −2.79, and −3.50 for YR 2, YR 3, YR 4, and YR 5, respectively.

The following supplies the results of the analyses of each index for Company 1:

- DSRI testing shows that all years, except for YR 5, are over the general benchmark of 1.
- GMI testing shows YR 2 and YR 3 over the general benchmark of 1.
- AQI testing is reasonable.
- SGI testing shows that YR 3 and YR 5 are over the general benchmark of 1.
- DEPI testing shows that YR 2 and YR 4 are over the general benchmark of 1.
- SGAI testing shows that all years, except YR 3, are over the general benchmark of 1.
- TATA is positive for YR 2.
- LVGI is over the general benchmark of 1 for all years, except YR 2, with YR 3 significantly over the benchmark.

In comparing the indices testing with other tests already performed, accounts receivable, sales, depreciation, cost of sales, and general and administrative expenses are areas already identified as needing further investigative work.

Knowing that accrual testing includes more than just liabilities, these analytical techniques allow the financial forensic examiner to review the reasonableness of accruals in the financial statements. Remember that accruals are the non-cash components of the financial information and easily allow management to manipulate earnings. The following explains the results of the three types of accrual testing for Company 1.

Dechow–Dichev Accrual Quality

- Low accrual quality in YR 2 and YR 3.
- Implied earnings indicate decreased earnings in YR 2 and YR 5.

Sloan's Accruals

- YR 3 shows net income as positive, but when subtracting the accrual component, net income is negative.
- YR 2 and YR 4 also have positive accrual components, but net income is already negative, so subtracting the accrual components reduces net income even further.
- YR 5 shows a negative accrual component that reduces the loss of net income.

Jones Nondiscretionary Accruals

- YR 2 shows nondiscretionary accruals decreasing, suggesting increases in discretionary accruals.
- YR 3, YR 4, and YR 5 remain comparatively consistent.

From these tests, the financial forensic examiner suspects the financial statements in YR 2 and YR 3 to have significant accruals that may not produce future cash flows. Even though YR 3 shows positive net income, the accrual components reduce net income to a net loss. In YR 5, however, accrual components reduce the net loss for the year.

The last set of analytical tools relate to statistical techniques that allow the financial forensic examiner to determine the reasonableness of the information in the financial statements. The results of the Z-score testing for Company 1 follow:

- Both YR 1 and YR 4 show inconsistencies in accounts receivable compared to the other years.
- Both YR 1 and YR 2 show inconsistencies in sales compared to the other years
- YR 3 shows inconsistencies in depreciation compared to the other years.
- YR 5 shows inconsistencies in general and administrative expenses compared to the other years.

In addition, the regression analysis test to determine the reasonableness of accounts receivable based on sales shows differences in projections running from 25% to 8%.

When reviewing the results of all of the testing, much of it points to accounts receivable, sales, depreciation, accounts payable, and general and administrative expenses as areas that require further investigative work. Remembering account relationships, it makes sense that sales and accounts receivable, along with accounts payable and general and administrative expenses, are areas requiring additional investigative work. Now that the financial forensic examiner has a roadmap showing the direction of the additional work based on multiple analytical techniques and tools confirming areas of inconsistencies, the investigation process requires detailed analysis of the underlying data of these areas. This also allows the financial forensic examiner to bypass other areas of financial information that did not show unusual variations in the testing.

Remembering the general information of the case study for Company 1, the crux of the embezzlement was to reduce the net worth of the company so that one of the shareholders could purchase the shares of another shareholder at a fraction of their true worth. To reduce the net worth of the company, the shareholder manipulated the earnings using several tactics. In many instances, the off-book bank account diverted cash sales and new customer sales to prevent recording the sales and receivables on the books. In other instances, an old account receivable, previously recorded as a bad debt but not written off the books, included reductions that were actually new cash sales. To increase general and administrative expenses, the shareholder recorded personal expenses in the books so the company would pay them, while taking a modest salary, explaining that the modest salary was the result of the company's operations not producing sufficient net income. Depreciation expenses increased one year so that additional deductions on the tax returns would reduce the net worth of each shareholder's shares. Thus, the bottom line is that the analytical techniques and tools used to analyze the financial statements pointed to areas suggesting the possibility of fraud, and further detailed examination found fraudulent activity and multiple fraudulent transactions occurring in several areas of the financial statements.

COMPANY 2

Since most of the discussions concerning the overview of the tools and techniques used in the analysis of the financial statements are included in the analysis of Company 1, beginning with Company 2, these discussions are not required and are therefore omitted in the analysis. Just like Company 1, the forensic analysis for Company 2 begins with the basic, preliminary liquidity and profitability ratios. The outcome of these tests follows.

- The liquidity ratio testing produces mixed signals.
  - The working capital indices vary significantly from year to year, although working capital does not.
  - After YR 1, working capital remains comparatively stable for YR 2 and YR 3 while increasing in YR 4 and YR 5, indicating management is effectively managing the operations of the company.
  - Working capital turnover calculations vary from year to year, similar to the working capital indices.
  - Current ratio calculations increase from year to year.
- The profitability ratios also produce mixed signals.
  - Gross profit increases in all years except YR 5, suggesting effective operations management.
  - Gross profit margins vary from year to year, with only YR 4 and YR 5 showing consistency.
  - Stock sales ratios vary significantly from year to year.
  - Return on equity ratios vary from year to year.

These preliminary analytics are inconclusive for Company 2 as well, but there is the subtle clue of inconsistency within the testing that should attract the interest of a prudent financial forensic examiner, such as gross profit increases and gross profit margins.

Since the first two analytics did not provide consistent outcomes, the next step is horizontal analysis. The following shows the outcome of this testing.

- Changes for accounts receivable vary from year to year, with significant changes from YR 1 to YR 2.
- Changes in inventory vary from year to year, with significant changes from YR 1 to YR 2.
- Although the changes in prepaid expenses increase from YR 1 to YR 2, there are significant decreases in the changes in both YR 3 and YR 4.
- Changes in fixed assets increase from YR 1 to YR 4, with a minor decrease in the change for YR 5.
- Changes for accounts payable vary from year to year, with significant changes in YR 2, YR 3, and YR 5.
- Changes in other liabilities vary from year to year, with significant changes in YR 2 and YR 5.

- Changes in sales vary from year to year, with significant changes in YR 2 and YR 5.
- Changes in cost of sales vary significantly from year to year.
- Changes in general and administrative expenses vary from year to year.
- Changes in depreciation occur in both YR 2 and YR 3 but are comparatively stable for YR 4 and YR 5.
- Miscellaneous income varies from year to year.

At this point, the testing opens a vast number of areas with possible anomalies in the financial statements, so the financial forensic examiner needs to reduce the scope of the testing to concentrated areas showing anomalies from more than one analytical technique in order to be efficient and effective.

The logical next step is to perform a vertical analysis of the financial statements for Company 2. The end results of this testing follow.

- Accounts receivable varies from year to year, fluctuating between 19% and 35% of total assets.
- Inventory fluctuates between 35% and 45% of total assets.
- Prepaid expenses remain relatively stable from year to year when compared to total assets.
- Fixed assets varies from year to year, ranging between 21% and 34% of total assets.
- Accounts payable varies from year to year, fluctuating between 12% and 32%.
- Other liabilities remain relatively stable from year to year.
- Cost of sales varies only slightly from year to year, ranging from 80% to 83%.
- General and administrative expenses varies from year to year, fluctuating from 11% to 16%.
- Depreciation expenses remain comparatively stable.
- Miscellaneous income stays relatively stable.

Once again, the oscillation of the testing results makes it difficult for the financial forensic examiner to target specific areas to investigate, but both depreciation and miscellaneous income are relatively stable, suggesting these accounts may not require additional study. However, to the trained eye, the changes in cost of sales warrant further study, starting with other analytical techniques to determine whether the changes require investigating the underlying data that makes up the balances on the financial statements.

Like Company 1, Company 2 did not prepare cash flow statements as part of its financial statement preparations. In building the cash flow statements for Company 2, the analysis shows differences in the ending cash reported in the financial statements compared to the calculated ending cash balance, with the exception of YR 5. In analyzing the cash realized from operations, the calculations for YR 3 are greater than those for YR 1, suggesting variability in the financial statements. At this point in the testing, the most significant technique used thus far is the visual presentation of cash realized from operations compared to net income, showing inverse relationships from YR 3 to YR 4. Knowing that inverse relationships are warning signs of unusual variations between cash flows and net income, the financial forensic examiner now has more evidence that further analytical techniques are necessary to determine just where these variations are occurring.

Both Piotroski's F-Score and Lev–Thiagarajan's 12 Signals give the financial forensic examiner additional information about Company 2's financial statements. The outcomes of these tests follow.

Piotroski's F-Score

- Both YR 3 and YR 4 exhibit average financial position, while YR 1 shows a weak financial position.
- YR 5 is marginal average financial position with an overall score of four.
- Operating cash flows do not exceed net income in all years except YR 3.
- The percentage increase in sales does not exceed the percentage increase in total assets.
- Gross margins exceed the prior-year gross margins in YR 2 and YR 3 only.

Lev–Thiagarajan's 12 Signals

- Inventory signals are negative in YR 4 and YR 5, noting that inventory increases exceed sales increases.
- Accounts receivable shows positive signals for all years analyzed.
- Negative signals for capital expenditures are in both YR 4 and YR 5.
- General and administrative expenses has a negative signal in YR 4.
- The allowance for doubtful accounts shows negative signals in both YR 3 and YR 5.
- Gross margin shows negative signals in both YR 3 and YR 4.

For the first time, the financial forensic examiner has additional information confirming some the changes noted in both the horizontal and vertical analyses that warrant additional study, including accounts receivable, cost of sales, inventory, and general and administrative expenses.

The next step is to use Benford's Law to determine whether the actual frequencies of the first two digits of the numbers in the account balances within the financial statements meet the expected frequencies of Benford's Law. This allows the financial forensic examiner to review the financial statements of each individual year to see if there are consistencies from year to year in any anomalies found in the testing. The actual frequencies of first two digits of the account balances that exceeded the threshold follow.

Findings for YR 1

▪ No variations exceeding the expected frequencies of the first two digits test of the account balances.

Findings for YR 2

▪ Accounts receivable
▪ Accounts payable
▪ Fixed assets
▪ Miscellaneous income

Findings for YR 3

▪ Cash
▪ Sales

Findings for YR 4

▪ Inventory
▪ Sales

Findings for YR 5

▪ Fixed assets
▪ Cost of sales

Findings for All Years Combined

▪ Allowance for doubtful accounts
▪ Deferred taxes
▪ Depreciation

- Stockholder's equity
- Sales

The one account that is consistent throughout the Benford's Law testing is sales, although cost of sales, inventory, and accounts receivable show inconsistencies in other testing.

In order to determine consistency in the outcomes of the other testing, the Beneish M-Score and the component indices are techniques generally required for all financial statement analyses. The outcomes of the Beneish M-Score techniques follow.

- The DSRI index is greater than the benchmark in YR 5.
- The GMI index is greater than the benchmark in both YR 2 and YR 5.
- The AQI index is comparatively stable and within the guidelines of the benchmark.
- The SGI index is significantly above the general benchmark in YR 2 and greater than the benchmark in YR 3.
- The DEPI index is greater than the benchmark in YR 2.
- The SGAI index is greater than the benchmark in YR 5.
- The TATA index is positive in YR 2 and YR 4.
- The LVGI index is greater than the benchmark in YR 2.
- The overall score is $-.70$ in YR 2 and -1.53 in YR 5.

These techniques show inconsistencies in accounts receivable, cost of sales, general and administrative expenses, depreciation, and sales. Other techniques have identified these accounts as having areas of inconsistencies already.

The next step is the accrual testing, discussed in Chapter 6. The outcomes of the accrual testing for Company 2 follow.

Dechow–Dichev Accrual Quality

- Overall testing indicates a comparatively stable relationship, suggesting that accruals relate to cash flows.
- Dechow–Dichev earnings follow the same trends as net income, except in YR 4.
- In YR 4, net income increases while the Dechow–Dichev earnings decrease, representing a significant warning sign for the financial forensic examiner.

Sloan's Accruals

- YR 3 and YR 4 show higher implied cash components to net income.
- Both YR 2 and YR 5 have high accrual components that positively affect net income, with YR 5 showing that net income is mostly the accrual component.
- The accrual component for YR 2 changes a net loss into net income.

Jones Nondiscretionary Accruals

- Nondiscretionary accruals decrease from year to year, suggesting increases in discretionary accruals.
- Nondiscretionary accruals are negative in YR 5.

The accrual testing shows that the financial statements include accruals not related to future cash flows, and they have the potential of manipulating earnings. In this instance, the accruals that need additional analysis relate to both accounts receivable and the allowance for doubtful accounts due to the outcome of the accrual testing.

The final testing for Company 2 relates to the statistical testing of the Z-scores, correlation, and regression analysis. The outcomes of these tests follow.

Z-Score Testing

- Both YR 1 and YR 2 show significant inconsistencies in all Z-scores for the specific accounts tested, except accounts receivable.
- Inventory shows inconsistency in both YR 1 and YR 5 compared to the other years.
- Sales show inconsistencies in both YR 1 and YR 3 compared to the other years.
- Cost of sales shows inconsistency in YR 1 and YR 3 compared to the other years.
- Depreciation shows inconsistency in both YR 1 and YR 5 compared to the other years.
- General and administrative expenses shows inconsistency in both YR 1 and YR 3 compared to the other years.

Correlation and Regression Analysis

- The correlation analysis shows changes in the relationship between sales and cost of sales.

▪ The regression analysis implies that the amounts recorded for cost of sales may not be reasonable.

These tests also support other testing showing unusual variations in sales, cost of sales, inventory, and general and administrative expenses. Now the financial forensic examiner can proceed with detailed studies of the underlying data that makes up these account balances on the financial statements. Noting that these areas appear to be consistent but vary across all years under study, the testing suggests that all of the financial statements under study have anomalies that may relate to possible fraudulent activity.

Once more, the analytical tools and techniques point to areas of inconsistencies suggesting possible fraudulent activity. However, the financial forensic examiner must remember that all inconsistencies are not fraudulent activity, such as the anomaly with depreciation expense, but might come from unusual business transactions that are appropriate for the situation. When investigating the underlying transactions to determine the possibility of fraudulent activity, the financial forensic examiner will discover unusual, but proper, transactions related to the operations of the company and then set those aside and move to other areas. Analytical techniques and tools merely find variances, so it is up to the financial forensic examiner to determine whether the variances are proper or improper.

As for Company 2, the embezzlement activities occurred over a rather long time, and the activity is included in all of the years under study. Remember, the embezzlement was discovered in YR 5, so the financial statements for YR 5 include only nine months of fraudulent activity with corrections made to record the fraudulent activity as a bad debt for that year. Cost of sales hid the majority of the embezzled funds, along with fraudulent invoices also in general and administrative expenses. To cover up the increases in cost of sales, fictitious invoices increased sales in order to maintain a comparatively reasonable relationship that otherwise might alert management to the fraudulent activities. To hide the embezzled funds in general and administrative expenses, the office manager duplicated invoice amounts from various vendors, changing invoice numbers and vendors throughout the course of the embezzlement. The company also sold scrap material and these sales were diverted, reducing miscellaneous income. However, these amounts were minor, so management did not consider any of these changes consequential. More important, the analytical tools and techniques focused on these areas of inconsistencies, thereby allowing detailed investigative work to uncover the embezzlement.

 **COMPANY 3**

Since Company 3 includes two separate sets of financial statements, most of the tools and techniques separately test each set of financial statements to find specific variations even though the primary government's financial statements include some of the information found in the governmental funds' financial statements. However, the preliminary ratios test only the primary government's financial statements. The outcomes of those tests follow.

Liquidity Ratios

- Working capital decreases from YR 2 forward, with significant decreases each year.
- Working capital indices decrease significantly from year to year, remaining in a negative position after YR 2.
- Working capital turnover increases each year beginning with YR 2.
- Current ratios decrease year over year.

Profitability Ratios

- Generally, gross profit margins do not apply to governmental entities, but reclassifying the financial information for this purpose shows variations in gross profit from year to year.
- Gross profit margins also vary significantly from year to year.
- Stock sales are comparatively stable.
- Return on equity also fluctuates from year to year.

While governments tend to have stability in their financial statements, variations are possible, so the financial forensic examiner needs to perform additional analytical techniques to determine if the variations have reasonable explanations or if they are indicative of possible fraudulent activity.

In testing the changes in the financial statements using horizontal analysis, the outcomes for both the primary government's and the governmental funds' financial statements follow:

Primary Government

- Changes in accounts receivable vary from −8% to 20%.
- Changes in inventory vary from −22% to 23%.

- Changes in prepaid expenses vary from −53% to 23%.
- Changes in fixed assets vary from 3% to 13%.
- Changes in investments vary from −85% to 127%.
- Changes in accounts payable vary from −51% to 121%.
- Changes in accrued liabilities vary little, ranging from 10% to 14%.
- Changes in deferred revenues vary from −13% to 4%.
- Changes in charges for services vary from −6% to 19%.
- Changes in taxes vary from −4% to 15%.
- Changes in other revenues vary from −54% to 172%.
- Changes in general and administrative expenses vary from −11% to 24%.

Governmental Funds

- Changes in accounts receivable vary from 2% to 12%.
- Changes in due-from-other funds vary from 19% to 64%.
- Changes in inventory vary from −47% to 139%.
- Changes in prepaid expenses vary from −68% to 14%.
- Changes in accounts payable vary −50% to 202%.
- Changes in accrued liabilities vary from 7% to 29%.
- Changes in due-to-other funds vary from 20% to 76%.
- Changes in deferred revenues vary from 1% to 9%.
- Changes in charges for services vary from −6% to 5%.
- Changes in taxes vary from 1% to 6%.
- Changes in other revenues vary from −53% to 96%.
- Changes in general and administrative expenses vary from −6% to 23%.

Both sets of financial statements include wide swings in change from year to year, which does not provide the financial forensic examiner with any one area that may include unusual variations. Therefore, other analytical techniques are necessary.

The natural next step is to use vertical analysis on both sets of financial statements. The outcomes of the vertical analysis follow:

Primary Government

- Investments compared to total assets vary from year to year.
- Fixed assets compared to total assets varies from 78% to 91%.
- Most of the remaining balance sheet accounts are relatively consistent from year to year.
- Taxes compared to total revenues vary from 49% to 55%.

- Charges for services compared to total revenues vary from 31% to 36%.
- General and administrative expenses compared to total sales varies from 57% to 76%.

Governmental Funds

- Accounts receivable compared to total assets varies from 26% to 35%.
- Due-from-other funds compared to total assets varies from 21% to 59%.
- Due-to-other funds compared to total assets varies from 18% to 55%, increasing every year.
- Deferred revenues compared to total assets vary from 19% to 26%.
- Most of the remaining balance sheet accounts are relatively consistent from year to year.
- Taxes compared to total revenues vary from 24% to 30%.
- General and administrative expenses varies from 60% to 78%
- Operating transfers in varies from 48% to 65%.
- Operating transfers out varies from 30% to 43%.

Grant revenues in the primary government and intergovernmental revenues in the governmental funds are excluded from the analysis, since these accounts normally include significant changes from year to year, depending on the number and types of grants issued to the government. The financial forensic examiner should expect variability in these accounts, but possible fraudulent activity can still occur related to compliance with grant covenants and require further study regardless of outcomes of analytical techniques. Notice the similarities in the outcomes between the primary government and the governmental funds vertical analyses. Both taxes and general and administrative expenses show unusual variances in both the primary government's and the governmental funds' financial statements.

Since governmental financial statements only show cash flow statements for the business activities, any cash flow analysis requires the preparation of a simple cash flow statement. The cash realized from operations ratio for the primary government shows cash from operations exceeding net income as it should, but with significant increases that are unusual. The comparison of net income to CRO shows CRO decreasing in YR 5 while net income increases, definitely a warning sign for the financial forensic examiner. Since the only non-cash transaction in the governmental funds relates to deferred revenues, any significant increase in CRO compared to net income is associated with this account and requires further investigation. More important, the comparison of CRO to net income shows inverse relationships for all years, signaling the financial statements have some unusual variations that require additional analysis.

Since the comparison of CRO to net income shows inverse relationships, the next analytical techniques that may point to specific areas of inconsistencies are Piotroski's F-Score and Lev–Thiagarajan's 12 Signals. The outcomes of these tests for both the primary government and the governmental funds follow.

Piotroski's F-Score for the Primary Government

- Overall scores show an average financial position, improving from YR 2 and maintaining stability in YR 4 and YR 5.
- Signals associated with the primary government's ability to meet future debt obligations are weak for all years.
- Signals associated with the operating efficiency of the primary government are weak for all years, yet the profitability signals are average.

Piotroski's F-Score for the Governmental Funds

- Overall scores show a weak financial position in YR 4 for the governmental funds, with the other years' total scores barely reaching the average status.
- Signals associated with the governmental funds' ability to meet future debt obligations are weak for all years.
- Signals associated with the operating efficiency of the governmental funds are weak for all years.

Lev–Thiagarajan's 12 Signals for the Primary Government

- Inventory has a negative signal in all years except YR 3.
- Accounts receivable has positive signals in YR 2 and YR 3 while showing negative signals in YR 4 and YR 5.
- General and administrative expenses has positive signals for all years except YR 2.
- The allowance for doubtful accounts has positive signals in all years except YR 3.
- The audit opinion has positive signals for all years.

Lev–Thiagarajan's 12 Signals for the Governmental Funds

- Inventory has a negative signal in all years except YR 3.
- Accounts receivable has negative signals in YR 2 and YR 4 while having positive signals in YR 3 and YR 5.

- General and administrative expenses have negative signals in YR 2 and YR 4 while having positive signals in YR 3 and YR 5.
- The audit opinion has positive signals for all years.

The only consistencies between the primary government and the governmental funds in the Lev–Thiagarajan's 12 Signals analysis are the signals for inventory, the same signals for accounts receivable in YR 2, and the negative signal for general and administrative expenses in YR 2. Under Piotroski's F-Score model, there are no consistencies between the primary government and the governmental funds.

The Benford's Law analysis applies to both the primary government's and the governmental funds' financial statements. Thus far, the different analytical techniques used on the governmental funds' financial statements suggest these financial statements have more inconsistencies compared to the primary government's financial statements. The outcomes of the Benford's Law analysis follow, showing the account balances where the actual frequencies of the first two digits of the account balances exceed the threshold of the expected frequencies in Benford's Law:

Findings for YR 1 of the Primary Government

- Notes receivable
- Fixed assets

Findings for YR 2 of the Primary Government

- Interest income
- Interest expense
- Fixed assets
- Grant revenues
- Deferred revenues
- Other revenues

Findings for YR 3 of the Primary Government

- Investments
- Net assets

Findings for YR 4 of the Primary Government

- Fixed assets
- Accrued liabilities

Findings for YR 5 of the Primary Government

- Notes receivable
- Allowance for doubtful accounts

Findings for all years of the Primary Government

- Net assets
- Investments
- Depreciation expenses

Findings for YR 1 of the Governmental Funds

- Other revenues
- Debt service payments
- Cash
- Inventory
- Due-to-other funds
- Due-from-other funds
- Accrued liabilities

Findings for YR 2 of the Governmental Funds

- Due-to-other funds
- Interest expense
- Inventory
- Notes receivable
- Due-from-other funds
- Debt service payments

Findings for YR 3 of the Governmental Funds

- Capital outlay
- General and administrative expenses

Findings for YR 4 of the Governmental Funds

- Investments
- Accounts receivable
- Prepaid expenses
- Accounts payable
- Charges for services

Findings for YR 5 of the Governmental Funds

▪ Cash
▪ Accrued liabilities

Findings for all years of the Governmental Funds

▪ Interest expense
▪ Accrued liabilities
▪ Deferred revenues
▪ Tax revenues
▪ Accounts receivable
▪ Charges for services
▪ Accounts payable
▪ Other revenues
▪ Investments
▪ Prepaid expenses
▪ Capital outlay

The common account of the primary government shown as an exception in more than one year's analysis concerns fixed assets. Chapter 7 discusses the inference to interest income and interest expense. For the governmental funds, common accounts include due-to-other funds, due-from-other funds, inventory, and debt service payments. However, when combining both the primary government findings and the governmental funds findings, common accounts include other revenues, deferred revenues, investments, and accrued liabilities.

The Beneish M-Score is the next analytical technique to use in order to find specific areas within the financial statements of both the primary government and the governmental funds containing inconsistencies. All of the previous analytical techniques tell the financial forensic examiner the financial statements, in general, have multiple areas suggesting unusual variations and unusual relationships, but further analytical tests should point to specific areas for detailed study. The outcomes of the Beneish M-Score model follow.

Primary Government

▪ The overall Beneish M-Scores fall within the guidelines of the threshold of −2.22.
▪ The DRSI index is greater than the benchmark in YR 4 and YR 5.

- The AQI index is comparatively stable and within the guidelines of the threshold.
- The SGI index is greater than the threshold in all years except YR 4.
- The DEPI index is greater than the threshold in YR 3 only.
- The SGAI index is greater than the threshold in YR 2 only.
- The TATA index is positive in YR 2.
- The LVGI index is greater than the threshold in all years except YR 4.

Governmental Funds

- The overall Beneish M-Scores for YR 2 and YR 5 do not fall within the benchmark of -2.22, suggesting the possibility of manipulation.
- The DSRI index is greater than the threshold in both YR 2 and YR 4.
- The AQI index is comparatively stable and within the guidelines of the threshold.
- The SGI index is greater than the threshold in all years except YR 4.
- The SGAI index is greater than the threshold in both YR 2 and YR 4
- The TATA index is positive in all years except YR 3.
- The LVGI index is greater than the threshold in all years except YR 2.

Although the governmental funds do not record debt like the primary government, remember that the due-to accounts are advances to other funds and included in the LVGI calculations. Even though the primary government records other debts, the due-to-other funds are included in the total debt numbers.

Since the due-to-other funds and the due-from-other funds are accruals on the governmental funds, these financial statements are appropriate for the accrual analytical techniques. The outcomes of the accrual testing follow:

Dechow–Dichev Accrual Quality

- Primary Government
  - In YR2 and YR 3, the accrual quality remains relatively stable while income increases significantly.
  - In both YR 2 and YR 3, the Dechow–Dichev earnings remain comparatively stable with significant changes in net income.
- Governmental Funds
  - The accrual quality follows the trends of net income, suggesting accruals are not representative of future cash flows.

- The Dechow–Dichev earnings suggest significant differences from net income in all years except YR 5.

Sloan's Accruals

- Primary Government
  - In YR 2, the accrual component positively affects net income.
  - For the remaining years, the accrual component negatively affects net income.
- Governmental Funds
  - In YR 2, the accrual component positively affects net income, as in the finding for the primary government.
  - In YR 5, the accrual component positively affects net income.
  - In both YR 3 and YR 4, the accrual components negatively affect net income.

Jones Nondiscretionary Accruals

- Primary Government
  - Nondiscretionary accruals are rather stable from year to year.

The Jones Nondiscretionary accrual analytical technique is not appropriate for the governmental funds, since these statements do not include property, plant, and equipment. However, the other accrual analytical techniques do imply that the accruals significantly affect net income, requiring additional study.

Lastly, the outcomes of the Z-score analysis and the regression analysis follow:

Primary Government

- Accounts receivable shows inconsistency in YR 5 compared to the other years.
- Accounts payable shows inconsistencies in YR 1, YR 3, and YR 5 compared to the other years.
- Tax revenues show inconsistency in YR 1 compared to the other years.
- General and administrative expenses shows inconsistencies in YR 1 and YR 3 compared to the other years.
- Depreciation shows inconsistencies in YR 1 and YR 5 compared to the other years.

- Property, plant, and equipment shows inconsistencies in YR 1 and YR 5 compared to the other years.
- Accumulated depreciation shows inconsistencies in YR 1 and YR 5 compared to the other years.
- Changes in adjusted accumulated depreciation totals from year to year do not match the changes in depreciation expenses from year to year.

Governmental Funds

- Accounts receivable shows inconsistencies in both YR 1 and YR 5 compared to the other years.
- Due-from-other funds shows inconsistencies in both YR 1 and YR 5 compared to the other years.
- Due-to-other funds shows inconsistencies in both YR 1 and YR 5 compared to the other years.
- Deferred revenues show inconsistencies in both YR 1 and YR 5 compared to the other years.
- Tax revenues show inconsistencies in both YR 1 and YR 5 compared to the other years.
- General and administrative expenses shows inconsistency in YR 1 compared to the other years.
- Transfers in shows inconsistencies in both YR 2 and YR 4 compared to the other years
- Transfers out shows inconsistencies in both YR 3 and YR 5 compared to the other years.

By using regression analysis for both transfers in and transfers out, the predicted amounts question the reasonableness of the amounts when comparing these accounts to the due-from-other-funds and due-to-other-funds accounts.

By using multiple analytical techniques on both the primary government's financial statements and the governmental funds' financial statements, it is determined that areas that continually show unusual variations and relationships include accounts receivable, tax revenues, and all sales in general; general and administrative expenses; and deferred revenues. Unique to the primary government, areas that continually show unusual variations include fixed assets and depreciation. Accounts unique to the governmental funds that continually show unusual variations include due-from-other funds and due-to-other funds.

The off-book bank account is the center of this rather complex embezzlement scheme. Transferring governmental funds through various governmental bank accounts into this off-book account created the inconsistencies in the due-from-other-funds and due-to-other-funds accounts. The manager created fictitious invoices to hide the embezzlement, recording these invoices in general and administrative expenses as well as capital outlay, thus creating inconsistencies in the fixed assets and accumulated depreciation accounts. In an attempt to cover up the embezzlement, the manager stated that tax revenues were consistently late. When the outside accounting firm compiled the financial statements and converted the statements to full accrual, adjustments to deferred revenues created the inconsistencies in this account, since inconsistencies also existed in tax revenues and tax receivables. The analytical techniques discussed above pointed to areas of unusual relationships and inconsistencies in the financial statements, warranting further investigations that ultimately found the embezzlement.

 ## COMPANY 4

Company 4 is a prime example of a company having unusual relationships and inconsistencies in its financial statements, with these anomalies being not the result of fraudulent activity. It is up to the financial forensic examiner to determine whether these anomalies are the result of fraudulent activity. Yet, even with some inconsistency in its financial statements, the testing serves as a comparison for the other three companies, whose financial statements contain fraudulent activity. The outcomes of the basic, preliminary analytical techniques concerning liquidity and profitability ratios follow:

Liquidity Ratios

- Working capital increases year over year.
- After YR 2, working capital indices are rather consistent for YR 3 and YR 4 while decreasing in YR 5.
- After YR 1, working capital turnover calculations decrease year over year.
- Current ratio calculations increase year over year.

Profitability Ratios

- Gross profit increases every year, except YR 5, which shows a decrease.
- Gross profit margins are comparatively stable.

- Stock sales ratios are comparatively stable.
- Return on equity shows significant increases in YR 3 and YR 4.

The bankrupt subsidiary's financial statements requiring consolidation with the company's financial statements easily explains the changes. Remember, the deconsolidation of the financial statements did not occur until YR 4, and it was YR 5 before the financial statements no longer showed amounts related to discontinued operations.

Once again, horizontal analysis shows a range of variability from year to year. The outcomes of this test follow:

- Changes in account receivable balances vary from −21% to 34%.
- Changes in the allowance balances vary from −34% to 64%.
- Changes in inventory balances vary from −9% to 31%.
- Changes in prepaid balances vary from −52% to 181%.
- Changes in other asset balances vary from −48% to 71%.
- Changes in accounts payable balances vary from −32% to 29%.
- Changes in other liabilities balances vary from −51% to −13%.
- Changes in sales balances vary from −2% to 50%.
- Changes in cost of sales balances vary from −2% to 47%.
- Changes in general and administrative balances vary from −1% to 36%.
- Changes in depreciation balances vary from −13% to 20%.
- Changes in other expenses balances vary from −26% to −4%.

The changes in the account balances do not point to any specific areas, so the financial forensic examiner must perform additional analytical techniques to determine whether the financial statements include inconsistencies.

The vertical analysis for Company 4 shows more stability compared to the horizontal analysis. The outcomes of the vertical analysis test follow.

- Cash compared to total assets is comparatively stable, except for YR 5.
- Accounts receivable compared to total assets varies from 30% to 47%.
- The allowance for bad debts compared to total assets is consistent from year to year.
- Inventory compared to total assets varies from 20% to 27%.
- Prepaid expenses compared to total assets are consistent from year to year.
- Other assets compared to total assets varies from 11% to 30%.
- Fixed assets compared to total assets varies from 12% to 18%.
- Accounts payable compared to total assets varies from 21% to 31%.

- Other liabilities compared to total assets vary from 6% to 29%.
- Cost of sales compared to sales is comparatively stable from year to year.
- General and administrative expenses compared to sales is relatively stable from year to year.
- Depreciation expense compared to sales is rather stable from year to year.
- Other expenses compared to sales are rather stable from year to year.

The vertical analysis of Company 4 shows consistency in the financial statements, especially the income statement. The financial forensic examiner can easily see the difference of this outcome compared to the outcomes of the vertical analyses of the other companies.

The cash flow statement of Company 4 is the perfect example of when not to use the simple cash flow method as with Company 1, Company 2, and Company 3. When consolidated financial statements include foreign subsidiaries with currency translation adjustments, the cash flow statements become more complex. Therefore, the comparison of cash realized from operations compared to net income is a better choice of analytical technique. The comparison of CRO to net income also presents an excellent example where an inverse relationship actually has a legitimate business reason for the inconsistency. Again, this reminds the financial forensic examiner that not all inconsistencies and inverse relationships are fraud related, but to determine that fraud does not exist, the financial forensic examiner must investigate further.

Both Piotroski's F-Score model and the Lev–Thiagarajan's 12 Signals offer other analytical techniques to examine the financial statements of Company 4. The outcomes of these tests follow.

Piotroski's F-Score

- The overall scores show an average financial position for the company.
- YR 2 shows the lowest profitability scores.
- Scores for liquidity show the company is able to meet its future obligations, giving the impression of a strong financial position in this area.
- The scores measuring profitability show an average financial position.

Lev–Thiagarajan's 12 Signals

- Inventory signals are positive in all years except YR 2.
- Accounts receivable signals are positive in both YR 3 and YR 5 and negative for YR 2 and YR 4.

- Capital expenditure signals are negative in YR 2 and YR 3 and positive for YR 4 and YR 5.
- General and administrative expenses signals are positive in all years except YR 5.
- Gross margin signals are negative in all years except YR 5.
- The allowance signals are negative in YR 2 and YR 5 and positive in YR 3 and YR 4.
- The effective tax rate signals are negative in YR 2 and YR 4 and positive in YR 3 and YR 5.
- LIFO signals are negative for all years.
- The audit opinion signals are positive for all years.

Even the outcomes of these tests follow the known information concerning the operations of Company 4. In addition, the tests do not show any unusual variations in the financial statements.

The next logical test to apply to the financial statements is the Benford's Law analysis to determine whether the actual frequencies of the first two digits in the numbers in the account balances meet the expected frequencies of Benford's Law. The outcomes of this test follow:

Findings for YR 1

- Fixed assets
- Current portion of long-term debt
- Sales
- Accounts receivable
- Other assets

Findings for YR 2

- Other assets
- Current portion of long-term debt
- Cost of sales
- Stockholder's equity
- Other expenses
- Prepaid expenses
- Miscellaneous income
- General and administrative expenses

Findings for YR 3

- Other assets
- Other liabilities
- Notes payable

Findings for YR 4

- Allowance for doubtful accounts
- Income tax expense
- General and administrative expenses

Findings for YR 5

- Cash
- Other assets
- General and administrative expenses
- Inventory
- Accounts payable
- Fixed assets
- Other expenses

Findings for All Years

- Fixed assets
- Current portion of long-term debt
- Sales
- Other assets
- Cost of sales
- Prepaid expenses
- Inventory
- Accounts payable
- Accounts receivable

The account balances for other assets appear in all of the testing except for YR 4. Although Benford's Law is a test for reasonableness, the account balance for other assets includes deferred tax assets, and the financial forensic examiner should expect some variability in this account, along with other liabilities that include deferred tax liabilities.

The next sequence of testing concerns the Beneish M-Score model. The outcomes of the testing follow.

- The overall Beneish M-Score totals do not meet the guidelines of the -2.22 in all years, except YR 5.
- The DRSI index exceeds the general benchmark in YR 2 and YR 4.
- The GMI index exceeds the general benchmark in YR 5.
- The AQI index exceeds the general benchmark in all years except YR 4.
- The SGI index exceeds the general benchmark in all years except YR 5.
- The DEPI index exceeds the general benchmark in all years except YR 5.
- The SGAI index exceeds the general benchmark in YR 5 only.
- The TATA index is positive in all years except YR 5.
- The LVGI index is below the benchmark for all years.

While there will always be some variability in the Beneish M-Score from year to year based on the operations and management of the company, the indices' calculations for Company 4 relate to the unusual period in the company's operations where the bankrupt subsidiary financial information is included in the general operations for the rest of the company. Chapter 4 includes discussions related to the Beneish M-Score calculations and findings for Company 4.

The accruals testing for Company 4 also points to variations that are easily explainable based on the operations of the company. The outcomes of the accruals testing follow:

Dechow–Dichev Accrual Quality

- The Dechow–Dichev accrual quality is reasonably stable with the exception of YR 3, where income increases while the accrual quality remains stable.
- The Dechow–Dichev earnings follow the same trend as net income with the exception of YR 3, where net income increases and the Dechow–Dichev earnings show a slight decrease.

Sloan's Accruals

- The accrual component positively affects net income for all years.
- In YR 5, the accrual component is a relatively minor influence on net income.
- In YR 2, the accrual component converts net income into a net loss.

Jones Nondiscretionary Accruals

- Nondiscretionary accruals either remain relatively stable or increase in all years, except YR 5, suggesting low discretionary accruals.
- In YR 5, nondiscretionary accruals decrease, suggesting the increase of discretionary accruals.

The anomalies found in the accrual testing point to the years where the financial statements included the discontinued operations of the bankrupt subsidiary. In YR 5, the reduction in the nondiscretionary accruals relates to the deconsolidation of the subsidiary's financial information in the financial statements.

While the Z-score calculations for Company 4 show inconsistencies in the first four years under study, the calculations for YR 5 show more consistency in the financial statements with little extreme variability. Once more, the operations of the company of the prior four years easily explain the extreme variability. Remember that some variability is normal in the course of normal company operations and that the financial forensic examiner needs to focus on areas of *extreme* variability. The more years the financial forensic examiner studies using the Z-score calculations, the easier it is to define the variability within normal operating cycles.

 SUMMARY

The roadmaps drawn by the analytical techniques used for Company 1, Company 2, and Company 3 found pervasive fraudulent activity within each of the companies' financial statements resulting from embezzlement activities and the attempted coverup of the embezzlement. Yet, in Company 4, the analytical tests found anomalies and unusual variations in the financial statements relating to specific events within the company's operational cycle. This type of discovery is also important, because the tests did point to variations that are unusual to the normal operational activities of the company, presenting important knowledge for existing and potential investors, even though the testing did not find fraudulent activity. However, if Company 4 did not disclose these variations from its normal operations to its investors, the possibility of financial statement manipulation exists. Continued use of these analytical techniques and tools allows the financial forensic examiner to develop and perfect not only an analytical mindset but also the visual presentation skills often necessary for prosecution.

By using the various analytical techniques in the case studies of the four companies, the financial forensic examiner begins to see the importance of developing an efficient and effective investigative process to determine the possibilities of fraudulent activities. In each case study, a combination of these various analytical tools found inconsistencies within the financial statements that warranted further investigations, drilling down to specific areas within the financial statements compared to just a "hunt-and-peck" method of trying to find possible fraud. When any of these tools are used by themselves and not combined with other techniques, an individual technique may produce *false-positive* results; but the false-positive results diminish and areas associated with true anomalies will appear more than once throughout the outcome of testing when using multiple analytical tools. These forensic indices are just a few of the many that are available to the financial forensic examiner. However, in reviewing the outcomes of the testing for each of the four companies, these do provide powerful results for the small amount of time invested in doing the calculations. In essence, the analytical tools enable the financial forensic examiner to find either fraudulent activity or unusual events occurring within an operating cycle of a company.

Bibliography

Beneish, Messod D. "The Detection of Earnings Manipulation,"*Financial Analyst Journal*, 55, No. 5 (September/October 1999).

Benford, Frank. "The Law of Anomalous Numbers," *Proceedings of the American Philosophical Society*, 78, No. 4 (March 1938).

Carslaw, Charles. "Anomalies in Income Numbers: Evidence of Goal Oriented Behavior," *Accounting Review*, 63, No. 2 (April 1998).

Dechow, Patricia M., and Illia D. Dichev. "The Quality of Accruals and Earnings: The Role of Accrual Estimation Errors," *The Accounting Review*, 77, Supplement: Quality of Earnings Conference (2002).

Dorrell, Darrell D., and Gregory A. Gadawaski. *Financial Forensics Body of Knowledge*. Hoboken, NJ: John Wiley & Sons, 2012.

Dorrell, Darrell D., Gregory A. Gadawaski, Heidi Bowen, and Janet F. Hunt. "Financial Intelligence: People and Money Techniques to Prosecute Fraud, Corruption, and Earnings Manipulation," *U.S. Attorney Bulletin*, 60, No. 2 (March 2012).

Haynes, Allyn H."Detecting Fraud in Bankrupt Municipalities Using Benford's Law," *Scripps Senior Theses*, Paper 42 (2012).

Jones, Jennifer J. "Earnings Management During Import Relief Investigations," *Journal of Accounting Research*, 29, No. 2 (Autumn 1991).

Lev, Baruch, and S. Ramu Thiagarajan. "Fundamental Information Analysis," *Journal of Accounting Research*, 31, No 2 (Autumn 1993).

Nigrini, Mark J. "A Taxpayers Compliance Application of Benford's Law," *Journal of the American Taxation Association*, 18 (Spring 1996).

Nigrini, Mark J., and Linda J. Mittermaier. "The Use of Benford's Law as an Aid in Analytical Procedures," *Auditing: A Journal of Practice and Theory*, 16, No. 2 (Fall 1997).

Piotroski, Joseph D. "Value Investing: The Use of Historical Financial Statement Information to Separate Winners from Losers," *Journal of Accounting Research*, 38, Supplement (January 2002).

Sloan, Richard D. "Do Stock Prices Fully Reflect Information in Accruals and Cash Flows About Future Earnings?," *Accounting Review*, 71, No. 3 (July 1996).

About the Author

Pamela S. Mantone, CPA, CFE, CFF, CITP, CGMA, FCPA, is a senior assurance manager of Joseph Decosimo and Company, PLLC, a leading regional accounting firm that provides multiple services to both businesses and individuals. She performs both audit and attestation services and forensic accounting services to various types of organizations. She also provides consulting services regarding implementation of fraud prevention and detection internal control systems, especially for small and mid-sized businesses. She manages and performs audits of internal control systems for various types of business entities.

In practicing in the areas of audit and attestation services, Ms. Mantone manages and supervises these services for financial institutions, nonprofit organizations, governmental entities, small businesses, and publicly traded companies. Her fraud and forensic services primarily relate to the gathering of forensic evidence and testifying to findings, with an emphasis on embezzlement and fraudulent financial statement reporting, along with her ability to find patterns in financial information suggesting possible fraudulent activity.

Ms. Mantone is also active in various professional societies. She participates in the Tennessee Society of Certified Public Accountants (TSCPA) high school liaison program, promoting accounting career choices to high school students. She is an active member of the TSCPA Forensic Valuation Services Committee. She currently services as an officer of the Chattanooga Chapter of the TSCPA. As an active member of the AICPA, she is a Certified in Financial Forensics (CFF) champion for the state of Tennessee, promoting an accounting career choice and the opportunity of becoming a CFF to college students. She also serves on the ACFE Advisory Council, promoting educational resources for certified fraud examiners.

She makes presentations to various organizations on a variety of topics, including fraud and forensic techniques, internal control design and weaknesses, and auditing techniques. She also trains staff at her company in both auditing and forensic techniques. She is a well-known regional speaker and has been a presenter at the Tennessee FVS Conference for two years and for one year at the TSCPA Annual Conference. She has also made multiple presentations to the various local chapters of the TSCPA and has also presented at the 2012 Annual Consultant's Conference. Ms. Mantone has written numerous articles for local associations and had an article published in the January/ February 2013 issue of the ACFE's *Fraud* magazine relating to using analytical techniques in a case study involving embezzlement.

Index

A

Accruals, 171–198
  Dechow-Dichev Accrual Quality
    model, 173–183
    component abbreviations, 174
    four companies, 175–183
  Jones Nondiscretionary Accruals
    model, 191–196
    Company 1, 193
    Company 2, 193–194
    Company 3, 194–195
    Company 4, 195–196
    component abbreviations, 192
    gross PPE, 192
  Sloan's Accruals model, 184–191
    Company 1, 185–186
    Company 2, 186–187
    Company 3, 188–189
    Company 4, 190–191
Aging, 294
Analysis techniques using historical
    financial statements and other
    company information,
    199–235
  Lev-Thiagarajan's 12 Signals,
    215–233
    Company 1, 220–222
    Company 2, 222–225
    Company 3, 225–230
    Company 4, 230–233

  Piotroski F-Score model, 200–215
    Company 1, 203–205
    Company 2, 205–207
    Company 3, 207–212
    Company 4, 212–215
"Anomalies in Income Numbers:
    Evidence of Goal Oriented
    Behavior" (Carslaw), 241
Asset quality index (AQI), 122, 269

B

Beneish M-Score model, 119–170,
    269, 270, 271
  Company 1, 124–133
    calculations of eight indices, 125
    DEPI, 129
    DEPTA, 132
    DSRI, 126
    GMI, 127
    LVGI, 130
    overall M-Score calculations,
    125
    SGAI, 129
    SGI, 128
    TAPTA, 132
    TATA, 131
  Company 2, 133–143
    calculations of eight indices, 134
    DEPI, 137
    DSRI, 134

Beneish M-Score model (*Continued*)
   GMI, 135, 142
   overall M-Score calculations,
     133
   SGAI, 137
   SGI, 136, 142
   TAPTA, 141
   TARTA, 139
   TATA, 138
   TITA, 140
   Company 3, 143–158
     calculations for six of eight
      indices for governmental
      funds, 145
     calculations for seven of eight
      indices for primary
      government, 144
     indices of governmental funds,
      151–158
     indices of primary government,
      145–151
     overall M-Scores for primary
      government and
      governmental funds financial
      statements, 143
   Company 4, 158–165
     AQI, 162
     calculations of eight indices, 159
     DEPI, 163
     DSRI, 160
     GMI, 160
     GMI comparisons with Company
      2, 161
     LVGI, 165
     overall M-Score calculations,
      158
     SGAI, 164
     SGI, 162
     TATA, 165

component abbreviations,
   121–124
formula for, 120
formulas for each component,
   120–121
summary, 166–170
Benford's Law, 237–272, 290–291
   Company 1, 243–249
     first-digit test of YR 1, 243
     first-two-digits test of all 5 years,
      248
     first-two-digits test of YR 1, 244
     first-two-digits test of YR 3, 245
     first-two-digits test of YR 4, 246
     first-two-digits test of YR 5, 247
   Company 2, 249–255
     first-two-digits test of all 5 years,
      254
     first-two-digits test of YR 2, 250
     first-two-digits test of YR 3, 251
     first-two-digits test of YR 4, 252
     first-two-digits test of YR 5, 253
   Company 3, 255–267
     first-two-digits test of YR 1 for
      governmental funds, 261
     first-two-digits test of YR 1 for
      primary government, 255
     first-two-digits test of YR 2 for
      governmental funds, 262
     first-two-digits test of YR 2 for
      primary government, 257
     first-two-digits test of YR 3 for
      governmental funds, 263
     first-two-digits test of YR 3 for
      primary government, 258
     first-two-digits test of YR 4 for
      governmental funds, 264
     first-two-digits test of YR 4 for
      primary government, 259

first-two-digits test of YR 5 for
    governmental funds, 265
first-two-digits test of YR 5 for
    primary government, 260
Company 4, 267–272
    first-two-digits test of YR 1, 267
    first-two-digits test of YR 2, 268
    first-two-digits test of YR 5, 270
expected digital frequencies, 239

C

Cash flows and cash flow statements,
        importance of, 83–118
and net income, 85–100
    Company 1, 87–89
    Company 2, 89–92
    Company 3, 92–97
    Company 4, 97–100
other cash flow techniques,
        100–118
    Company 1, 101–104
    Company 2, 104–107
    Company 3, 107–114
    Company 4, 114–117
Chebyshev's Theorem, 277–278,
        280, 282, 291–292
Companies, overview of, 1–17. *See
        also* Grading the companies
Company 1 (communications), 2–5
    condensed balance sheets for, 3
    condensed income statements
        for, 4
Company 2 (manufacturing), 5–8,
        9
    condensed balance sheets for, 8
    condensed income statements
        for, 9
Company 3 (local governmental
        entity), 8–10, 11, 12, 13

governmental funds balance
        sheets for, 12
    primary government balance
        sheets for, 11
    primary government income
        statements for, 13
Company 4 (benchmark), 10–16
    condensed balance sheets for, 15
    condensed income statements
        for, 16
Correlation analysis, 291

D

Dechow-Dichev Accrual Quality
        model, 173–183
    component abbreviations, 174
    four companies, 175–183
        accrual quality, 175
        accrual quality and net income
            for Company 1, 176
        accrual quality and net income
            for Company 2, 177
        accrual quality and net income
            for Company 4, 182
        accrual quality and net income
            for governmental funds of
            Company 3, 180
        accrual quality and net income
            for primary government of
            Company 3, 179
        earnings to net income for
            Company 1, 176
        earnings to net income for
            Company 2, 178
        earnings and net income for
            Company 4, 183
        earnings and net income for
            government funds of
            Company 3, 181

Dechow-Dichev Accrual (*Continued*)
    earnings and net income for
        primary government of
        Company 3, 179
    implied cash earnings compared
        to net income, 175
Depreciation index (DEPI), 122

E

*Earnings Management During Import
    Relief Investigations* (Jones),
    191
Empirical Rule, 274–275, 277, 282,
    291–292

F

Financial forensic examiner, defined, 1
"Fundamental Information Analysis"
    (Lev & Thiagarajan), 215

G

Grading the companies, 293–327
    Company 1, 294–302
        Beneish M-Score, 300
        Benford's Law, 298–299
        cash realization ratio, 297–298
        Dechow-Dichev Accrual
            Quality, 301
        horizontal analysis, 295–296
        Jones Nondiscretionary
            Accruals, 301
        Lev-Thiagarajan's 12 Signals,
            298
        liquidity ratio analyses,
            294–295
        Piotroski's F-Score model, 298
        profitability ratios, 295
        regression analysis test, 301
        Sloan's Accruals, 301

    vertical analysis, 296–297
    Company 2, 302–309
        Benford's Law, 306–307
        correlation and regression
            analysis, 308–309
        Dechow-Dichev Accrual
            Quality, 307
        horizontal analysis, 303–304
        Lev-Thiagarajan's 12 Signals,
            305
        liquidity ratio testing, 303
        Piotroski's F-Score, 305
        profitability ratios, 303
        Sloan's Accruals, 308
        vertical analysis, 304–297
        Z-Score testing, 308
    Company 3, 310–320
        Beneish M-Score, 316–317
        Benford's Law analysis, 314
        Dechow-Dichev Accrual
            Quality, 317–318
        governmental funds, 311,
            312–313
        Jones Nondiscretionary
            Accruals, 318–319
        Lev-Thiagarajan's 12 Signals
            for governmental funds,
            313–314
        Lev-Thiagarajan's 12 Signals for
            primary government, 313
        liquidity ratios, 310
        Piotroski's F-Score for
            governmental funds, 313
        Piotroski's F-Score for primary
            government, 313
        primary government, 310–312
        profitability ratios, 310
        Sloan's Accruals, 318
    Company 4, 320–326

Benford's Law, 323–325
Dechow-Dichev Accrual
    Quality, 325
Jones Nondiscretionary
    Accruals, 326
Lev-Thiagarajan's 12 Signals,
    322–323
liquidity ratios, 320
Piotroski's F-Score, 322
profitability ratios, 320–322
Sloan's Accruals, 325
Gross margin index (GMI), 121–122

H
Horizontal analysis, 36–66
    Company 1, 36–43
        balance sheet, 37–38, 40
        big-picture concepts, 40–43
        income statement, 39, 40
        YR 1 to YR 2, 41
        YR 2 to YR 3, 42
        YR 3 to YR4, 42–43
        YR 4 to YR 5, 43
    Company 2, 43–50
        balance sheet, 44
        income statement, 45
        sales and cost of sales, 49
        YR 1 to YR 2, 46
        YR 2 to YR 3, 46–47
        YR 3 to YR 4, 47–48
        YR 4 to YR 5, 48–50
    Company 3, 50–61
        governmental funds balance
            sheet, 57
        governmental funds income
            statement, 58
        inter-fund analysis, 61
        primary government balance
            sheet, 51–52

primary government income
    statement, 53
sales and cost of sales, 50
YR 1 to YR 2, 54, 56, 59
YR 2 to YR 3, 54–55, 59–60
YR 3 to YR 4, 55, 60
YR 4 to YR 5, 55–56, 60–61
Company 4, 61–66
    balance sheet, 62
    income statement, 63
    YR 1 to YR 2, 64
    YR 2 to YR 3, 64–65
    YR 3 to YR 4, 65
    YR 4 to YR 5, 65–66

J
Jones Nondiscretionary Accruals
    model, 191–196, 218–219,
    270
    Company 1, 193
    Company 2, 193–194
    Company 3, 194–195
    Company 4, 195–196
    component abbreviations, 192
    gross PPE, 192

L
"The Law of Anomalous Numbers"
    (Benford), 240
Lev-Thiagarajan's 12 Signals,
    215–233
    Company 1, 220–222
    Company 2, 222–225
    Company 3, 225–230
        for governmental funds, 229,
            230
        for primary government, 226,
            228
    Company 4, 230–233

Liquidity ratios, 20–25
case studies, 22–25
current ratio, 22
calculations, 25
working capital, 21
calculations, 23
working capital index, 21
calculations, 23
working capital turnover, 22
calculations, 24

M
Monte Carlo simulation, 294

N
Net income and cash flows, 85–100
Company 1, 87–89
cash flows, 88
cash realized from operations vs.
net income, 89
CRO calculations, 88
Company 2, 89–92
cash flows, 90
cash realized from operations vs.
net income, 92
CRO calculations, 91
Company 3, 92–97
cash realized from operations vs.
net income of governmental
funds, 96
cash realized from operations vs.
net income of primary
government, 94
CRO calculations of
governmental funds, 96
CRO calculations of primary
government, 94
governmental funds cash flow
statements, 95

primary government cash flows,
93
Company 4, 97–100
cash flows, 98–99
cash realized from operations vs.
net income, 100
CRO calculations, 99

P
Piotroski F-Score model, 200–215
Company 1, 203–205
Company 2, 205–207
Company 3, 207–212
Company 4, 212–215
Preliminary analytics, "norm" and
"forensic," 19–82
horizontal analysis, 36–66
Company 1, 36–43
Company 2, 43–50
Company 3, 50–61
Company 4, 61–66
liquidity ratios, 20–25
case studies, 22–25
current ratio, 22
working capital, 21
working capital index, 21
working capital turnover, 22
profitability ratios, 25–36
case studies, 27–36
gross profit, 26
gross profit margin, 26
return on equity, 27
stock sales, 26–27
testing results, 31–36
vertical analysis, 66–79, 80–81
Company 1, 66–70
Company 2, 70–73
Company 3, 73–79
Company 4, 79, 80–81

Profitability ratios, 25–36
  case studies, 27–36
  gross profit, 26
    calculations, 28
  gross profit margin, 26
    calculations, 28, 29
  return on equity, 27
    calculations, 30
  stock sales, 26–27
    ratios, 30
  testing results, 31–36
    Company 1, 31–33
    Company 2, 33–34
    Company 3, 34–35
    Company 4, 35–36

S
Sales, general and administrative
    expenses index (SGAI), 123,
    270
Scatter plot, 277, 291
Sloan's Accruals model, 184–191,
    224
  Company 1, 185–186
    comparison, 186
  Company 2, 186–187
    comparison, 187
  Company 3, 188–189
    comparison for governmental
      funds, 189
    comparison for primary
      government, 188
    for governmental funds, 189
    for primary government,
      188
  Company 4, 190–191
    comparison, 190
Statement of Cash Flows, Topic AU
    230, 83

Statistics, simple, 272–292
  Company 1, 277–281
    AR scatter plot for, 278
    comparison of actual and
      projected receivables, 280
    scatter plot for AR and sales,
      279
    Z-scores for specific financial
      statement balances, 281
  Company 2, 281–284
    general and administrative
      expenses and Z-scores, 284
    regression analysis of cost of
      sales, 283
    sales and cost of sales, 283
    Z-scores for specific financial
      statement balances, 282
  Company 3, 284–288
    comparison of A/D and
      depreciation of primary
      government, 286
    comparison of changes in A/D
      and depreciation of primary
      government, 286
    regression analysis of transfers
      in balances of governmental
      funds, 288
    regression analysis of transfers
      out balances of governmental
      funds, 288
    Z-scores for specific financial
      statement balances of
      governmental funds, 287
    Z-scores for specific financial
      statement balances of primary
      government, 285
  Company 4, 289–290
    scatter plot of sales and cost of
      sales, 20

Statistics, simple (*Continued*)
　　Z-scores for specific financial
　　　statement balances, 289
　　pie chart for different type of
　　　distribution, 276
　　pie chart of normal distribution,
　　　275
　　scatter plot for different type of
　　　distribution, 276
　　scatter plot of normal distribution,
　　　274
Stratification, 294

T

Total accounts payable to total
　　accruals (TAPTA), 271
Total accruals to total assets index
　　(TATA), 123, 171–172
Total inventory to total assets (TITA),
　　271
Trend analysis, 294

V

"Value Investing: The Use of
　　Historical Financial Statement
　　Information to Separate
　　Winners from Losers"
　　(Piotroski), 200

Vertical analysis, 66–79, 80–81,
　　101–117
Company 1, 66–70, 101–104
　　balance sheet, 67
　　cash flows, 101–104
　　income statement, 68–69
Company 2, 70–73, 104–107
　　balance sheet, 71
　　cash flows, 104–107
　　income statement, 72
Company 3, 73–79, 107–114
　　cash flows of governmental
　　　funds, 110–114
　　cash flows of primary
　　　government, 107–110
　　governmental funds balance
　　　sheet, 77
　　governmental funds income
　　　statement, 78
　　primary government balance
　　　sheet, 74–75
　　primary government income
　　　statement, 76
Company 4, 79, 80–81,
　　114–117
　　balance sheet, 80
　　cash flows, 114–117
　　income statement, 81